UNITED KINGDOM OF BEER

250 Top Beers in Bottle and Can

ADRIAN TIERNEY-JONES

CAMRA
BOOKS

For James, may your beers always be awesome

Published by the Campaign for Real Ale Ltd
230 Hatfield Road, St Albans, Hertfordshire AL1 4LW
www.camra.org.uk/books

© Campaign for Real Ale Ltd. 2022
First published 2022

ISBN 978-1-85249-378-3

A CIP catalogue record for this book is available from the British Library

Printed in the UK by Cambrian Printers Ltd, part of The Pensord Group

FSC MIX
Paper from responsible sources
FSC® C004116

Managing Editor: Alan Murphy
Design / typography: Dale Tomlinson
Sales & Marketing: Toby Langdon
Cover: David Wardle

PHOTO CREDITS

The publisher would like to thank all the breweries and others who kindly
granted permission for their photography to be used in this book.

Specific thanks go to: **Brad Evans** (page 15); **Chris Coulson** (Exale Der Titan);
Drew Worthley (Unbarred TropicSoda); **Jason Chetwynd-Cox** (Campervan
Salted Speyside Wee Heavy); **Jonny Garrett** (pages 14, 16, 40, 68, 176);
Mark Newton Photography (Abbeydale Daily Bread and Black Mass;
Hop Hideout, Sheffield); **Nicci Peet** (Campervan Leith Porter); **Zbyněk Pecák**.

‘"Come round to my place,
I'll get some beer in."
Often the words are spoken,
often the beer is
unworthy of the occasion.
Good conversation,
good companionship,
warrant good beer.’

ANDREW CAMPBELL,
The Book of Beer. 1956

CONTENTS

IPA

LAGER

LOW- AND NO-ALCOHOL

SPECIALITY

STRONG

INTRODUCTION

There is a thirst for good beer on these islands,
a thirst for beer that satisfies the soul and quenches
the thirst and leaves the drinker glowing with
satisfaction. These beers are legion in their appeal.
You might be moved by a muscular Best Bitter, a
thrilling showcase for the boisterously booming
aromatics of English hops and the deep-set, biscuity
character of Maris Otter malt. You could be in the
mood for philosophy with a brooding, midnight-black,
herculean Imperial Stout, or maybe it's all about
wanting to hang out with friends and chat and laugh
and clink glasses with a crisp and briskly amiable
lager based on the brewing traditions of central
Europe. Whatever the avenue your desire takes
you down, be assured that there is a beer for you,
which is what the theme of this book is about.

The home, the garden, the riverbank or the top of
a hill are all wonderful spaces in which to drink beer.
When friends are gathered, whether on a sunny
afternoon while the zephyrs of grilled meat or fish
drift across the garden, or around a table all snug and
comfortable on a cold winter's night, there will be
the desire for a good beer that suits the occasion –
which is also what this book is about.

Adrian Tierney

THE CANNED BEER REVOLUTION

The onset of the Covid-19 pandemic and the resulting chain of lockdowns brought sharply into focus the quality of British beers available in can and bottle, as breweries were forced to focus on website sales, selling at the brewery door or making home deliveries. The take-home market has always been in existence (in the years before World War One it was common for children to appear at the Jug and Bottle part of a pub to pick up beer for the family table), but for those of us forced to stay home it was time to enjoy a variety of beers from breweries across the UK, a time of travel when we couldn't travel.

The quality of beers in bottle and can is glorious these days. Bottle-conditioned beer has long been a given for quality, though beers that have been unfiltered and unpasteurised also dare to be delicious. However, it is the quality of beer in a can that has really soared into the stratosphere of taste and quality in the past few years. Before that, canned beer was either an excitable carbonated lager that tasted of dishwater or an ale into which some gadget has been popped to enable it to foam out of the can with the velocity of a fire extinguisher.

That has all changed. Thanks to technological advances over the past few years, which have given the inside of cans a micro-thin, water-based lining, the dire canned beers of the past have been consigned to the recycling bin of history. There are even can-conditioned beers.

The influence for the canned beer trend initially came from across the Atlantic, where American craft breweries such as Oskar Blues (an early pioneer), Sierra Nevada, Firestone Walker and Ballast Point started putting their exemplary beers in cans towards the end of the noughties.

Their enthusiasm was also about more than the flavour improvement: brewers are happy with cans because they are environmentally sound, easy to package together for distribution and there is little or no chance of light or air affecting the beer. The 360° wraparound nature of the can also gives them the chance to experiment with colourful and vivid branding.

For those of us who love the outdoors, this new wave of cans is an ideal companion to take along on that summer's day hike (though cool in a mountain stream first) or put in a cool box and carry on down to the beach.

ABOUT THE BOOK

For this book I have tried to speak with the brewers of each beer (though it wasn't always possible as they are brewers who spend their time brewing first and foremost) and get the stories on the motivations that drove them to create their beers, how they came to develop the recipe and sometimes how they felt on first tasting the beer. Obviously I have included my own tasting notes: the beers are here because they taste good, not just because they have interesting back stories. I am afraid you won't learn how to brew in reading this book, and you won't always find out which hops are used. For me, writing about beer has always been about people and stories and that is why I want to let the brewers tell the tales (tall or otherwise) behind their beers, while the writer will try and paint a picture about what my impression is. I hope I have achieved what I set out to do, but that will be up to you to let me know.

I have broken the book into nine chapters: Amber; Bitter; IPA (in all its peacock-like variants); the family of lager beers; Pale Ale; Porter and Stout; speciality beers; strong beers; and low- and no-alcohol beers, a sector of beer that you wouldn't expect to read that much about until recently (this section highlights the leaps and bounds these kinds of beers have made in recent years). I have tried to broadly keep within the parameters of beer styles, but given the increasing fracture of some styles, especially that of IPA, you might find some cross-channel cooperation.

Each entry will have the brewery's website and information on how regular the beer is released (there is also a list of independent stockists at the end of the book, they all deserve your custom, especially as they, along with the breweries, kept us stocked with takeaway beers during the lockdowns).

One of the characteristics of contemporary beer is that many breweries have stepped away from the tradition of having a core range and instead concentrate on releasing a range of one-offs, a result perhaps of Generation Untapped's need for constant novelty. Some beers that I considered essential for the book might not be available, but I felt this gave a good impression of what the brewery brewed and would encourage the reader to search them out.

All I can say now is that this is a book for travel and exploration, for outdoor drinking and indoor contemplation. I hope you enjoy it and get to try as many of the beers within these pages as you can.

cheers

STORAGE AND SERVING TEMPERATURES

Beer is a food product and how it is stored affects its condition. Both bottled and canned beers should be kept at a cool temperature, ideally around 8–10°C, though lagers can go straight in the fridge, and not subject to extremes of heat (e.g., not stored next to radiators). Strong smells and direct sunlight should also be avoided. The latter can speed up the ageing of the beer, and if the beer is in either clear or green glass bottles (thankfully becoming much rarer) it will develop what is called a 'skunky' aroma, which is as unpleasant as it sounds. Beers with corks in them should be laid on their side to avoid cork leakage letting in oxygen. Those with metal crown caps should be stored upright. Bottle-conditioned beers should be kept still for at least 24 hours before serving and should never be shaken. Depending on how many bottles you are storing you may want to organise them by style and strength. Put the ones that are in for the long haul at the back, while the ones you want to drink soon go to the front. Some beers, usually over 8% ABV, age well with time, with a depth of flavour developing.

The temperature at which you drink your beer is very much a personal choice, but here are certain suggestions that could help enrich your drinking experience even more. Do remember, a beer served too cool is not a disaster as it will warm up and start releasing its precious aromatics; on the other hand a beer served too warm cannot be salvaged.

Serve lagers between 5–8°C with darker ones such as Märzen, Dunkel and Doppelbock towards the warmer end of the scale. Pale Ales are perfect between 7–9°C, as are IPAs. Store Stouts and Porters between 7–9°C, which is the same for strong beers, with DIPAs towards the lower end and Barley Wines higher; this also goes for Amber beers. For Bitter the traditional pub cellar temperature of 10–12°C is ideal, while with speciality beers serve between 7–12°C depending on the style.

BEST WITH ...

...cheese

Buxton Brewery · Axe Edge *(page 78)*
Cheddar Ales · Gorge Best *(page 50)*
Fallen Brewing · Chew Chew *(page 189)*
Lacons · Audit Ale *(page 259)*
Runaway Brewery · ESB *(page 62)*
Unbarred · Tropic Soda *(page 239)*

...seafood and fish

Adnams · Ghost Ship Alcohol Free *(page 134)*
Anspach & Hobday · The Sea Salt Chilli Stout *(page 178)*
Camden Town Brewery · Hells Lager *(page 110)*
Wild Horse Brewing · The Serpent and the Worm *(page 244)*
Windsor & Eton Brewery · Guardsman Best Bitter *(page 66)*
Yeastie Boys · Gunnamatta Earl Grey IPA *(page 102)*

...friends

Attic Brew · Mild *(page 18)*
Bristol Beer Factory · Clear Head *(page 137)*
DEYA Brewing · Best Foot Forward *(page 51)*
Lacada Brewery · East the Beast *(page 86)*
Lost and Grounded · No Rest for Dancers *(page 27)*
Triple Point Brewing · Žatec *(page 127)*

...a comfy armchair

Adnams · Tally-Ho *(page 250)*
Bohem Brewery · Amos *(page 107)*
Harviestoun Brewery · Wheesht *(page 139)*
Heaney Farmhouse Brewery · Irish Stout *(page 193)*
Orbit Brewery · Nico *(page 167)*
Tring Brewery · Death or Glory *(page 276)*

...Christmas Day

Coniston Brewery · Nº 9 Barley Wine *(page 253)*
Elgood's Brewery · Coolship Sour Ale *(page 222)*
Hammerton Brewery · Crunch *(page 223)*
Ramsgate Brewery · Gadds' Nº 5 *(page 60)*
Ridgeway Brewing · Imperial Barley Wine *(page 266)*
Thornbridge Brewery · Bracia *(page 273)*

...a bracing walk

71 Brewing · Outer Galactic *(page 104)*
Duration Beer · Turtles All The Way Down *(page 155)*
Elusive Brewing · Oregon Trail *(page 82)*
Geipel Brewing · Bock *(page 116)*
Harviestoun Brewery · Ola Dubh *(page 224)*
Theakston · Old Peculier *(page 37)*

AMBER

Whether Brown Ale,
Mild or Amber Ale,
you will find beers with
a more pronounced malt
accent in this chapter.

ATTIC BREW
Mild

3.8% Occasional

Stirchley, Birmingham
atticbrewco.com

Spend some time in the company of a classic Midlands beer style

We drink beer for a variety of reasons. It's the thirst quencher that spreads across the palate with the simplicity of the spoken word; it's the thoughtful quest for complexity that comes with a beer whose method of brewing has brought in layers of flavour that torment and taunt the tongue with the potency of pleasure. It is also the chatty, friendly companion with whom we like to spend time, secure in the knowledge that time spent in this company will be sociable and comfortable.

When approaching a glass of Attic's smooth-talking Mild it is the latter reason and sequence of thoughts that will bring the beer to our presence. It is a beer that you can drink several cans of, an easy-going beer that friends can enjoy without concern for the passage of time.

For brewery founder Oli Hurlow developing a Mild had always been an ambition: 'As a proud Birmingham brewery, we've always wanted to brew one. It's a style so intertwined with the beer culture of the Midlands and it has remained very relevant here, even if the style is drunk less. We wanted to do our bit to keep it in people's minds, because it deserves a place at the table.'

Mahogany in colour, there is a flurry of chocolate and sweet caramel on the nose with hints of hazelnut in the background. There is more of the same on the palate, with a low bitterness, that never dominates, or as Hurlow says, 'the end result is something that has plenty of complexity to interest the keen drinker, but after a couple of pints it just fades into the background to accompany good conversation – just as it's supposed to.'

Goes well with... The company of good friends and salted peanuts

BLACK ISLE BREWING
Red Kite

4.2%   Core

Munlochy, Ross and Cromarty, Scotland
blackislebrewery.com

Black Isle's debut beer
continues to shine

Beers change over time as tastes take different paths and breweries decide that the beer they once brewed at the start of its life needs to develop and grow as the years roll on by. Red Kite is no exception, having being first brewed by founder David Gladwin in 1998, when it was Black Isle's debut commercial brew – though Gladwin's original aim of using organic raw materials has remained the same.

'It was very different to its current incarnation,' he says, 'it had far more malt and fewer hops. What I wanted was what I got, a malt-driven beer with enough bittering hop character to take the edge off the sweetness. What the first brew was like I couldn't say, it was 23 years ago, but I dare say I was bitterly disappointed, because we all are when we brew a beer, aren't we? We are always striving for better. The time you think you've perfected it is the time to give up. Today's beer is more akin to a US Amber, it's still got that malt backbone, but is far more heavily hopped with Simcoe, Cascade and Palisade making up the hop profile.'

The current incarnation is dark amber in colour, with shades of malt and caramel rising from the glass alongside a delicate fruitiness, plus hints of chocolate and bourbon biscuit. The palate is in possession of a moderate sweetness, caramel softness and a hint of toffee, red fruit and light citrus before finishing dry alongside a subtle bitterness. Despite its relatively low alcoholic strength there is a generous warmth in the beer that makes it an engaging comfort on a cold winter's night.

Goes well with… Venison burger and game chips

BOXCAR BREWERY
Dark Mild

3.6% Occasional

Bethnal Green, London
boxcarbrewery.co.uk

A thoroughly modern Mild

Mild is the English beer style that refuses to die. It has been deemed unfashionable and – perhaps wrongly – seen as redolent of a past England featuring factory chimneys belching smoke, men in flat caps with cigarettes dangling like chains from their lips and women drinking port and lemon in the saloon bar. It is a stubborn creature though and this low-hopped, moderately alcoholic ale of a bygone age still remains a popular pint in pockets of the United Kingdom. A further sign of its slow, Lazarus-like resurrection is its emergence on the beer list of breweries whose activities usually involve a lot of juicy, hazy NEIPAs, with East London-based Boxcar getting a lot of notice for their Dark Mild, which is made every few months.

'Both our Bitter and Dark Mild took inspiration from New England IPA techniques for creating a softer, fuller beer in can and keg,' says brewery founder and head brewer Sam Dickison. 'They both contain oats and wheat, and rely heavily on our house yeast strain,

which we also use for our IPAs. I wanted to counteract the high carbonation and low temperature of keg, which can mask more subtle flavours.'

The result is a lush and full-bodied dark mahogany-coloured beer with plenty of chocolate, mocha coffee, caramel and hints of toffee on the nose. The palate provides more of the same, along with a restrained sweetness and a moderately dry finish. Dickison also hopes to produce a Double Dark Mild once a year, which is luxurious, rich and elegant. Mild – somehow – lives!

Goes well with… Sunday lunch of chicken and plenty of roast potatoes

BRICK BREWERY
Peckham Rye

4.7% Core

Peckham, London
brickbrewery.co.uk

A luscious Red Ale with
malted rye in the mix

Over in Bavaria a small group of breweries adds rye to some of the beers they make, which they then call *Roggenbier*. The ones I've tried have been delicious, and bring a spicy, earthy and bittersweet character to the glass. In the UK, if we think about rye it is American whiskey rather than beer that springs to mind, though a small but growing number of breweries are adding malted rye to their brewing box of tricks and Brick is one of them (though this is styled as a Red Ale rather than a *Roggenbier*).

For the brewery's co-founder Ian Stewart, having started the brewery in Peckham Rye, it was obvious that a beer playing on the name of the location had to be made. 'I like all types of beer,' he says, 'but a Red Ale has a bit of a special place for me. I remember drinking a fair amount of Killian's Irish Red when I lived in the US back in the late 80s and early 90s and I enjoyed the malty character of it. I remember cooking up the very first Rye on our original 1000-litre brew kit alongside Peckham Pils. I loved the colour of it and was pleased to pick up on the caramel malts and hop character.'

Pouring a smooth mahogany-red in colour, there are notes of caramel, wafer biscuits and orange on the nose, which brings to mind a particularly exotic, if boozy, afternoon tea. Each sip reveals more biscuit and orange alongside a luscious bittersweetness and a bracing dry and bitter finish.

Goes well with… A couple of chocolate digestives on a quiet Sunday afternoon

BROUGHTON ALES
Old Jock

6.7% Core

Biggar, South Lanarkshire, Scotland
broughtonales.co.uk

A rich and nutritious Wee Heavy

First brewed in 1980, a year after Broughton was founded, this is a superb example of the old Scottish beer standard, the 'Wee Heavy' (though the brewery has Scotch Ale on the label), which was a strong and nutritious ale that was often drunk with a whisky chaser, a case of malt meeting malt and seeing how each expression got on with the other. It is dark chestnut in colour, as impenetrably dark as the mind of a magician (and some might think that magic has something to do with the richness of the beer). The nose is a powerful punch of dark roasted malt, warming alcohol and fruitcake. On the palate each drop of the beer is equally potent, with a cavalcade of rich malt sweetness, hints of liquorice, the smooth warmth of alcohol and an easy-going bitterness in the finish. It is a beer that you take your time with, appreciate like a fine wine and then notice you have finished one bottle and might just take your time with another one.

'Old Jock was inspired by the Scottish brewing history of strong/Wee Heavy style beers,' says Broughton's managing director David McGowan, 'whilst the brand imagery encapsulated rugged Scotsmen who were famous for their honesty and bravery. There is a rumour that one of the founders of the brewery wanted to name one of his children "Jock" but instead opted for calling his new beer Old Jock. We have always felt that this is a beer to savour and enjoy at the end of the day.'

Goes well with… Roast lamb and mash

CUMBRIAN ALES
Grasmoor Dark Ale

4.3% Core

Loweswater, Cumbria
cumbrianales.com

A rich, dark mahogany ale whose home is the Cumbrian hills

All beers possess a sense of place, even if they have been produced in a bleak, post-modernist industrial unit just off a busy motorway. For Grasmoor Dark Ale, the sense of place is accompanied more by a lullaby than the roar of passing traffic, as it is brewed at the Kirkstile Inn in Loweswater, a place overlooked by the heart-fluttering views of Cumbrian hills.

Dark mahogany in colour, perhaps reminiscent of a moonless night spent flitting across the surrounding fells, there are warm, lush zephyrs of chocolate and caramel on the nose, as comforting and cosy as a winter's evening spent in front of a blazing log fire. There is more of this richness on the palate alongside a gentle bitterness that lingers in the finish.

'We were aiming for a dark beer that would use English malt and hops but would not be a Stout,' recalls managing director Roger Humphreys. 'It was one of the first beers we brewed at the Kirkstile Inn. The first brew tasted lovely but a little dry. We tweaked the level of crystal malt and this balanced

the beer beautifully and provided some sweetness and a hint of caramel. It will always remain the same. There isn't a large choice of dark beers in Cumbria and this has a good following.'

So when you pour this beer into your glass, whether you are in the centre of Nottingham or on the outskirts of Newton Abbot, think of its sense of place – the chill of the Cumbrian night, the looming shadows of the hills and the cheery light in the distance, which you call home, where a beer like this one is waiting.

Goes well with... A good book, in your favourite armchair on a cold night

ELGOOD'S BREWERY
Black Dog

3.6%   Core

Wisbech, Cambridgeshire
elgoods-brewery.co.uk

A Fenland classic

Fancy a drop of Dark Mild? This classic, traditional beer lost its dominance at the bar in the 1950s when drinkers decided that they wanted Bitter, for after all, that was what their bosses drank and of course they'd never had it so good. I imagine that the family owners of Elgood's, happily making their beer in the Fenland town of Wisbech, would have noticed a change in tempo in their pubs, and over the next couple of decades perhaps life for their traditional Dark Mild Black Dog might have become a little precarious. However, here it still remains, an award winner and a standard-bearer for this most neglected of beer styles. So pour yourself a glass of history.

Out of the bottle it pours reddish brown in colour, certainly dark, but maybe not as dark as a sinister Fenland moonless night when the hellhound Black Shuck might be abroad. There is a slight suggestion of roastiness on the nose, light and delicate, ingenious in its appeal to the senses. There are also hints of chocolate, caramel sweetness and dark fruits (ripe plums perhaps), all of which add a welcome complexity. On the palate there is more of the stone fruitiness, chocolate and roastiness, with a gentle bitterness before it finishes dry and fruity. There is character, taste and adventure in this beer, which demonstrates that sometimes you don't need a big boost of alcohol for a beer to slide its way into your heart.

Goes well with… A packet of pork scratchings and your favourite TV drama

FYNE ALES
Highlander

4.8% Core

Cairndow, Argyll and Bute, Scotland
fyneales.com

*Fyne's first beer has stood
the test of time*

Every beer has a story, from its motivation to inception to how it has changed or weathered the passage of years. Highlander is no different as we travel back to 2001 when Fyne Ales was set up by Jonny and Tuggy Delap, after returning from England to Glen Fyne in Argyll and Bute and setting up a farm. A brewery was installed and Highlander was the first beer to be brewed on 30 November, which of course is St Andrews Day; on the same day a consignment of Highland cattle also arrived, hence the name of the beer.

The inspiration for the taste and style of the beer was Gale's HSB, which Jonny Delap had enjoyed during the couple's time living in England. To appeal to local drinkers who mostly enjoyed pints of Heavy, however, the recipe was developed to be malt forward, with a complementary hop profile that added flavour without dominating.

The beer remains a constant part of Fyne's core range, a bridge between tradition and modernity, which marks the brewery out to be one of the most forward thinking in the UK. It is dark amber in colour and has a pronounced malt-centric nose with hints of toffee, the slightest whisper of chocolate, a brief flash of nuttiness and a faint suggestion of citrus in the background. There is more malt and toffee on the palate, alongside a gentle toastiness, followed by a shine of citrus that beams like a shy smile on the mid palate before it finishes bittersweet and bracingly dry.

Goes well with… A ripe Stilton and oatmeal biscuits

HOWLING HOPS
We Buy Teeth

5.5% Occasional

Hackney Wick, London
howlinghops.co.uk

A rich and full-flavoured
American-style Brown Ale

Let's get the curious name of the beer out of the way first. Even though its name sounds like it came about after an evening's session in the taproom, its origins are more down to earth. 'I think Pete (brewery owner) imagined "WE BUY TEETH" being on a poster bill layers and layers beneath the ones covering the walls of Hackney now,' says the brewery's marketing manager Chris Hall. 'If you kept peeling them off eventually you'd find the weird Victoriana beneath. A sort of Dickensian Cash4Gold of its time!'

Whether this is true or not, we do know that We Buy Teeth is an American-style Brown Ale, a far cry from the traditionally sweetish style that was the norm once upon a time. This kind of Brown Ale is robust and well-hopped, turning its back on sweetness and the use of crystal malt that was common in more traditional versions of the style.

It certainly pours its colour, coming out as dark, opaque chestnut, though there are crimson tints at the edges on which sits a crema-coloured head of foam. On the nose there are notes of chocolate, nuts (hazelnuts?), a rye-like spiciness (though no rye is used), a herbal lemoniness and even a hint of black pepper. Each swig reveals more chocolate, caramel, pine/resin with a background of citrus and tropical fruit. It is spicy and peppery, bittersweet and dry in the finish, possessed of a full mouthfeel; chewy, virtuous and a big hitter of a beer, even though it is only 5.5%. Savour this rich and full-flavoured version of the style as the aromatics of the hops tumble out of the glass like acrobats in search of teeth to buy.

Goes well with... Chicken satay

LOST AND GROUNDED
No Rest For Dancers

6.2% Core

Bristol
lostandgrounded.co.uk

A beer with which to relax and ponder on life

The original inspiration for this sleek beast of a beer, which the brewery styles as a Red Ale, was to re-imagine a Belgian-style Dubbel and then boost it with Chinook and Mosaic. It was also given a huge amount of specialty malts as well as dextrose, a neutral sugar that helps to lighten the body. According to brewery co-founder Alex Troncoso, 'this beer formed part of our opening line-up and it was a revelation of how one could carefully use Belgian yeast to craft all manner of styles, and have them appeal to drinkers who typically don't explore that particular beer culture. We have great memories watching typical ale drinkers in our taproom loving the beer, and probably not realising the Belgian notes in its DNA.'

There is a vivid, hop-charged nose about this dark-chestnut beer, along with plenty of toasted malt (brown bread crust almost), and rich citrus marmalade; there is also an earthiness (think woodiness, barnyard, red Burgundy, cherry even) in the background. This is a beer where complexity rules on the nose. The flavours are robust, rugged even, with sticky, resiny hop, a toastiness, a sweetness and biscuity graininess, alongside citrus notes and a smoothness with the dryness in the finish somehow reminiscent of the aridity of crispbread or a cracker.

'This is a great beer to relax with and ponder life and all of its glory,' says Troncoso. 'When one embarks on an epic journey of creating something special, there is literally no time to rest until the book is written. There's a happiness and freedom in this beer in knowing that sometimes rules are meant to be broken.'

Goes well with... Sitting in the garden with friends

MANCHESTER UNION BREWERY
Alt Beer

4.5% Occasional

Manchester
manchesterunionbrewery.com

*Manchester meets Düsseldorf
and all goes well*

Pint of lager? As yellow as a Van Gogh sunflower, and as fizzy and as cold as a bath in well-chilled lemonade. A beer as shy of taste and flavour as Donald Trump is of humility. Let's reverse this: the reality of lager is of a diverse family of beer styles, ranging from the classic Czech Pilsner to the powerful Doppelbock and not forgetting the esoteric smoke-bomb of Bamberg's Rauchbier. Furthermore, just like a family, these beers are diverse and varied, with some as dark as despair and others as hoppy as an overgrown millennial on a pogo stick.

Then there is Alt, whose home is Düsseldorf and which is lagered, but here is the crucial difference – a top-fermenting yeast is used, so you could argue that an Alt is a hybrid. However, whatever the theological debates, Manchester Union's Alt is a fine and thoroughbred beer.

'At Manchester Union Brewery, we want to showcase a huge variety of flavours within the lager category and enjoy challenging the perception of lager as a light tasting beer,' says sales director and co-founder Will Evans. 'While we appreciate this beer is more a lager/ale hybrid we want the drinker to actually think about lager while drinking it.'

Amber with a slight nod to crimson, there is a delicate sonata of caramel sweetness on the nose, which aligns itself willingly with a citrus fruitiness. There is more light citrus fruitiness on the palate, while a caramel sweetness comes in midway before leading to a refreshingly bitter finish that engages and sets you up for another swig.

Goes well with... A well-ripened Cheddar

NEPTUNE BREWERY
Sirens Song

5.2% Seasonal

Liverpool
neptunebrewery.com

*A subtly sweet, bracingly dry
and full-bodied gem of a beer*

There's an element of a glorious accident about the genesis of this beer as Neptune co-founder Julie O'Grady explains: 'It was brewed in collaboration with a Montana-based brewery called Neptune's Brewery after we kept being accidentally tagged in to each others' social media, so eventually conversations started up on how it would be great to do a collaboration sometime. Twelve months later the US outfit messaged to say they were visiting the UK in early 2020, which fitted perfectly with our fifth birthday. We discussed what beer to brew, and it was decided one of their best sellers, Siren Song, would be a great fit, so we tweaked the recipe to suit us.'

The American Siren Song uses honey and rye in the mix, but the Merseysiders' Sirens Song avoids honey, substituting it with a malted barley variety called honey malt alongside the rye, which O'Grady believes gives it, 'the right amount from the malts. It is not too sweet, very moreish and highly drinkable'.

Sleek red-amber in colour, there is a soft honey note and rye bread spiciness on the nose, almost reminiscent of breakfast toast spread with honey. On the palate there is a subtle sweetness, rye spiciness, suggestions of milk chocolate and a full-bodied mouthfeel. The finish is bracingly dry alongside more rye spiciness and a delicious bittersweetness. There is an ease about the way the beer slips down. It is a big flavoured beer, muscular, with a general spiciness that is almost like a mixture of pepper, coriander, and possibly even fennel and clove, while the rye gives a sandpaper dryness in the finish. A beer that deserves your complete attention and which grows in character as you drink it.

Goes well with… A salt beef sandwich with gherkins on the side

THE PARK BREWERY
Isabella

4.3% Occasional

Kingston upon Thames, London
theparkbrewery.com

*A beer that is ideal for
drinking in the great outdoors*

As you might guess, the sylvan surroundings of the great outdoors has rather a large part to play in the naming of this husband-and-wife run brewery. The park in question is Richmond, in south-west London, which is close to the brewery's home in Kingston upon Thames. It also provides inspiration and emotional sustenance for the names of its beers as well. This American-style Brown Ale (where the traditional sweetness of an English Brown Ale is dialled down to be replaced by a blast of citrus fruitiness courtesy of US hops) is named after Isabella Plantation, a 40-acre woodland garden set within a Victorian plantation dating from the 1830s. I can just imagine a place where the whisper of a breeze glides through a glade of trees and the sound of morning birdsong acts as a cool relaxing hand on the brow.

'It's a beer that's close to my heart and a style I now love,' says co-founder Josh Kearns. 'It was inspired by a beer made by the much-missed Mad Hatter brewery back in 2016, Something About Words. This is my take on it.'

And after contemplation in the great outdoors, why not pour yourself a glass of Isabella? Dark amber in colour, it has aromas of caramel, bourbon biscuit, Nutella and citrus, all of which entice you deeper into the beer's embrace. The palate is crisp and biscuity, with more caramel, plus hints of hazelnut, mocha coffee, a gentle toastiness and a delicate citrusy fruitiness. The finish is long, dry and bittersweet and exceptionally appetising with hints of caramel and chocolate in the ascendancy. Just like its woodland namesake, this is an occasion you should take time in enjoying.

Goes well with... A quiet and reflective time spent in a sunny woodland glade

PILOT BEER
Vienna Pale

4.6%   Core

Edinburgh, Scotland
pilotbeer.co.uk

*A well-balanced and
sessionable ale-lager hybrid*

Each beer has an origin story, whether it was created by accident or deliberation. For Pilot's ale-lager hybrid Vienna Pale, the story pre-dates the formation of the brewery, being a survivor of co-founder and brewer Patrick Jones' home-brewing days.

'My best mate was getting married and wanted to brew a beer for table favours,' he recalls. 'He asked me if I could do something like Brooklyn Lager, but not having chilled FVs on the home-brew setup we decided to go with an ale yeast, a fairly classic Vienna lager malt base, Saaz in the dry hop for noble character, together with a wee bit of Cascade and Citra just to lift it a bit.

'The very first brew on the home-brew kit was magic, just me and my best mate hanging out. Similarly, drinking it at the wedding of my two greatest friends was also magic. The first brew on the full-scale kit, our first ever brew on the secondhand brew kit we'd bought and cobbled together, was far from magic. Let's just say we learned a lot and the beer is better now.'

Light amber in colour, there is a malt-fringed sweetness about the nose, with sparkles of tropical fruit and citrus also in the mix. On the palate it is clean and crisp with light citrus, a brush of honeyed malt sweetness and a gentle toastiness, before a bittersweetness takes over, leading to a biscuity, dry finish.

'The drinker should just expect a really good pint,' says Jones. 'All those words that seem quaint and old fashioned now, like balanced and sessionable. It's a beer that isn't meant to blow your socks off, it's meant to be there for the next pint, and the next.'

Goes well with... A hearty dish of cocido with plenty of chorizo

POPPYLAND BREWERY
Sweet Chestnut Ale

6.7% Core

Cromer, Norfolk
poppylandbrewery.com

*A bold, malt-driven beer
with sweet chestnuts added*

You come to Cromer to experience this
windswept part of north Norfolk and
sample the delicious crabs. You also
come to Cromer to enjoy the beers of
Poppyland, which is located in part of
a former garage near the town centre
(which is why there is a fascia board on
the front saying 'Ales Gas n Lager').

Run by Dave Cornell since 2019,
when he bought the business from
founder Martin Warren, this small
outfit produces a variety of intriguing
beers that feature equally intriguing
ingredients. The award-winning Sweet
Chestnut Ale is one of these outliers, a
boldly flavoured, malt-driven beer that
has sweet chestnuts added in the mix.

According to Cornell, the idea came
about when 'we were some months
away from Christmas and the thought
of a beer containing sweet chestnuts
roasted over an open brazier on a cold
winter's afternoon appealed to our
sense of a traditional Christmas beer.
On developing the recipe we tried
several Italian chestnut beers which
convinced us we were on the right track

for something different. The first brew
was delightful, we hit the starting original
gravity we were aiming for, the colour
was spot on and the nose was divine.'

Densely dark amber in colour,
this has sweet barley, ripe dark fruit
and chestnut on the nose, the latter
conjuring up images of glowing braziers
on long-ago London street corners.
On the palate there is a fruitcake
sweetness, perhaps currants and raisins
in a generous Christmas cake, balanced
by a light earthiness and a creamy
mouthfeel followed by a lingering dry
finish. A beer with which to toast your
good fortune come Christmas, or any
time of the year for that matter.

Goes well with… A bowl of freshly roasted chestnuts and a pinch of salt

PURPLE MOOSE
Dark Side of the Moose

4.6%   Core

Porthmadog, North Wales
purplemoose.co.uk

*A rich, dark Bitter that
sings with malt character*

As you might have guessed from this beer's name, brewery founder Lawrence Washington is a Pink Floyd fan. It might be somewhat of a painful pun perhaps, but there's no doubting the thoughtful and exemplary nature of this rich, dark Bitter (or is it an Amber?) with its complex aromatic grid of grain, roast barley and citrus fruit, followed by a blast of coffee beans, smoke, caramel, rich citrusy fruitiness on the palate and finally ending its sojourn in the sun with a dry finish in which the flavour of fruit gums briefly appears.

The genesis of this beer began in Washington's mother's kitchen, when he began home brewing and developed a liking for dark ales and Bitters of all strengths. Over the years, he kept tweaking the recipe for one mid-strength dark Bitter with a rich malt character, which eventually became Dark Side when brewed for the first time in 2005.

'I can recall being enthralled by the deep, malty aromas coming from the beautiful dark wort as it ran through the under-back on its way from the mash tun to the copper,' says Washington, 'it is something which still inspires my senses today. It has also won the most prestigious and highest number of awards, by far, of all of our beers we've ever produced.'

Purple Moose make their beers in the town of Porthmadog, which lies in the shadow of Snowdonia, with the brewery diagonally opposite a chapel, a location that always makes me think of the irony of the twin attractions of pub and pulpit that, from the evidence of my family history, often used to get the Welsh in such a lather.

Goes well with... Toasted and well-buttered Bara Brith

ROUND CORNER BREWING
Mackinaw

5.4% Core

Melton Mowbray, Leicestershire
roundcornerbrewing.com

*Sessionable American-style
Brown Ale named after a textile*

First a bit of textile history: the name of
this rugged American-style Brown Ale is
a reference to a Michigan town famous
for producing a thick, felt-like cloth that
is similar to Melton cloth, which was
used to make that ubiquitous fashion
statement, the donkey jacket. Oh, and
Melton is where Round Corner is based.
There's nothing donkey-like about
the beer though, as it shines and
gleams, chestnut-amber in the glass,
beneath a firm, off-white head of
foam. There's a perfectly balanced
bustle of caramel, chocolate, a rich
biscuitiness and dried fruit on the
nose, which continues onto the palate
before its dry and bittersweet finish.

'We had produced an Imperial Brown
Ale for a customer, which they loved and
then asked us to make a more sessionable
version as a one-off,' says co-founder
and head brewer Colin Paige. 'It has not
been out of production since. We love
Brown Ales and the American-style is
one we love. They tend to be a little more
hoppy and slightly higher in alcohol than
UK Brown Ales. We loved the thought
of taking an American iteration of a UK
style and bringing it back home, which
is what the name Mackinaw conveys.

'We loved it right from the start.
It is a smoothly balanced beer, brown
in colour but not in personality, and
has a great amount of appeal across
the spectrum of drinkers. We think
the balanced hoppiness and malt
characters make it simultaneously
complex yet very drinkable.'

Goes well with... A Melton Mowbray pork pie

RUDGATE BREWERY
Ruby Mild

4.4%   Core

Tockwith, North Yorkshire
rudgatebrewery.co.uk

An appetising Yorkshire Mild with a surprisingly bitter finish

Mild is the beer style that can confound, spread confusion and see minds struggling to make themselves up. It's supposed to be dark and weak right? Yes, it is, but then there are several light-coloured Milds, and I was once told by Timothy Taylor's head brewer Andrew Leman that, 'light Milds were traditional in the Pennine area'. As for the strength, there are also strong Milds from the likes of Sarah Hughes and Boxcar, whose traditional Mild has been joined by a Double Mild.

Then there is the issue of the hopping rate. Back in 2009, York-based Rudgate's Ruby Mild became the Champion Beer of Britain, a rare change from the usual array of Golden Ales that kept winning throughout that decade. However, not everyone was happy. According to a couple of letter writers to CAMRA's *What's Brewing*, Ruby Mild was a hoppier Mild than what they were used to. On the other hand, you could fire a counter-argument back that Mild, like every other beer style, is a canvas upon which the brewer can make their own interpretation, which is what Rudgate's brewers did.

Whatever the controversy, Ruby Mild is certainly in the right colour zone, a very deep reddish/ruby brown, which gleams like a fiery beacon in the glass. On the nose there is mocha, chocolate and a nuttiness that could hint at hazelnut. And yes, when tasted there is a bitterness in the finish alongside an appetising dryness, but before that there is a light roastiness, sweet toffee, caramel, a medium-bodied mouthfeel before returning to that bitterness that Mild is not supposed to have. Confounding and captivating and not for the mild-mannered perhaps?

Goes well with... A mid-afternoon slice of parkin

SIMPLE THINGS FERMENTATIONS
No 8 Scottish Export

5.5% Seasonal

Glasgow, Scotland
simplethingsfermentations.com

A soothing yet punchy Scottish Export with spruce tips in the mix

Sometimes it pays to turn your whole life around and take a totally different path, which is what Phil Sisson did in 2016 when he quit a music industry job in London and moved north to Edinburgh to take a Masters in brewing at Heriot-Watt University. Two years at Harviestoun followed until he set up Simple Things Fermentation in 2019 in Glasgow, motivated to 'produce beer that celebrates the variety of possibilities within brewing, and for that to have at least a loose sense of place. It's not good to define yourself by what you are not, but I don't see any point in trying to be another Scottish brewery that turns out US-style beers, when there are already plenty of people making a great job of that and so many other fabulous styles, ingredients and processes to delve into.'

Scottish Export is a good example of what he is trying to do, taking a beer style that is often seen as bland and overly sweet and giving it some care and attention to change people's perception of it. Spruce tips are also added to the mix, an ingredient Sisson had brewed

with before and which are also amply available in and around Glasgow. 'Because it's a fairly malty style,' he says, 'the spruce tips are just a background note really but they add a level of complexity and lift the beer up a notch.'

Chestnut-brown in colour, there is the sweetness of malt on the nose, while the palate has a smooth and creamy malt-driven character with suggestions of graininess, an earthiness and citrus fruitiness. Soothing but yet also punchy in its mouthfeel, there is crisp dryness in the finish all of which make this a temptation of a beer.

Goes well with… Grilled lemon chicken

THEAKSTON
Old Peculier

5.6%   Core

Masham, North Yorkshire
theakstons.co.uk

Classic English ale with its roots in the 19th century

Old Peculier is one of those English ales that even the most dedicated followers of the latest in beer fashions might have heard of, even if only to ask what a Peculier is (apparently it's something to do with a medieval ecclesiastical court in the beer's home town of Masham in North Yorkshire). During the 1970s when CAMRA emerged and focused its members' energies on cask beer, Old Peculier was one of the mainstays of the Campaign, a beer whose 5.6% strength made it seem like a titan on the bar-top and to be treated with the utmost respect, though its origins are said to go back to the late 19th century where the brewery believes the name might have referred to a stock ale, which was commonly made then.

In the glass it gleams with a mahogany-coloured sleekness beneath an ample, snow-white collar of foam. On the nose there is caramel, toffee and a rich sense of biscuitiness, while its full-bodied surge of flavour brings up more toffee and caramel, alongside a luscious fruitiness and a muscular bitterness that perks up the palate in anticipation of another sip. It's an atmospheric beer, a beer that can conjure up visions of sitting by the fireside while the weather does its worst outside; or maybe it should be a gracious companion to a slice of Wensleydale and fruit cake. Whichever way you drink it, this is a beer that gives you faith in the virtues and visions of greatness that good beer can bring.

Goes well with… A hearty toad in the hole on an autumnal Sunday afternoon

TINY REBEL
Cwtch

4.6% Core

Newport, South Wales
tinyrebel.co.uk

*Award-winning Red Ale
with a bouncy drinkability*

Let's get the meaning of the beer's name out of the way first. *Cwtch* is Welsh for a cuddle or a hug and is pronounced 'butch', but with a C. It's one of those words that most people born in Wales will have heard, especially when they were young. It's an affectionate word, an endearing one, a word that connects people. Beer is also about connections between people, those sharing moments, the clink of glasses topped with foaming pints and the gasps of appreciation as it makes its impression on the palate. No wonder Dylan Thomas wrote, 'I liked the taste of beer'. He could have been writing about Cwtch, Tiny Rebel's award-winning Red Ale, which won Champion Beer of Britain in 2015.

'We're super proud of being Welsh,' says Tiny Rebel co-founder Bradley Cummings, 'but we never wanted Tiny Rebel to be all about dragons, daffodils and pretty basic traditional beer. So if there was one beer that was going to have a hint of Welshness to it then it was going to be Cwtch. That naturally led us to a beer that would be red in colour, while the abv came

from us wanting this to be sessionable. We wanted to blend traditional with craft and that led us to a flavour profile of a really malty and caramel-like backbone injected with citrus kick that would come from the Citra hop.'

Reddish-amber in colour, there are heady flights of caramel and joyous citrus mingling on the nose, with more of this collaboration on the palate, creating a bouncy drinkability, which is as harmonic as a Valleys choir, while the delicate bitterness in the finish tingles the throat and invites you to take another swig.

Goes well with… Watching Wales win their next rugby Grand Slam

WESTERHAM BREWERY
Audit Ale

6.2% Regular, part of the brewery's Heritage Range

Westerham, Kent
westerhambrewery.co.uk

Masterful recreation of a beer style once brewed for Oxbridge colleges

Along with Lacon's Brewery in Great Yarmouth (*see page 259*), Westerham is unique in that it also produces an Audit Ale, a beer that historically was especially brewed for Oxbridge colleges when it came to produce the annual audit. An idle thought: you would hope that the auditors would have laid off the specially brewed ale until they had done their work otherwise mistakes might have been made.

Anyway, back to the beer. Westerham's version is based on the Audit Ale that the Black Eagle Brewery (based in Westerham, closed in 1965) made in 1938, using the same ingredients and having the same strength, though technical changes in brewing since the 1930s would mean that the modern beer would only have a slight resemblance to the original.

Tawny-copper in colour, there are bold aromatics of stewed fruit (dark plums perhaps?) on the nose, with the sweetness of barley and hints of almond, Bakewell tart and a tannic-like woodiness in the background all joining in the fun. Naturally, this complex and fascinating brush of aromatics gets the appetite going and makes you impatient to take a taste. On the palate there is a restrained vinous-like sweetness (suggestive of port), raisins and currants steeped in booze, a whisper of chocolate, a hint of banana, with all of these components successfully integrating and working together in the beer. The finish is dry, but also initially weighty before it becomes dry and bitter and descends in an easy-going finish of barley sweetness. Pour yourself a glass of this fine and eloquent beer next time you do your accounts and celebrate a little-known but fascinating footnote in British brewing.

Goes well with… A well matured chunk of Stilton cheese with plum chutney on the side

BITTER

Feeling like a Bitter?
This is the chapter
where the great
British beer style goes
under the spotlight.

ABBEYDALE BREWERY
Daily Bread

3.8% Core

Sheffield
abbeydalebrewery.co.uk

An invigorating and insightful traditional Bitter

If we think about the word 'bitter', we think of bitter people and the bitterness that encases them like a shroud, the bitter coldness of a winter's day when the trumpet blast of spring seems far away, or maybe it is the bitter truth of a revelation that wrecks relationships. On the other hand, we could think about bitter in the context of the socially blessed beer that is Bitter, the beer that acts as a social glue for friendships as well as strangers who briefly become friends. Our Daily Bread even, which is how Abbeydale's traditional Bitter came to be born.

'It was very much created to fulfil a particular aim,' says Abbeydale's sales director Dan Baxter, 'which was that of converting the John Smith's drinkers in our pub, the Rising Sun, when we acquired it in 2005. So it was designed as a traditional and straightforward Bitter, but one which was still lovingly crafted by an independent business. It came into being as a result of extensive quizzing of our new regulars and the recipe was built from their feedback.

There wasn't much enthusiasm for brewing a Bitter initially, so Pat (Morton, founder) snuck in on a Sunday to create it for the first time! It's since become a beer the team has a great fondness for.'

Light brown in colour, there is caramel and a lightly toasted, smooth-talking breadiness on the nose. On the palate it is crisp, biscuity, soothing in its caramel note, refreshed by a mid-palate hint of citrus and a light pepperiness, before sliding into a dry and bitter finish that clangs on and on like an old-time fire engine ringing its way to an incident.

Goes well with... A Waterall Brothers pork pie from their stall at Sheffield's Moor Market

ACORN BREWERY
Barnsley Bitter

3.8%   Core

Barnsley, South Yorkshire
acorn-brewery.co.uk

*Full-bodied, copper-coloured,
old-school masterpiece*

When Barnsley Brewery was closed by Courage in the mid-1970s, local beer-lovers, including TV chat show host Michael Parkinson, were aghast at the loss of what was by all accounts a notably characterful Best Bitter. However, all was not lost and if we fast forward to 2003 here come Dave and Judi Hughes with the foundation of Acorn Brewery and the use of the original Barnsley Brewery yeast strain to resurrect the kind of Bitter that Yorkshire has always been famous for.

Using the classic malt variety Maris Otter and opting for English hops, the result is a gleaming, well-polished, copper-coloured masterpiece that if it were a trophy would easily take pride of place on any self-respecting mantlepiece. This is a full-bodied, old-school beer with a rich, malt-flecked flurry of notes on the nose, which are joined by hints of toffee, a light and divine roastiness as well as fleeting suggestions of chocolate and citrus. Each swig, for this is a beer to drink deeply rather than approach with an undernourished sense of timidity, unveils waves of more rich malt, toffee, biscuity graininess and an undercurrent of light citrus before an intensely bitter finish that has the palate asking for more.

It goes without saying that this is a beer best drunk in the company of friends, perhaps in your front room with the telly on; a social beer that will accompany the to and fro of conversation as you roar your football team on and wonder why so much money was paid for a so-called striker who couldn't hit a barn door never mind the back of the net.

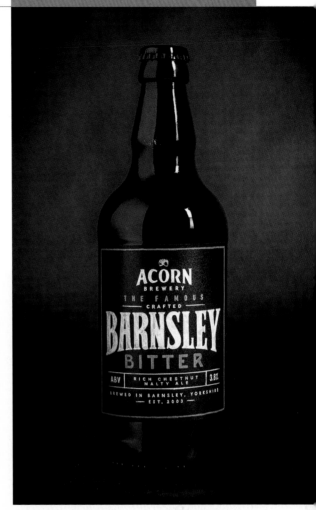

Goes well with... What else but a grilled Barnsley chop and mushy peas

ADNAMS
Southwold Bitter

4.1% Core

Southwold, Suffolk
adnams.co.uk

Superlative bottled version of Adnams' mighty Bitter

Even though the multi-monikered Irish writer and poet Flann O'Brien had it that a pint of plain (Porter) was 'your only man' when things went wrong, you could say the same thing for a pint of Bitter. When it is at its height of pure quality it's a reviving, chattering beer in the glass, a friend for the night, a sight that is wonderful to behold. I have often found the same thing when contemplating a glass of Adnams' superlative bottled version of its mighty Bitter, a beer that lifts the day's toil and trouble and dumps it in the North Sea, alongside which this iconic brewery produces its beers in the popular seaside bolthole of Southwold.

First brewed at the start of the swinging Sixties, this is a beer that makes no bones of its use of those classic English hop varieties, Fuggle and Golding, while its spine of malt is grown and malted in East Anglia, an area the Romans once called the granary of the province of Britain. It is chestnut brown in colour and its nose pulsates with a ripe and rich expression of malt, alongside the citrusy and earthy muscularity of the hops. On the palate, there is a restrained biscuity sweetness, a whisper of caramel, the murmur of citrus, followed by a delightful bittersweetness before it all tumbles down into a bracingly dry finish that speaks glowingly of a fun night with friends, whether sitting in the garden with or sharing stories round the dinner table.

Goes well with… Order in some fish and chips, a partnership that would entice Odin himself down from Valhalla

ANSPACH & HOBDAY
The Ordinary Bitter

3.7% Core

Croydon, Greater London
anspachandhobday.com

A far from ordinary classic Bitter

It's always a bit odd when you see a beer being described as Ordinary. It's as if the brewers using the word were somewhat shy in pushing their beer into the spotlight, and hope that by using Ordinary they will not be accused of being showy or arrogant. On the other hand, when a Bitter is as well made as Anspach & Hobday's, you can just ignore the use of the Ordinary prefix and marvel at the character of the liquid in the can.

Starting off in 2013 in a railway arch on the Bermondsey Brewing Mile (where they still have their taproom), Anspach & Hobday now make their superlative beers in a purpose-built facility in the romantic surroundings of Croydon. However, their move away from the throbbing heart of London's frenetic beer scene hasn't dampened their ardour or caused a dip in the quality of beers such as The IPA, The Porter and this easy-drinking, simply constructed version of one of the mainstay styles of British beer.

As soon as you have popped the can, be prepared to pour a beer that has a lovely gleam of copper, from which suggestions of caramel, biscuity graininess and pine drift up into the air before you dive straight into the glass. There is more caramel and biscuitiness on the palate alongside a light citrus caress before it plunges into a bold and bitter finish accompanied by a lingering dryness. At 3.7% it's also low enough in alcohol for you to enjoy several cans of without falling into bad company.

Goes well with… Mature Cheddar and a couple of slices of well-buttered, freshly baked artisanal farmhouse bread

BATEMANS
Victory Ale

6%      Core

Wainfleet All Saints, Lincolnshire
bateman.co.uk

*A beer pulsating with a strong
sense of its own character*

The landscape through which the train rattles its way across eastern Lincolnshire to Wainfleet, home of Batemans, is flat, as if a giant had come along with an electric iron and decided to smooth out any contours that got in its way. That done, another giant then came along and stitched this land with channels of water, dropped in fields and hedge lines and clumps of woodland, and as an afterthought added villages with their pillars of church towers. Did this imaginary giant, when it passed through Wainfleet, also drop in the windmill that is home to Batemans? Depends if you believe in giants.

On the other hand, you could argue that this open, flat landscape with its big skies engenders a sense of freedom, and when it comes to brewing, this freedom is evident in the glorious stubbornness that Batemans demonstrate when it comes to their core range of beers. Yes, there are coffee Porters and fruity things elsewhere, but with Victory Ale you are in the presence of a beer that pulsates with a strong sense of its own character.

It is light amber in colour and there are suggestions of the sweet umami of toffee, the rampart of nuttiness and the muscle of an earthy hoppiness with the shadow of citrus fruitiness in the background. On the palate I spy a breadiness, more toffee and light citrus before it descends into a finish that combines bitterness, sweetness and dryness, with all of these constituent parts creating a chewy, vociferous beer that is the ideal metaphor for the openness and potency of the landscape in which it is brewed.

Goes well with… A mixed grill (remember them?) and make sure you have some black pudding next to the baked beans

BATHAMS
Best Bitter

4.3% Core

Brierley Hill, West Midlands
bathams.co.uk

Classic Black Country Best Bitter

Whether you are in the Outer Hebrides or in the middle of London, a single bottle of Bathams Best Bitter will have the power to transport you straight to the heartland of Black Country drinking, where pale-coloured Bitters with a sugary sweetness from the likes of Bathams and Holden's still fly a precarious flag for regional beer tastes.

First brewed in 1954 and still at the heart of the brewery's identity, this is the only Bathams beer to be bottled, but it will still manage to give you an idea of the company's approach to making beer, even if you have never ever been anywhere near the Black Country. It is straw-gold in colour, and there are delicate hints of caramel, a soft breadiness and a suggestion of freshly cut grass on the nose, while the mouthfeel is sprightly with a brief touch of malt sweetness at the start alongside a gentle floral note. It finishes with a lingering bitterness and cream cracker-like dryness, and before you know where you are it is time to take another refreshing gulp.

This is very much a beer that has its own fan club amongst aficionados, such as Beavertown founder Logan Plant, who once told me about his time growing up in the Midlands and how he was 'dragged from Banks' to Bathams' pubs as a youth. The classic Black Country Bitter got me at about 18.' It is even said that the brewery's Neck Oil was originally based on Bathams Best Bitter before it became an American Pale Ale.

Goes well with... Pork scratchings, from the Black Country, naturally

BLACK SHEEP BREWERY
Ale

4.4% Core

Masham, North Yorkshire
blacksheepbrewery.com

Yorkshire in a glass

For a long time I resisted the lure of
Black Sheep's Ale, but then finally in
2007 I really understood and fell for the
beautifully wrought lattice-work of malt
and hops. It was, I thought, yet another
great expression of an English Bitter, to
be ranked alongside another favourite,
that of Adnams. This is a beer that has
a heft and weight on the palate, a beer to
be considered and celebrated, with its
bittersweetness, bitterness and dryness.

Black Sheep was famously set up
by Paul Theakston in Masham in the
early 1990s when the family brewery
Theakston's was sold, hence the black
sheep. Ale is one of the brewery's flagship
beers, which, as Theakston recalls,
'was about being a proper Yorkshire ale
brewed in a traditional way using the
best possible ingredients we could lay
our hands on – whole flower English
hops, Maris Otter malted barley and
water from our own source. We also
knew that our Yorkshire Square
fermentation system would give the
beer an interesting flavour angle.

'The beer should speak (or shout)
Yorkshire to you. Its taste is in the best
tradition of a Yorkshire ale – so that is a
lovely sweetness on first taste, with rich
body and the fruity aromas of Golding
hops, which runs through into a crisp
and dry refreshing finish. The dryness
keeps you thirsty and wanting more!
It's actually quite a bitter beer, but the
sweetness of the malt masks this. In
other words it's beautifully balanced.'

And sometimes all we want in the
beer that we drink is that sense of
balance on the palate.

Goes well with... A chunk of artisanal Wensleydale cheese and a couple of slices of Yorkshire parkin

BOXCAR + MILLS BREWING
Best Bitter

4.6%   Occasional

Bethnal Green, London
boxcarbrewery.co.uk

Fascinating collaboration that sings like a siren in the glass

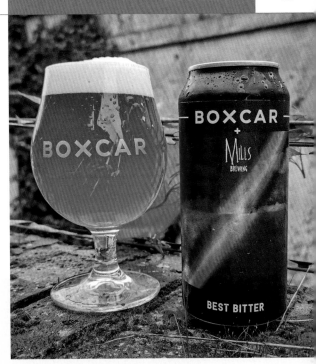

What does it mean to collaborate? One version is collaborating with an enemy, as Marshal Petain and Vidkun Quisling leap to the front of the queue and remind us of one of the darkest patches of 20th-century European history. On the other hand, the idea of collaboration is about the magnificence of like-minded people working together to create music, art, buildings and, of course, beer.

Some might see brewing collaboration as a commercial gimmick, the craft beer world looking in the mirror and preening itself like Bowie in his Thin White Duke period and liking what they see. On the other hand, I see it as the positive sign of an alliance between similar souls who are interested in experiencing what happens when they brew together.

When East London's Boxcar got together with rural-based Mills Brewing to produce a Best Bitter, there was a definite sense of intrigue as to what the two breweries would come up with. For a start, they chose one of the most traditional of beer styles, which might have surprised a lot of people as Boxcar specialise in juicy, hazy pales and Jonny Mills is a wizard at mixed fermentation (his Sat on Rhubarb Sour was exceptional).

'Jonny helped formulate the exact recipe of the Best Bitter with his experience in brewing the style,' says Boxcar's Sam Dickison. 'It is fruity and spicy from the yeast and hops. The Golden Promise malt provides a lot of biscuit and we use crystal malt to increase the complexity of sugary flavours. We love modern New England IPAs, but naturally as beer lovers we're passionate about the more traditional styles, too. I love classical music and also love drum 'n' bass. Beer shouldn't have to be any different.'

This is definitely a beer that will be occasionally produced but it is worth looking out for.

Goes well with… Slow-cooked beef brisket and plenty of roast potatoes

CHEDDAR ALES
Gorge Best

4% Core

Cheddar, North Somerset
cheddarales.co.uk

*A philosophical search for
the meaning of Best Bitter*

Sometimes the question has to be asked: what on earth is a Best Bitter? We have Bitter, Best Bitter, Premium Bitter and Strong Bitter, but the term Best Bitter has always puzzled me. Does it mean that any brewery who dubs one of their beers a Best Bitter is saying that every other Bitter they brew is sub-standard? Such is the intellectual curiosity that beer can induce.

In the course of my search for the meaning of Best Bitter, I decided to try Cheddar Ales' Gorge Best, which has the words 'Best Bitter' emblazoned on its label. According to brewery founder and managing director Jem Ham, he developed the beer in 2005 with a view to improving on other local Best Bitters.

'I sought to increase both malt flavour by using a variety of kilned malts alongside the usual pale malt base,' he says, 'and an overall increase in mouthfeel by building the hop profile through stage-by-stage introductions rather than the more traditional "hops for bitterness at the start of boil followed by hops for aroma at the end of boil". I stayed loyal and to this day still have traditional English hop varieties like Golding and Challenger and use around four times the amount that I had previously brewed with.'

The beer is copper coloured with a toffee-like sweetness on the palate, which conjoins with a peppery hop character (white pepper?), plus a whisper of orange marmalade – all coming together like a diabolic dance. It is bitter, chewy, dusty (as in a hay barn during a rainless summer) and there is a bracing dryness in the finish. It's a Best Bitter and I rather enjoy it.

Goes well with… A toasted cheese sandwich, Cheddar naturally

DEYA BREWING
Best Foot Forward

4.4% Core

Cheltenham, Gloucestershire
deyabrewing.com

*Modern Best Bitter with a
long and lingering dry finish*

Success for a new brewery is when it gets known for its expertise with a certain beer style. For DEYA renown came in the shape of its juicy, lip-smackingly fruity Pale Ales, but as a freshly poured glass of their Best Bitter demonstrates, there are no one-trick ponies wandering around its brewing site close to Cheltenham railway station.

'Having become known for modern hazy beers,' brewery founder Theo Frayne says, 'we wanted to brew some more traditional UK styles, a desire that came about from a love and appreciation of those beers – and we like drinking them! Best Foot Forward allowed us to work closely with Brook House Hops, and try and really nail our take on a Best Bitter. It was originally brewed for the CASK Beer Festival in London and it is what we want to drink in the pub.'

Dark orange-gold in the glass, this beer is about the aroma of the crunch of buttery biscuits, caramel, and an earthiness that suggests the warp and weft of classic English hops. The palate has more of that childhood-evoking biscuitiness, caramel, a light fruitiness in the background, which is almost berry meets citrus, alongside a full-bodied mouthfeel followed by a lasting bitterness in the finish with an accompanying grainy dryness. This is a fabulous example of a modern Best Bitter, especially with its finish that lingers like the scent of blossom in an English country garden.

Oh, and if you're wondering about the striking image on the can of a character striding forward, Frayne explains that the design idea, 'came from the Keep On Truckin' poster by Robert Crumb. It's my favourite DEYA design!'.

Goes well with... Fried chicken tacos and several friends

FIVE POINTS BREWING
Best

4.1%   Core

Hackney, London
fivepointsbrewing.co.uk

*Best Bitter that showcases
English hops and malt*

Such a simple name, such a simple aim. Best is all about balance, a showcase for the Fuggle hop and Maris Otter malt, no more, no less. This is a beer that brings together a biscuity sweetness, a floral and citrus brightness and a roistering bitterness, a collaboration and togetherness that reminds me of a favourite tram ride through a much-loved Central European city, a journey that links together some of its most beautiful parts. It is a handsome looking beer, a glorious amber-copper colour with grain, Ovaltine, malt and citrus marmalade on its well-constructed nose. Each gulp of this beer brings forth a biscuity graininess, a citrus fruitiness, a bittersweetness and a bitterness and dryness in the finish that is both soulful and mindful, with everything in order as it should be.

For Five Points head brewer Greg Hobbs, launching a Bitter had long been on the agenda for him and co-founder Ed Mason, but there were fears that the mood amongst modern beer drinkers wasn't there for such a beer.

Finally, in 2019 it was launched. 'As a brewer I've learnt to be patient when developing new recipes,' he says, 'with the usual wait of a few weeks until the beer is finished and conditioned before finally tasting how it has all come together – having said that, the wait for Five Points Best felt particularly painfully slow. We initially released the beer on cask only, so we rolled the firkin across the road to the Pembury Tavern and the first sip was a day or so later, properly cellared and poured with a sparkler – it was an absolute joy.'

Goes well with… The simple, unconfined joy of ham, egg and chips

FULLER SMITH & TURNER
ESB

5.5% Core

Chiswick, London
fullersbrewery.co.uk

A true classic of British beer

Several years ago I wrote an update of Fuller Smith & Turner's history (*Crafting A Company*). This meant that I spent a lot of time at the brewery, interviewing key personnel and going through brewing records that went back to the 19th century. These are massive bound volumes that recorded (and still do presumably) every daily brew. You might be surprised to read that many of the beers brewed before World War One had American hops and malt from Smyrna (now Izmir) in the mix, but one of the biggest thrills for me was discovering the record of the brew day when ESB was first brewed in 1971 (though its genesis went back to 1969 when Fuller's Old Burton Ale was replaced by Winter Brew, which went onto become ESB). I was so excited that when I left the archives room to go and interview the then chairman Michael Turner, I only just realised in time that my suit was covered in dust.

Even though Fuller's is now owned by Asahi, it is still anchored into its Chiswick site, and some great beers remain in its portfolio, including ESB.

This was the first Extra Special Bitter and went on to inspire a beer style of its very own through the work of American craft brewers. Amber in colour, it has a rich surge of biscuity maltiness and Seville orange hoppiness on the nose (though it is often claimed that this marmalade oranginess also comes from the house yeast), while on the palate there is a richness of citrus, marmalade, crisp biscuit dryness and a bracing bitterness in the finish. This is a true classic of the last 50 years of British brewing and rightly deserves its place in history.

Goes well with… Roast pheasant and all the trimmings

HARVEY'S BREWERY
Sussex Best Bitter

4%   Core

Lewes, East Sussex
harveys.org.uk

*One of the most magnificent
examples of an English Bitter*

Balance is the foundation upon which a great Bitter is created. A balance between the biscuity, cereal-like suggestion of malt conjoined with the light citrusiness and earthiness of English hops, leading this bountiful balance to be anchored together with a bitterness in the finish.

So let us salute Sussex Best Bitter, perhaps one of the most magnificent examples of an English Bitter, a beer that has a muscular and musky hop presence on the nose, which might be something to do with a hop selction of Fuggle, Golding, Progress and Bramling Cross, while the palate is full-bodied without being intrusive, showing off its effortless balance between rich maltiness and more hoppiness. There's also a slight sweetness in the background, which head brewer and joint managing director Miles Jenner once told me was the result of the way the local palate developed in the years after World War Two, which was when the beer was launched.

'This was when we stabilised our beer flavour profile with a good hop character and a slight sweetness which was very moreish,' he said. 'The sweetness happened because in many ways there was a postwar liking for slightly sweet things. We are also in a traditional hop growing area and we always well-hopped our beers.'

The beer was initially developed by Harveys' then head brewer Anthony Jenner, and was originally just called Best Bitter with the prefix Sussex added in 1970. It has always been a mainstay of the brewery pub trade, but in 2017 the beer joined the canned beer revolution and the result is an exceedingly satisfying link to Harvey's beautiful home town of Lewes.

Goes well with... A plate of fried calamari, believe it or not, is an ideal match

HOOK NORTON BREWERY
Old Hooky

4.6%   Core

Hook Norton, Oxfordshire
hooky.co.uk

*A beer that demands
to be taken seriously*

It's been the kind of working day you would like to forget and it is definitely time for a beer so pour yourself a glass of Old Hooky. Take a glance at the beer in the glass and admire its burnished chestnut-brown colour, suggestive of an late autumn walk in the park as the leaves fall and the promise of the home fireside quickens the steps.

You are home and the beer has a sweet, biscuity, grainy aroma with a suggestion of ripe orange in the background, a quiet, subtle kind of citrusy note, not the big blasts of noise that New World hops produce. There is a light chocolate note, a chocolate wafer biscuit perhaps that has been lightly flavoured with orange; it is crisp and warming on the palate, full-bodied in that it fills the mouth in the same way as some have thought God (or the idea of God) fills the interior of a great cathedral.

There is a bittersweet and dry finish that lingers and leaves its mark like the dry flutter of wings in the eaves of a dovecot; this is a beer that demands to be taken seriously. The poet Anne Sexton once wrote: 'God has a brown voice, as soft and full as beer,' and as I read those words once more I think of Hook Norton's Old Hooky, a study in brown and a beer that has its own voice and special place in the many varied halls of British brewing.

Goes well with... Steak and kidney pie, chips and peas with a side helping of gravy

LONDON BEER LAB
Bitter

3.9%   Core

Brixton, London
londonbeerlab.com

A classic English Bitter with everything in balance

London Beer Lab's 15-barrel brewhouse is based in Brixton, London. It was set up by home-brewers Bruno Alajouanine and Karl Durand O'Connor in 2013, and the brewery's fulsome and well-balanced Bitter is, according to the latter, something of an exercise in nostalgia.

'Neither of us grew up in countries where this particular style holds any popularity,' he says, 'but it is as classically English as fish and chips at the seaside so we always knew we'd give it a crack. Through our brewing workshops we'd explored the style on a small scale and after a handful of iterations we were happy with where we'd got the recipe to, but the idea of brewing on a larger commercial basis was shelved till early 2021.

'With the first taste we were blown away by the fruity esters achieved by the London ESB yeast strain and how it played with the sweet caramel of the grains. I'll admit to a moment of panic with the bitterness of the first sips but it develops subtly and lingers, which just rounds the whole beer off.'

Dark amber in colour, there are suggestions of chocolate, caramel and light citrus on the generous nose, while the palate resonates with malt-derived sweetness, caramel, citrus and a delightful bittersweetness before a stately dry and bitter finish. A highly accomplished, well-defined beer that hits all points of the Bitter compass, or as Durand O'Connor says, 'for me the mood of this beer would be contentment and satisfaction'.

Goes well with... Sitting at home in front of the fire after an exhilarating walk in the country

MARBLE BREWERY
ESB

5.5% Seasonal

Manchester
marblebeers.com

*A gloriously malty and
well-rounded ESB*

Here's a conundrum you might want to consider whilst engaging in your latest glass of beer. Both Pint and Manchester Bitter are Marble's flagship examples of the style but beer pedants in the south can be often found likening them to Pale Ales, according to the brewery's head of production Joe Ince: 'I took this somewhat personally as they are brewed like Bitters and are what we could consider Bitters in the north. Paler, yes, than in the south, hoppier, yes, but still, I would consider them Bitters. From this I started playing around with recipe ideas for Bitters that more echo the southern style of higher gravity and being more malt forward.'

The result of these criticisms was this ESB, which should do more than enough to silence the cries of those with a regional bias, but as is often said (or should be), the truth is in what is poured into the glass. So here it is. A gleaming beacon of amber in the glass, this has a richness of malt character on the nose, redolent of caramel, light toffee and a delicate nuttiness; be also prepared

for a cross-current of rich citrus in the background. Take a deep swig of the beer and recognise more of this glorious malt certainty alongside a benevolent swipe of orange marmalade and light citrus, before it descends into a crisp, bitter and dry finish. Well-rounded and balanced, this is a welcome addition to the ESB canon.

'The ethos and thought behind the beer will stay the same,' adds Ince, 'but how we achieve it might change slightly over time as we discover new ingredients such as hop varieties or processes within the brewery. We are always looking at self improvement.'

Goes well with… An indulgent dessert such as a homemade sticky chocolate brownie and a scoop of vanilla ice cream

MARBLE BREWERY
Manchester Bitter

4.2% Core

Manchester
marblebeers.com

Juicy, dry and crisp Bitter

Bitter is a social beer style, a chatterer in the glass, an easy-going companion that tells stories, exchanges jokes and makes life that little bit more humane and happy. It is a plain spoken pint that speaks its mind with no recourse to spin or angles, and it certainly won't take any nonsense. When you drink deeply of a Bitter (for you must drink deeply not sip), you are entering a world of sociability and serendipity, for this is a beer style that you must drink before you die otherwise your life will have been just that little bit poorer.

Marble's exuberant, straw-gold-coloured Manchester Bitter is that kind of beer, an exclamation mark in a glass, a liquid philosophy and a tale told of the city's beer culture, which was once dominated by a Bitter that sadly fell from grace when its brewery was sold and the new owners turned it into an ice cream. That was then, so let us drink the Bitter of now.

This is a beer whose nose pulsates with notes of orange, ripe blueberry and lightly toasted grains. It is a juicy, dry and crisp Bitter, full-bodied and bitter (naturally), and a mainstay of one of Manchester's most enduring and much-loved craft breweries, which was set up at the back of the Marble Tavern in 1997 by then owner Vance Debachval, who reputedly wasn't sure whether to put in a karaoke room or a microbrewery. Thankfully, the latter option won and Marble is a glittering, gleaming success whose beers, like Manchester Bitter, are authoritative and precise in their appeal to the palate.

Goes well with… A homemade Scotch egg with some black pudding in the mix

NEPTUNE BREWERY
Silenus ESB

5.6% Seasonal

Liverpool
neptunebrewery.com

*A malt-forward,
dry and bitter ESB*

Silenus was a Greek god as well as a drinking pal of Dionysus. He was also instrumental in giving Midas his unwise wish of being able to turn everything to gold. Hopefully, he would have enjoyed several cups of this characterful ESB, which Neptune brewed especially for a local bar that was celebrating a birthday. 'We decided upon an ESB, as it is a beer style we very much enjoy,' says brewery co-founder Julie O'Grady. 'Given that Silenus was a Greek god known for his drunkenness, it seemed apt and very tongue in cheek to celebrate a birthday and hold a party. This beer exceeded our expectations and turned out so well, while the feedback we received was great with many who haven't tried a Bitter before saying that they very much enjoyed it.'

Reddish copper in colour with a rocky head of foam, it is a mesmeric beer to watch as tightly packed together bubbles reach towards the top of the glass. There is a medium malt character alongside a biscuitiness on the nose, a richness which you would expect from

an ESB. It is full-bodied in the mouthfeel – thanks to the use of Chevallier heritage malt perhaps? – with plenty of biscuity graininess alongside flurries of toffee, caramel, citrus fruitiness and orange marmalade before it descends to a bitter finish that is accompanied by a bracing dryness. It's a chewy, dry, bitter beer that you could describe as muscular, not because of its alcoholic strength but because of its impact on the palate, and the glorious exchange between the malt and the subtle fruitiness of the hops.

Goes well with... A comfortable armchair and a copy of Robert Graves' classic *The Greek Myths*

RAMSGATE BREWERY
GADDS' N°5

4.4% Core

Ramsgate, Kent
ramsgatebrewery.co.uk

A classic Kentish Best Bitter

Eddie Gadd learnt his brewing trade at the Firkin chain of pubs in the 1990s and he was one of the team that developed the award-winning Dogbolter, a beer that he still produces. When made redundant in 2001 he began building his own brewery, which eventually opened a year later. It was initially based at the back of a Ramsgate pub, which he once described as being full of 'louts and ne'er-do-wells', but then moved to the current home in 2006. His reputation as a brewer who you can rely on for superb beers has soared ever since (quite a few awards have come his way as well).

If Gadds N° 3 was the beer that launched Ramsgate, N° 5 was the one that helped it to celebrate its first birthday. It was developed very much as a Kentish Best Bitter, though, according to Gadd, 'one with a slightly higher hop profile'. Nearly two decades on, the beer remains at the heart of the brewery, a beer with a citrusy slow build of sweetness, hints of toffee and hop spice, a full-bodied mouthfeel and a blistering bitterness that echoes the siren call of English hops, especially East Kent Goldings, which Gadd once said that he believed were the classiest hops in the world.

'I'm a simple brewer,' he says, 'but this was a deliberately finicky malt bill to give the beer an out-of-character complexity. We went through nine kilderkins on the launch (birthday) night – that doesn't happen often these days.'

Goes well with... Roast beef, roast potatoes and Yorkshire pudding for Sunday lunch

ROOSTER'S BREWING
Capability Brown

4% Core

Harrogate, North Yorkshire
roosters.co.uk

*Well-rounded Best Bitter
with a subtle fruitiness*

Capability Brown has been described as one of the greatest gardeners of England, but I bet he couldn't brew a beer to save his life. On the other hand, we don't know what the gardening capabilities of the brewing team at Rooster's are like, but they certainly make good beer. This is one of them, an amber-daubed Best Bitter that shines in the glass like a well-polished ancient sideboard that was left to you by an eccentric great-aunt you hadn't seen since childhood.

For Rooster's commercial manager Tom Fozzard, there was a simple motivation in producing the beer: 'When moving to our new brewery in Harrogate, which allowed us space to open an onsite taproom for the first time, we wanted to offer our customers a wide variety of styles of beer and we recognised one thing missing from our line-up at that stage was a year-round traditional Best Bitter, so Capability Brown was developed. The balance of the various malts and the way they harmonised with our house yeast strain and the English hop varieties we chose to use turned out exactly as planned.'

Thanks to the use of Challenger, Fuggle and Whitbread Goldings Variety, the beer has an array of spicy, earthy, biscuity and sweetish caramel notes on the nose, with the well-rounded palate displaying a light roastiness, more caramel, floral and fruity notes before its bittersweet and dry finish. This is a complete and eminently approachable beer that is just right for settling down with and enjoying several glasses of after a stint in the garden.

Goes well with... Mac and cheese with pieces of chorizo scattered on the top

THE RUNAWAY BREWERY
ESB

5.8% Core

Manchester
therunawaybrewery.com

*Full-bodied ESB which has
speciality Belgian malts added*

Let's jump straight into the origins story of this ESB. Back in 2014 the London restaurant chain Hawksmoor opened up in Runaway's home city, Manchester, and its owners were looking for a local beer to use in their Shakey Pete's Ginger Brew cocktail. Runaway's American-style Brown Ale was initially used but was eventually deemed too hoppy and the brewery was asked if it would consider something less hoppy.

'We (politely) refused,' recalls Runaway's co-founder and head brewer Mark Welsby, 'something along the lines of "if you want London Pride, perhaps you should go and speak to bloody Fuller's!" However, after reining in our obvious disdain (we're a hip modern brewery don't you know!), we suggested brewing a beer that would take inspiration from another Fuller's classic, but something specifically designed to complement the flavours in their cult cocktail – gin, ginger and lemon. So, in the era of IPA, we set out to brew our first proper Bitter ... and we knew it had to be Extra Special!'

The result was this full-bodied strong Bitter that had speciality Belgian malts added to the mix, which sees the beer lie somewhere between a Bitter and a Belgian Dubbel. There is a whoosh of sweet and rich caramel, light treacle and dried fruit on the nose and palate, before it descends to a finish that pulsates with a light hoppiness, dryness and bitterness.

'We wanted to create a twist on a classic,' says Welsby, 'it's what I enjoy most – modernising a style that has fallen a bit out of fashion. The aim was not to reinvent the ESB, but to celebrate it in a modern way.'

Goes well with... A trio of English cheeses: Cheshire, Stilton and Single Gloucester

SALOPIAN BREWERY
Darwin's Origin

4.3%   Core

Shrewsbury, Shropshire
salopianbrewery.co.uk

Hoppy and refreshing with a good belt of bitterness

Beers are brewed to commemorate all sorts of historical occasions, and Darwin's Origin was first produced in 2009 on the 200th anniversary of his birth in Salopian's home town of Shrewsbury. However, there was more to just brewing a beer to celebrate Darwin. According to the brewery's chairman, Wilf Nelson, 'the original idea behind the beer was to commemorate the bi-centenary of Charles Darwin's birth at Shrewsbury. We decided to use the idea of evolution as the theme for the beer so it's a composite of a traditional Best Bitter from the malt grist, but with a contemporary hopping using mainly New World hops.

'We were really pleased with it. In its original form I think it had Riwaka, Brewers Gold, Galaxy and Centennial, which all combined to give it a lovely orangey, spicy flavour. The beer has evolved over 12 years to be more hop led and less malty, so overall it is hoppy and refreshing, with a good belt of bitterness, great drinkability and a balanced malty body.'

The beer is copper coloured with a fine, firm head of foam and has a thrilling counterpoint on the nose between rich biscuity notes and a chiming, tingling fruitiness that is reminiscent of a lemon-flavoured fruit gum. This is an enticing and enchanting nose, though perhaps the word enchantment would be one Darwin would never use in his scientific work. There is more sweet biscuitiness and sprightly citrus on the palate, followed by a bracing bitterness and dryness in the finish alongside a peppery spiciness.

Goes well with… An evening with friends discussing evolution (or just the latest hit series on Netflix)

SALTAIRE BREWERY
Saltaire Best

4.4% Core

Shipley, West Yorkshire
saltairebrewery.com

A down-to-earth, plain-speaking, bracingly dry Best Bitter

There's a simplicity about Best Bitter, a purity, an invocation of honesty even. This is a beer without frills, a beer that sits in the glass and lets the essence of its raw materials do all the talking, and when it talks you listen. It's the everyman and woman of beer, dependable, level-headed and not too hasty to come to conclusions: a friendly beer that is a great companion in the glass.

Saltaire Best is that kind of beer, a robust example of a Best Bitter that sings with the hymnals of malt, which is exactly what the brewery's production manager Ben Pearson wanted when he developed it.

'Our sales team had been requesting we brew a traditional British Bitter made from homegrown ingredients,' he recalls. 'As someone who enjoys Bitter I was happy to take up the challenge. This beer was actually my first ever commercial recipe, just to throw in a little added pressure to the mix. I just wanted to make a throwback to the type of beer I liked to enjoy with my Dad.

The reason why I started out in this job is because I wanted to make a beer I could sit and enjoy with friends and family, and when I tried Best, I knew I'd done that.'

Sit down and pour yourself a bottle. The colour is amber verging onto copper and there are aromatics of dark fruit, caramel and biscuity malt rising into the air, while each gulp reveals more of the malt biscuitiness, a hint of roastiness and delicate fruitiness before finishing bracingly dry and bitter.

Goes well with… A luscious and juicy burger that you bought in from the local, award-winning butcher's

WESTERHAM BREWERY
1965

4.8% Occasional (Heritage Range)

Westerham, Kent
westerhambrewery.co.uk

Full-bodied Bitter that was
originally brewed until the mid-60s

This is a beer about time, a survivor, a memento mori. In 1965 the Black Eagle Brewery in the Kentish town of Westerham shut its doors for good, another statistic in the attritional round of closures that happened during the decade. However, someone on the brewing team, presumably the head brewer, had the foresight to save its special yeast strain for the National Collection of Yeast Cultures in Norwich. Poignantly, the same year saw the death of Churchill, whose home was nearby, and it's a fair assumption that he might have enjoyed a drop of the local ale whenever he was at home. Forty years later the newly opened Westerham Brewery produced this classic full-bodied Bitter using the saved yeast strain and based on a similar recipe that was used for the last brew at the old brewery on 3 March 1965. The beer has gone on to become a regular member of the Westerham's well-mannered family of beers.

Copper coloured with tints of amber, this has a classic English Bitter nose of restrained citrus, hints of toffee, earthy hop character and suggestions of a crisp and perky graininess. Poured into the glass, it has toffee, citrus, the boom of Kentish hops and a bracingly dry and bitter finish that will have your tastebuds calling for more of the same. This classic, full-bodied Bitter is the kind of beer that is like a time machine for those of us who never drunk the original, and a muscular, heady anvil of a Bitter that speaks to us of a different time.

Goes well with… Glancing through the family's photo albums and remembering those who are no longer here

WINDSOR & ETON BREWERY
Guardsman Best Bitter

4.2% Core

Windsor, Berkshire
webrew.co.uk

*A classic, full-bodied and
sessionable Bitter*

Before a brewery comes into being, the people (or person) behind the project need to work out what the first beer will be. Can the market be tickled by a ferociously hoppy, DDH-ed-to-the-hilt pale, or will it be swayed by a clean and refreshing lager that looks to the traditions of Central European brewing? When Windsor & Eton were planning their first beer prior to opening in 2010, the four founder members spent some time thinking of what their debut should be, and as co-founder Paddy Johnson explains, 'whilst we had plans to do some "modern" beers we decided our first beer should be a "classic". As I explained to my three colleagues, producing something extreme like a "hop-bomb" was relatively easy – there were no clear reference points and flavour could mask a thousand faults. However, to produce a beer that was truly "quaffable" (our key objective) and that people would compare favourably to their much-loved "life-time" beers was a real challenge!'

Research amongst friends over a few pints soon revealed that their best drinking experiences involved pints of a sessionable beer in good company, a balanced and clean beer with plenty of malt character and a satisfying bitterness. The result of this market research was Guardsman, a robust, copper-coloured Best Bitter built on potent malt foundations, tingling with a fruity hoppiness, and most important of all, resonating with a bitterness in the finish that perks up the palate and demands another swig.

Guardsman is now the brewery's best-selling beer and according to Johnson, 'We now get "fans/supporters" telling us that this has become their bench-mark beer – the one that they compare all session beers to. Nothing gives us greater satisfaction on hearing that.'

Goes well with… Fish and chips on a Friday evening

YONDER BREWING & BLENDING
Boogie

3.8% Core

Radstock, Somerset
brewyonder.co.uk

*An appetisingly refreshing
and bitter beer from Somerset*

Somerset-based Yonder thrives on using foraged and local farmed ingredients, mixed culture fermentation and barrel ageing and blending, but there is none of this eclecticism when it comes to what they call a 'modern Bitter', unless you note the use of the Norwegian yeast strain kveik (rhymes with steak) in fermentation. Originating in the world of Scandinavian farmhouse brewing, champions cite its ability to ferment at high temperatures while also shortening fermentation time, something that Yonder co-founder Stuart Winstone says, 'can be great for achieving the flavours of traditional English beers'.

Boogie has obviously succeeded as it pours a hazy pale amber-gold from the can, with a zap of bitterness on the palate alongside a biscuity, malt-flecked backbone, hints of citrus, a sweet fruitiness that is almost like a peal of handbells, light, ethereal, but still evident. It is satisfyingly full-bodied for 3.8% and the finish is appetisingly bitter and dry, which lingers around for some time, an echo, a shadow, a memory.

'When it came to brewing it,' says Winstone, 'we looked to bring the South West's influence of beer with us. We wanted to combine elements of South West "Bitter" with a traditional Pale Ale, knowing that people's (and our) tastes these days leaned more towards hop flavour, including a good refreshing bitterness, despite how trends seem to be going at the moment.

'Boogie is our nod to the beers that started us on our journey.'

Goes well with... An autumnal day out in the country picking blackberries

IPA

The IPA is a coat of many colours and this chapter shines and glimmers with a whole variety of this most popular of beer styles.

ABYSS BREWING
Dank Marvin

5.8% Core

Lewes, East Sussex
abyssbrewing.co.uk

*Juicy, fruity, resiny and
dank-inclined IPA*

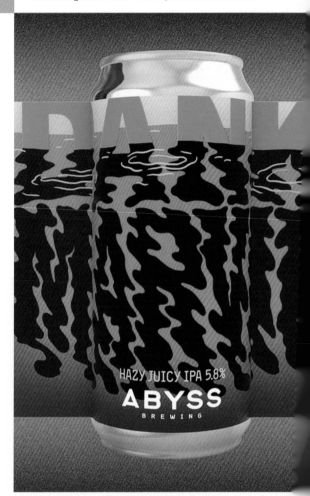

Lewes is a beer destination, not only for
the venerable Harvey's, but also for Beak
and Abyss, both of whom have taprooms
in the town where you can buy their cans.
Dank Marvin is Abyss's aptly punned
American-style IPA, which co-founder
Andy Bridge describes as a bridge between
East and West Coast styles, producing
'a smoother softer and mellow full body
with some piney, older school craft beer
hops and a hint of caramel in the malt.

    'The name came first,' he continues,
'a play on Hank Marvin, the much-lauded
innovator of the electric guitar, who is up
there with Jimi Hendrix and Les Paul.
True to Hank's legendary playing, the
beer had to be rock'n'roll, it had to be
piney and dank, and an IPA.'

    Dankness is a common description in
the world of IPA, usually meaning that any
beer described as dank will feature a piney,
resinous greenness somehow associated
with marijuana, something I suspect
Hank Marvin wasn't familiar with.

    Hazy gold-orange in colour, there is a
halo of resiny pine, an ethereal earthiness,
ripe mango and citrus on the nose, both

sweet and rugged in the appeal to the
drinker. The first sip reveals a juicy
ripeness of citrus, mango and stone fruit
plus a chunky resiny note followed by a
light sweetness and a gentle bitterness.
The mouthfeel is generous and pleasing.

    'This beer is always evolving, all our
beers are,' adds Bridge, 'but this one has
been a quite a quest for softness and
dankness. Two of the original hops,
Chinook and Columbus, remain the
same, others have come and gone,
it's had a few yeast changes, and
water profile evolutions … and the
journey is still far from over.'

Goes well with… Making a treat of it and serving with fish and chips

S ALLSOPP & SONS
Allsopp's India Pale Ale

5.6%   Core

Brewed in Sheffield at time of writing
allsopps.com

A history lesson in a bottle

Emerge from the railway station at Burton upon Trent and turn right onto Station Street and across the road you will see a great big fortress of a building, multi-windowed, rock solid and built in the 1920s when the town was the capital of British brewing. This was the offices and brewery for Allsopp's, which in the 1930s merged with Ind Coope, before its name was dropped in the 1950s. Ind Coope itself didn't survive long either – it was enveloped by Allied Breweries during the great brewing ram raids of the 1970s. One of Allsopp's notable beers was its India Pale Ale, another beer that vanished from history when its name was changed to Double Diamond in the late 1930s (and we know how wondrous that beer was, or wasn't).

Let's move onto now and Allsopp's India Pale Ale was resurrected in 2021 by Jamie Allsopp, who is seven-times great grandson of brewery founder Samuel Allsopp. Along with the help of a Burton-style brewing expert and the use of a surviving ledger of his family's original recipes, he has managed to recreate the IPA (a Pale Ale is also brewed).

In an era when the meaning of IPA could be said to be totally devalued, this recreation is both a history lesson and a solid, silver-tongued example of the style. Dark copper in colour, there are suggestions of ripe plum fruitiness and toffee on the nose, while the palate has a soft carbonation plus hints of caramel, toffee, bittersweetness and a peppery spiciness followed by a sharp lingering bitterness in the finish.

A welcome return.

Goes well with… Squid tacos and a positive attitude towards life

ARBOR ALES
Yakima Valley

7% Occasional

Bristol
arborales.co.uk

A big bruiser of a hoppy IPA from one of Bristol's star breweries

Sometimes it's almost as if the sky above Bristol is ablaze with brewing talent, a fiery constellation of switched-on brewers creating beers that amaze and collude with the palate to draw forth dazzling experiences. Arbor Ales is one of these stars in the sky, brought to life by former telephone engineer Jon Comer in 2007, when home was at the back of a pub until a move to the Easton part of the city. Since then the brewery's reputation as one of the most accomplished and exciting in England has grown with a natural, organic energy.

Yakima Valley is one of the brewery's earliest beers, first produced in 2010 and Comer's first attempt at an American IPA with just US hops, hence the name (Yakima Valley is the major hop-growing region in the USA). It pours golden amber and has zephyrs of citrus, orange marmalade and light caramel on the nose, while there is more orange marmalade, sweet citrus, delicate caramel and stone fruit followed by a bracing bitterness and dryness in the finish.

'We were aiming for a beer that had plenty of New World tropical fruit and citrus flavours,' he recalls, 'but with a discernible malt backbone. At 7%, we were able to add what at the time was considered a huge amount of hops without it tasting overly bitter. We learnt a lot about balancing bitterness to gravity whilst brewing Yakima Valley. We were very excited to try the first brew, having smelt it every day in the brewery while fermenting. It certainly didn't disappoint when we got to try it and we couldn't have been happier with the finished beer.'

Goes well with... An appreciation of the finer things in life

THE BEAK BREWERY
Gurr

7% Occasional

Lewes, East Sussex
beakbrewery.com

A peerless West Coast IPA with a bracing, grapefruit-like bitterness

West Coast IPA is the kind of beer style you could imagine roaring along a Californian freeway on its Harley/Guzzi/Triumph (delete where applicable, I used to have a Guzzi so I've got a dog in the fight), the Pacific breeze in its hair and the road ahead like an itinerary it intends to keep to – but then again might not. It is a style of unplumbed depths, loquacious in its hop character and absolute in the constituency of bitterness. All of this brings me neatly to The Beak Brewery's peerless West Coast IPA Gurr (lots of mango, dankness, grapefruit and lemon on both nose and palate plus an appealing bitterness), and whose label features a rather slapdash bear on its label, as if Picasso had decided that members of the family *Ursidae* needed a bit of a makeover.

'The beer was inspired by some of the classic Californian beers that got us into beer culture back in the early noughties,' says Daniel Tapper, who opened Beak in 2020 just as a certain pandemic started to take hold. 'These days, beers like Sierra Nevada Pale Ale can seem a little tame compared to modern NEIPAs, but there's so much we love about them, from their weedy aromas through to the bracing grapefruit bitterness.'

In common with a lot of new, hip, gunslinging breweries, Beak has a small core range of which Gurr is not part, but according to Tapper it will be back: 'We are always tinkering with our beers, even the core offerings. With this beer, I'd perhaps like to see it a little clearer with even more piney bitterness. I think it would be fun to do a DIPA version too.'

Goes well with… Spicy Italian sausages with the fennel seed tang making a robust match

BEAVERTOWN
Lupuloid

6.7% Core

Tottenham, London
beavertownbrewery.co.uk

*Fruity IPA that makes you get all
philosophical over the description 'fruitiness'*

When we call a beer fruity we don't really mean real fruit, it's more of a karaoke version of fruitiness, something that seems to taste similar to the real thing but is not the original (unless of course it has actual fruit in it, but then that's a different bowl of Kriek and Framboise). If I am going to be philosophical about it and generous in my observations, maybe the use of the word 'fruity' helps the drinker to get an idea of what the beer might taste like, a point of reference that will help them make a decision, but let's be honest, this is not part of your five-a-day as some souls might think.

This is a subject I think a lot about given that many beers, especially well-hopped Pale Ales and IPAs, are almost caricatures of fruit in the same way as the fruit-filled hat that Hollywood starlet Carmen Miranda would wear in her movies (I think I might have trademarked that description btw).

Take Beavertown's bright, gold-coloured Lupuloid IPA, which fairly bristles with fresh and slick imaginations of mango, papaya and grapefruit on the nose – Carmen Miranda sashaying across the big screen. The fruitiness also transfers over to the palate alongside a shimmer of bittersweetness and brisk carbonation before it finishes as dry as a pub wit making a clever remark. It's a fruity IPA, which, unlike the same brewery's Bloody 'ell, does not have fruit in the mix. It is a beer that entrances and delights the palate, but it's a fruitiness as imagined by hop merchants and brewers, which makes it all the more gorgeous in the glass. That's my thought for the day over.

Goes well with... Shellfish and a mango-dominated salsa

BRISTOL BEER FACTORY
Southville Hop

6.5% Core

Bristol
bristolbeerfactory.co.uk

A luscious old-school West Coast IPA with bitterness in the finish

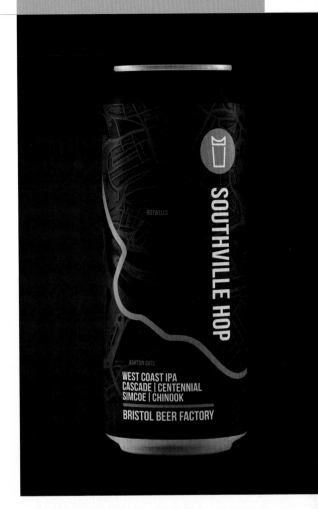

Bristol Beer Factory. Was there ever a brewery name that said it all? Based in the Southville district of the city, it brews beer and is located in a former industrial area whose old factories have been rebooted to other uses. Factory? All too often factory in the context of brewing has a negative connotation, suggesting a worker drone-like application to beer making, but the factory in this instance is the Tobacco Factory, a multi-media centre hosting a theatre and space for other arty and business-like things as well as various markets. No alienation here then.

Southville Hop is a luscious West Coast IPA. When the brewery first produced it at 6.5% such beasts of hoppiness were rare on the British beer scene, as the brewery's former managing director (and now a director) Simon Bartlett recalls: 'We wanted to emulate what was happening in the US at the time and not happening in the UK with hard-hitting IPAs. Influenced by Stone and Russian River, it felt like a big call

in 2010 to bring out a West Coast-style IPA at 6.5% in the UK, but exactly the sort of big call we wanted to make.'

Since then the beer has been a continuous part of the brewery's core range, with only its Milk Stout being brewed for a longer period of time. Over a decade on it still thrills the palate with its ripe peach skin and grapefruit notes on the nose, followed by a big blast of tropical fruit and citrus on the palate alongside a complex malt spine before finishing with a long and lingering bitter finish.

Goes well with... Chicken peri peri

BULLHOUSE BREW CO
Merc Bro

6.5% Core

Belfast, Northern Ireland
bullhousebeer.co.uk

A confident New England IPA

Like many beer names, there is a story behind Merc Bro, according to William Mayne who founded the Belfast-based brewery in 2016 (when it started off on a farm). 'In early 2019 we did a tour around Ireland to check out the beer scene. The first stop was Galway and then we went to Dingle in Kerry. As well as the brewery van, one of our brewers was driving a purple Merc, which when we were in Dingle wouldn't start and had to go to a garage. All the way back Mick had to sit on kegs in the van. He got the car back three weeks later and the name of this beer is our tribute to it.'

This is a confident New England IPA brimming with an abundance of tropical fruit and stone fruit, both on the nose and the palate, with a full body, a rounded and soft mouthfeel and a malt-derived sweetness towards the finish. Simcoe and Mosaic are the classic hop varieties used, and the beer was one of the first of its style brewed in Northern Ireland, back in 2019, as brewery founder Mayne recalls: 'We used pale malt, rather than extra pale, we wanted the beer to have a bit of backbone to it, though we didn't want it to be hop dominant and wanted a bit of malt sweetness for the finish. We had a high proportion of oats and wheat and used Vermont yeast. The thing about picking Simcoe and Mosaic is that you cannot go wrong with these two.'

As for the car, it gave up the ghost some time ago and is now at the brewery with Mayne saying there are plans to hang it from the ceiling one day as a tribute to its tireless motor.

Goes well with… Chargrilled chicken and a good appetite

BURNING SKY
Easy Answers

6% Core

Firle, East Sussex
burningskybeer.com

A well-accomplished and halo-inducing IPA

Sometimes you just want a beer that is easy to drink, that completely fits the parameters of whatever style it is supposed to be and brings a big smile to your face with every sip. Easy Answers is that kind of beer, a well-accomplished and halo-inducing IPA that Burning Sky founder and brewer Mark Tranter first developed in 2015.

'I just wanted a nice, easy-drinking IPA that showcased Simcoe hops,' he says, 'but like all our beers, if you look at the recipe then and now, it has changed, but that is how you keep beer tastes relevant in a changing world. Alongside the Simcoe I now add Centennial and Amarillo. There's always room for improvement with whatever you do. That is one of the joys of making core range beers – you can constantly evaluate them. One-offs are fun and easy to sell, but there is real symmetry with core range. I like drinkability in all of our beers, what people could expect with Easy Answers is a drinkable, full-flavoured IPA.'

The beer is pale gold in colour and has plenty of resinous, piney and tropically fruity notes on the nose, as well as hints of orange and grapefruit. There is more of this fruitiness on the palate, alongside a pine-like character that adds a light sweetness and delicate earthiness to the flavour profile. There is a bitterness and a full-bodied mouthfeel before it finishes dry and delicately bitter. Easy answers, easy drinking, what more can you say?

Goes well with... The ease and brunch-time splendour of a bacon sandwich

BUXTON BREWERY
Axe Edge

6.8%   Core

Buxton, Derbyshire
buxtonbrewery.co.uk

*A flagship of an IPA that thrills
with its complexity of flavours*

What do we talk about when we discuss a brewery's flagship beer? Is it the beer that the brewery wants to be most recognised for, that represents the beating heart of its aspirations, aims and ambitions? And, is it the beer that the brewery hopes drinkers will keep coming back for whenever they have it in their sights (and, of course, lead them onto trying other beers)? So many questions when it comes to thinking about flagship beers.

For Buxton, who make their beers in the eponymous town in the Peak District, it is Axe Edge that is often seen as their flagship. First brewed in 2011, two years after the brewery began (Buxton was part of a second wave of craft breweries that included the likes of Kernel, RedWillow and Magic Rock), this is a full-bodied IPA that has ripened tropical fruit and citrus (mango and grapefruit in the vanguard with a hint of papaya in the background) on the nose. It is a collection of aromatics that could be described as a gentle and almost Mediterranean burst of sunshine, or maybe reminiscent of that bowl of fruit

in the corner of the white-walled kitchen into which the sun pokes its gentle rays.

For the less romantic and more technical of us, this nose is a gentle reminder of the aroma of fresh hops in the brewery. On the palate there is more of this tropical fruit and citrus from the New World hops used, alongside a full-bodied mouthfeel and chimes of bittersweetness before it finishes with a furnace blast wave of bitterness and dryness. Yes, I think that this might be a flagship beer.

Goes well with... The pungency and the audacity of Stinking Bishop cheese

CHAPTER BREWING
Keystone

7.3%   Frequently available

Sutton Weaver, Cheshire
chapterbrewing.co.uk

Free-wheeling West Coast IPA that tastes of the freedom of the road

This is a ravening, orange-amber West Coast IPA, which, when I first drunk it, was what a West Coast IPA meant to me, with images of a 2015 trip down the coast from Seattle to Portland flitting through my mind. There were pulsations of tropical fruit and pine on the nose, the pine reminding me of the smell of a forest of conifers after rainfall, and again I travelled back to the West Coast of America, thinking of the sight of pine forests stretching up into the hills with the dexterity of a troupe of acrobats.

I took a swig and there was more of the tropical fruit (freshly cut ripe mango perhaps, a bite into the soft, juicy flesh of a guava), as well as the pine; there was the weight of alcohol on the tongue, a mid-palate bittersweetness before a finish that managed to be both dry and bitter. This was a beer that made its presence known on the palate, a beer that made me think of the freedom of the road, even though I sat outside a small bar in a seaside town.

The beer was brewed in collaboration with Liverpool pub the Keystone and intended as a one-off, but its popularity has seen it become a regular on the brewing schedule, which may be down to the creative instincts of brewery founder and head brewer Noah Torn.

'We wanted to make something with a bit of gob on it,' he says, 'it needed to have the slight chewiness of caramel in there, to be countered by the hopping as well as enough of a punch to really make itself known. This was not meant to be a shy iteration of a West Coast IPA but something that, whilst smooth and drinkable, wasn't hiding anywhere.'

I think he succeeded.

Goes well with… A mortadella sandwich overlooking the ocean

CHEDDAR ALES
Goat's Leap

5.5% Core

Cheddar, North Somerset
cheddarales.co.uk

A gorgeous-looking bottle-conditioned English-style IPA

There is a lustrous beauty about this beer in the glass, it is well-polished and as clear as one of those days when you can see forever from the top of the mountain, while its dark-amber hue gleams with the beneficence of a loved one's smile. It is a cliché that we are said to drink with our eyes, but on this occasion one glance at Goat's Leap as it stands in its glass should have you falling in love with it and ready to study it with intense devotion.

For head brewer and founder Jem Ham, the motivation behind the beer was to produce a traditional English-style IPA that would use English malted barley and hops. 'I can't remember the exact date when I first brewed it,' he says, 'but I think it was somewhere around 2008–09. I was fishing in India a lot in those days, looking for the elusive hump-backed bahseer, and one of the spots I fished was 150 feet above the river in a gorge, which was called *mekedatu* (this translates to the Goat's Leap). Legend had it that this was the place where a goat leapt across the river to escape a pack of chasing wild dogs. It seemed like a great name for a beer, which also tied into the gorge in Cheddar where it is brewed.'

After you have stopped looking at the beer, take note of the spicy, earthy notes on the nose, giving the aromatics a muscularity as well as a well-defined link between what is in the glass and the raw materials used. In the background, sighing with a long-drawn keen of love, there is the sweet, biscuity undertone of Maris Otter. On the palate there is citrus marmalade, pepperiness (white pepper), digestive biscuits and breakfast cereal graininess alongside hints of toffee before it slides into a striking dryness and bitterness in the finish.

Goes well with... a spicy chicken Madras and an action-packed Netflix thriller

CLOUDWATER BREW CO
Somewhere Within

6% Core

Manchester
cloudwaterbrew.co

An ebullient IPA that leaps into the glass with consummate ease

This is a harmonious, luminous and sparky IPA, a signature beer for Cloudwater if you like, a brewery known not only for its well-hopped beers but also for championing and supporting diversity and inclusivity in an industry that is not always supportive of these issues. It is also that rare Cloudwater beast, a frequently available beer, and according to brewery manager Mark Cotterrell, was the result of an extensive period of development, which demonstrates the brewing team's conscientious approach to making beer.

'We launched a Recipe Evolution series designed to trial new ingredients and processes with our IPA and two other signature styles,' he says, 'and asked our customers for their input into what they most enjoyed. Somewhere Within was born from that series, bringing together the elements drinkers enjoyed most from the four different trial recipes. As a result, it is dry hopped with a blend of US and New Zealand hops, with complementary characteristics from both, and is designed

to be impactful, hazy and rich in flavour, while light and refreshingly drinkable.'

Dark orange in colour, hazy in appearance and poured with a coherently firm collar of foam, there is a merging of fresh tropical fruit and delightful citrus on the nose. It is juicy and pithy in the statement it makes on the palate with tropical fruit, citrus and a suggestion of white pepper. The mouthfeel is smooth and the alcohol is adroitly levelled into the beer without any hint of booziness.

Asked if the beer will always remain the same, Cotterrell answers: 'It's probably more appropriate to say the intention of this beer will always remain the same. We always want to strive for that balance between impact and drinkability, between a super-soft body and a refreshingly dry finish.'

Goes well with... A generous helping of the Thai dish Pad Kra Pao

ELUSIVE BREWING
Oregon Trail

5.8%   Frequently available

Finchampstead, Berkshire
elusivebrewing.com

*An immensely gratifying
old-school West Coast IPA*

Just like tracing back the journey a wagon train would have taken along the Oregon Trail, you can track the genesis of this thrillingly hoppy throwback of a West Coast IPA to Andy Parker's first ever all-grain home-brew recipe in 2012. At the time, Parker, who opened Elusive in 2016, was still trying to understand beer and how all its ingredients worked, with the home-brew being influenced by Green Flash's West Coat IPA.

'The beer really grabbed my attention when I first tried it,' he recalls, 'with its sticky and resinous hop profile balanced really well against a sweet, slightly chewy malt composition. Oregon Trail was about applying everything I'd learned in the years since back to that original recipe to create something at a slightly lower ABV but with all that aroma and flavour.

'The first brew in 2019 landed close to my target but I felt it needed slightly more of that pine resin character on the nose. Since the first brew we've changed some minor things along the way such as hopping rates and experimenting with

different hop products to achieve the desired result. The target for the beer remains the same but we're exploring various tools to allow us to reach that.'

Sleek amber in colour, and, as Parker says, there is a burst of pine alongside citrus on the nose with a suggestion of caramel in the background. Each swig reveals more pine, citrus, a pepperiness and caramel in the background before its all-embracing bitter finish with a tingle of sweetness making an appearance. This is an immensely gratifying and fiery beer that preaches the gospel of old-school West Coast IPA.

Goes well with... The easy-to-make classic curry house favourite saag aloo

FALLEN BREWING
Platform C

6.3% Core

Stirling, Scotland
fallenbrewing.co.uk

Juicy, piney and fruity
West Coast IPA

Let's pour ourselves a glass of this West Coast IPA immediately. It's juicy, piney and fruity with a straitened dryness and bitterness in the background; there are slightly sweet lemon sherbet notes mid palate. There's a tropical fruit pithiness, a rawness of cut fruit rather than a sweetness, and there's an overt caramel maltiness. Yes, there's grapefruit and, yes, it's another IPA, but it has a demotic, gnarly, shoulder-shrugging sense of rebelliousness last seen when Wild One Marlon Brando was asked what he was rebelling at and he replied 'Whaddaya got?'

For brewery co-founder Paul Fallen, the epiphany for such a beer was tasting Stone's Levitation Ale on a visit to San Diego during the 2000s, which he recalls 'was my first experience of a super-fresh, sticky, resinous west-coaster. Each time I went back to San Diego I couldn't wait to get my fill of West Coast Pales and IPAs. It was only a matter of time in the evolution of the brewery that I was going to create my homage to these beers and Platform C was the one.'

First brewed in 2014, Fallen sees Platform C as his danger beer: 'It's so deliciously drinkable and moreish without any hint of its ABV. I've lost count of the number of nights with friends where I've just had one more of these than I should have! But it's also a beer to enjoy on its own merits. It won't sit well in a session alongside East Coast Pales and IPAs, but if you give it time, on its own, then you'll feel the pine and resin build on your palate, the refreshing bitterness and juicy malts bringing you back for another sip, then another, then another!'

Goes well with... A plate of prosciutto and goats' cheese

GIPSY HILL BREWING
Hepcat

4.6% Core

Norwood, London
gipsyhillbrew.com

*Juicy and easy-drinking
Session IPA*

Session beers are the bedrock of British pub drinking, the kind of beers that won't leave you reeling if you have two or three pints. Session IPAs are the craft beer world's equivalent, full of flavour, brimming with hoppy character but relatively low in alcohol, which brings us very neatly to the joyful embrace of Hepcat.

For Gipsy Hill co-founder and managing director Sam McMeekin, the magic of Hepcat 'is that the balance sits in such an exciting place. It smells amazing, it's got a good body that coats your mouth and makes you feel satisfied, the bitterness is just enough to keep the taste buds salivating. There are layers to it, from the tropical aroma to the tangerine body. But it's also simple enough to come back to.'

The aroma is juicy, orangey and reminiscent of the tinned mandarins I had instead of Christmas pudding as a child, while a slightly biscuity graininess keeps everything in line. Take a swig and you'll discover a crisp and refreshing mouthfeel, with more of that mandarin/orange character, alongside a delicious malt sweetness, before it finishes dry and bittersweet. Gorgeous and well worth having two or three of in the company of friends.

'I remember exactly where we were when we developed Hepcat,' recalls McMeekin. 'It was a boiling hot day in May 2015 and we were outside the brewery throwing hop combinations around on a whiteboard in between taking breaks from racking casks. We wanted something that would be absolutely refreshing, moreish, with tropical and fruity notes and a vein of bitterness to keep you coming back. An ABV that allowed you to session, but sitting just above a regular Pale Ale. We felt there was a sweet spot there, and we've been refining it ever since!'

Goes well with… Laughter and good company

GRAIN BREWERY
Lignum Vitae

6.5% Core

Alburgh, Norfolk
grainbrewery.co.uk

*A riotous, big-flavoured IPA
made in the middle of rural Norfolk*

Sometimes beer names can be confusing. Take the first expression of this exemplary IPA. It was called Tamarind IPA, but apparently somewhat confused drinkers who thought tamarind had been added (it hadn't). It was also a lower ABV at 5.5%, which the brewery felt didn't give it the body they wanted, so off back to the drawing board they went and Lignum Vitae was eventually brought into the world.

According to brewery co-founder Phil Halls, Jaipur was a big influence on the beer: 'I'd had Jaipur IPA for the first time at Norwich beer festival and it was way ahead of its time, long before any UK brewers had thought of craft as anything more than crêpe paper, lolly sticks and UHU glue. It then became my mission to create a beer as tasty and big as that experience. I wanted an eyebrow-raising, smile-inducing kind of beer.

'It is very rare that I taste one of my own beers and just "enjoy" it. That's not to say that it's not good, but that I am too used to analysing it and looking for faults, and that's what I did the first few times. However, in its early days someone sneakily passed me a half at a festival and asked me to try it. My praise for it was gushing, and I felt delighted, if a little foolish, when I discovered it was Lignum Vitae.'

Deep gold in colour, there is an immediate surge of tropical fruit on the nose, a juiciness and a friendliness that will set the palate tingling with anticipation. No disappointment there either, with more tropical fruit, a rich backbone of locally grown malt, followed by a bittersweetness and pepperiness before it finishes bitter and scorchingly dry.

Goes well with... Sitting in the sunny garden of your rented cottage in South Norfolk

LACADA BREWERY
East The Beast

6%   Core

Portrush, County Antrim, Northern Ireland
lacadabrewery.com

An irrepressible IPA that is one of the brewery's most popular beers

Lacada Brewery is based in Portrush where the waves crash in from the Atlantic and surfers turn up in all weathers to get in the water. This explains the name of this irrepressible IPA with East the Beast referring to a certain imperious wave at the East Strand of Portrush, which surfers both love and respect in equal measure. As for the brewery, it is a cooperative with over 400 members, which, as one of the directors Simon Boyle explains, has 'a motley crew of active members, ranging from very traditional CAMRA "real ale" enthusiasts to the now typical "craft" hipsters, all united by a love of big flavours, and, in this neck of the woods, surfing'.

The beer was initially brewed on a nano-kit and opinions were initially positive, but as Boyle explains, 'I felt like a right grinch delivering a negative verdict. It was clean, and generously hopped, but it was very one-dimensional. I still expected more from an IPA, and didn't think that it would remain interesting after the first half of the glass. We'd been promised an arc, and a ride, but had more of a trolley than a rollercoaster.'

East The Beast has come a long way since then and this rollercoaster is one of the brewery's most popular beers. Orange amber in colour, there are rich aromatics of ripe mango and freshly cut pineapple rising from the glass with a suggestion of lime and peach in the background as well as sweet malt. On the palate, grapefruit and orange combine as if in a tag match on the tongue, followed by a delicate, biscuity sweetness before it finishes dry and bittersweet with a wisp of sweet tropical fruitiness lingering.

Goes well with… That massive thirst you've developed after an afternoon spent surfing

LAKES BREW CO
West Coast IPA

5.6% Core

Kendal, Cumbria
lakesbrewco.com

*A handsome-looking West Coast IPA
that blazes away in the glass*

The four Lakes co-founders all worked at Hawkshead Brewery until the start of the first lockdown saw them being made redundant. However, out of adversity comes success. Lakes was founded in Kendal in 2021 and under the assured expertise of head brewer Matt Thompson a saintly selection of blisteringly bracing beers have emerged of which this rampart of flavour and bitterness is just one.

'If there were a style of beer I would go to drink, it would be West Coast,' says Thompson, 'I have always loved the classic West Coast style, so it would have always been in our starting line-up. I wanted the beer to be balanced with a clean finish, enough scope to show off the hop characters, and with those piney, resinous undertones that are synonymous with the style.'

Amber gold in colour, it's a handsome looking beer in the glass, a sight that is matched by its aromatics of the creamy fruitiness of freshly cut mango, the savoury spice of chives and the fresh whisper of resin. There is more of the

tropical fruit, chives and piney character on the palate with the suggestion of sweet orange and the firmness of graininess before it finishes dry and bittersweet, with the bitterness lingering.

'Being a brewer, I think with any first brew of a beer you are overly critical and analyse every aspect,' says Thompson, 'from the malt, to whether the hops have shone through enough. With this beer it was the one that I felt hit my expectations the most. The beer was piney, intense but not overpowering – definitely a happy beer for me.'

Goes well with… Mediterranean-style grilled salmon with a herby, spicy Moroccan chermoula on top

LEFT HANDED GIANT
Cheeseburger Cavalry

6.9% Seasonal/brewed at least four times a year

Bristol
lefthandedgiant.com

A boisterous and big-flavoured IPA

A figure reminiscent of a 19th-century hussar charges on his horse on the label of this boisterous IPA from Bristol's Left Handed Giant. There's just one thing: the figure has a cheeseburger instead of its head, which, as brewery co-founder Bruce Gray explains, goes back to the London Craft Beer Festival in 2017.

'At the after party Rich (our head brewery/co founder) did a McDonald's run with All Good Beer founder Libby,' he says. 'They returned with pockets, bags and socks stuffed full of cheeseburgers, which were sneaked into the bar we were in and devoured by a drunk, hungry and grateful crowd. They were dubbed the Cheeseburger Cavalry and we committed on the night to brew a beer in their honour. When we came to create the beer James Yeo had already done the artwork, and we tried to create something that was as bold and outrageous as the name and art.'

The beer is pale gold in colour and has a flurry of bright aromatics within which ripe peach, juicy citrus and the tropical thunder of papaya and mango

can be identified alongside a subtle chive-like note. This energetic ensemble also makes an appearance on the palate with a rounded, full-bodied mouthfeel before a finish as dry as the driest of wisecracks.

According to Gray the mood of the beer is 'pure fun' and he suggests that fans keep an eye on each release's label. 'We evolve all our recipes on a batch to batch basis, but the recipe never changes drastically. Anything we do will only improve the experience. James Yeo does the same with the label, and on a can to can basis you can see subtle changes and differences to the art.'

Goes well with... What else but a homemade cheeseburger

MOLSON COORS
Worthington's White Shield

5.6% Frequently available

Burton upon Trent, Staffordshire
molsoncoors.com

*A primal English-style IPA
with its roots in Burton*

Worthington's White Shield is a survivor, a hangover from Victorian Burton where a contemporary advert shows the words 'India Pale Ale' on the bottle label. It's an English-style IPA and has had a bit of a rocky time in the past couple of decades, at one time being farmed out of its home town to be brewed at the long-gone King & Barnes brewery in Sussex. Then there was the William Worthington brewery, where it was produced within the National Brewery Centre in Burton, before production came to a halt (that kit is now owned and used by Heritage Brewery). White Shield is now brewed at Molson Coors, where Carling is made. Curious companions, but at least it is still in Burton.

The man most associated with White Shield is former Bass brewer Steve Wellington, having first made it when starting in the industry in the 1960s. When I interviewed him several years ago he had firm ideas on what constituted an English-style IPA. 'To define it we have to go back to what an IPA was,' he said, 'a Pale Ale that was sent to India. I believe that American-style IPAs are nothing like what I would term an IPA, with all the double and triple versions and their exceptional bitterness. IPAs also had to be fairly strong to survive the sea voyage, between 6–7%, and there would be 2–3lb of hops per barrel, which is a lot.'

Amber in colour, it has a nuttiness, bittersweetness, Cointreau-like orange citrus on both the nose and the palate; there is an elegance about its taste, a sense that this is a beer that would hug you like a favourite grandparent and shower you with praise and warmth. It is also a beer that will age magnificently, with its flavours deepening and become even more grand.

Goes well with... Contemplation and silence

ROCK LEOPARD BREWING
Type Here To Search

6.8%   Frequently available

Welling, London
rockleopardbrewing.com

A West Coast IPA with plenty of fruitiness and a joyous bitter end

This is a West Coast IPA, a beer that knows its own mind about what it says to the palate and what it looks like in the glass. On the nose there is stone fruit (peach perhaps) and a sweet earthiness, while the palate is presented with a ripening citrus juiciness (orange, sweet lemon and grapefruit), a malt sweetness, a muscular mouthfeel thanks to the 7% addition of oats in the grist, with a lingering bitterness in the finish. This is a beer you will sip and pay supplication to right until the bitter end.

'In a blind taste I think the drinker would know straight away that it's a West Coast IPA,' says Rock Leopard founder and head brewer Stacey Ayeh. 'It is not trying to rejoin the bitterness arms race of the golden age of the modern version of the style but it still has what I believe is a near enough well-judged and appropriate bitterness. But to the connoisseur or specialist drinker of the style I think it brings a welcome challenge. I say that because it says on the label that it's a West Coast IPA and the drinker is expecting a clear liquid. But it is presented with a slight "haze" and some sweetness at the front and a clean, bitter finish, which sets it up for another sip.'

With the point about the haze in mind, Ayeh adds, 'when I first tasted it I was very happy mainly because I'm always happy to drink beer but also because I knew I could look people in the eye and say "yes". This is a well-made beer which is interesting because it's not what you'd expect from looking at it.'

Goes well with… The setting of the sun after a glorious day

ROOSTER'S BREWING
Baby-Faced Assassin

6.1%   Core

Harrogate, North Yorkshire
roosters.co.uk

An IPA in which the Citra hop shines in all its glorious, aromatic might

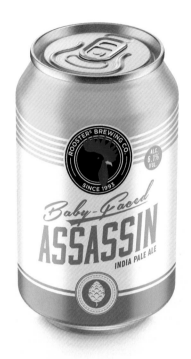

This bold, colourful, vividly flavoured IPA is a case of yin and yang as citrus orange, juicy mango and passion fruit juice notes leap out into the air, acrobatic and assertive, lubricious and luscious, to be balanced against a bracing bitterness and a grainy dryness in the finish. This is a beer in which the Citra hop shines with all its glorious, aromatic might and deserves your full attention when it comes to drinking it. When you enjoy this from the can you will discover how it can turn a commonplace day into an IPA day – and given that Rooster's make their mighty beers in Harrogate we could be talking about a Yorkshire IPA day.

'It was first made as a home-brew recipe in a bathroom in Leeds,' recalls Tom Fozard, Rooster's commercial manager, 'as the name suggests, it was conceived to be a deceptively drinkable IPA, with a striking hop character that ran through the beer from first sniff to the last gulp and showcased everything the Citra hop has to offer. I took a standard IPA recipe, chucked a load of late hop additions at it and dialled everything up to 11.

'As the then home-brewer who designed the beer, I couldn't have been more excited with how it turned out and remember syphoning off a sample from the fermentation bucket to share with my colleagues at the beer shop I worked in at the time.'

Since then the beer has won countless awards and become an integral part of Rooster's range of exemplary beers. And it all started in a bathroom in Leeds.

Goes well with… Some spicy sausages on the BBQ and a light salad

SALOPIAN BREWERY
Kashmir

5.5% Seasonal (Part of the 'Black Range')

Shrewsbury, Shropshire
salopianbrewery.co.uk

*A bright and vibrant IPA with
a lingering dry and bitter finish*

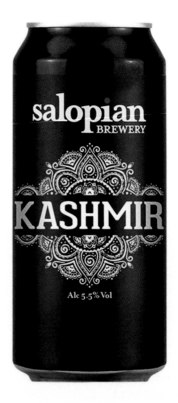

For me the name of this thrilling beer evokes the epic Led Zeppelin track of the same name from *Physical Graffiti,* a dense wall of orchestral rock that pile-drives its way onwards as Robert Plant's voice roars and soars to the heavens. Salopian's Kashmir is less of a piledriver, being more of a sensual counterpoint to the song in the way the use of Citra gives its nose suggestions of lime and an ur-tropical fruitiness, something that suggests sunlight and a bright vibrant ripeness, as well as a light chive-like savouriness. There is more of the tropical fruit on the palate, as well as pine-like and resinous notes, which somehow remind me of the white grape sprightliness of Riesling. There is also mango, some peppery hop, bittersweetness and a lingering dry and bitter finish, all of these components making for a complete IPA.

'It was originally just brewed as a cask beer to showcase the new wonder hop Citra in 2010,' recalls Salopian's Chairman Wilf Nelson, 'we were after the massive pungency of the hop, but wanted to make something massively flavoured but eminently drinkable, our normal mantra. It was brewed with whole hop flowers — no pellets, so the challenge was to get all that flavour without overpowering bitterness, which we achieved. The first brew came out exactly as we wanted it, and it felt great, as we had recently adopted a hop forward approach and this proved we were on the right track.'

When asked what the mood of the beer is, Nelson replies 'effervescent', which sounds like it could be the right accompaniment to a rendition of Led Zeppelin's monster of a musical triumph.

Goes well with... Reading *Led Zeppelin: The Biography* by Bob Spitz

SALT BEER FACTORY
Huckaback

5.5% Core

Saltaire, West Yorkshire
saltbeerfactory.co.uk

*A delectable and light-hearted
New England IPA*

Colin Stronge is Salt's head brewer and his approach to this beer and others is simple: 'I try to treat each brew like the most important beer you will ever make. Attention to detail, whether it is about selecting the malts and hops, choosing the combinations of flavours or the weighing out of salts, each piece of the puzzle must be meticulously handled.'

This New England IPA is a very drinkable beer. Hold on a minute though (sound of a description coming to a screeching halt). What do we mean by drinkability? What do we mean when we think about a beer that is so easy to drink that it can be downed in one? For a start, this is the essence of a well-made NEIPA (not a badly made one that has the bitterness of paracetamol in its finish). There is a joy in a style like this, thanks to its lightness of flavour, which doesn't mean there is no flavour but that it is not overwhelming. It is folk music rather than Wagner, a music that still has its roots in people's experiences but is not the entire human condition brought to you by an unsmiling orchestra. It is a story told, straightforward and bold rather than a bag of analogies and symbolisms from a writer whose tortured life is of more interest than their work. It is the comfort of a home-baked loaf of bread, a warm pasty from the local family butcher.

So with that in mind let us look at it in the glass, lemon gold in colour. It has a fresh, tropically fruity nose alongside ripe peach skin, almost as if a bag of ripe mangoes, guavas, lychees and peaches were dashed against a sun-frisked wall on a summer's day. There is more of this fruit salad on the palate, with a childlike juiciness joining in the fun before a light bitterness and dryness frisk about like young foals in the finish. Yes, this is a very drinkable beer.

Goes well with… Showing your culinary skills to friends with diced scallop ceviche

SIGNATURE BREW
Nocturne Black IPA

6.66% Occasional

Walthamstow, London
signaturebrew.co.uk

Black IPA with a multitude of flavours that perk up the palate

Black IPA is the beer style that causes eyes to roll and exclamations along the lines of 'how can there be such a thing as a black India *Pale* Ale?', to which I just shrug my shoulders and declare how much I love the style and how glad I am it is starting to be made again. But though various solutions to this conundrum of a name have been put forward, including Cascadian Dark Ale and India Dark Ale, Black IPA has stubbornly remained in use.

Not that any of this healthy debate should affect the quality of Signature's highly impressive Nocturne, which was brewed in collaboration with US hop merchants Yakima Chief Hops, who supplied the brewery with a new hop called Talus. Given the brewery's impressive track record of music-inspired beers (Roadie for starters) and band collaborations, you could be forgiven for thinking that Talus sounds more like a vintage prog rock band for which barrel-aged mellotrons are the very stuff of life.

That's the speculation and philosophy taken care of, so let's have a beer.

Nocturne, naturally, is dark, not just a faint-hearted kind of dark, but a deep, unshadowed darkness (incidentally, The Darkness collaborated with Signature on a beer), while a lightness of sorts is provided by the generous, rocky, crema-coloured head of foam. On the nose there is a cascade of grapefruit, soft butter toffee, some floral freshness and a delicate roastiness, with a deep, hefty gulp of beer revealing more soft roastiness, grapefruit, liquorice, caramel, toffee and a bitterness and dryness in the finish. Sometimes the debate has to end and the time for drinking begins.

Goes well with... A chargrilled steak with fries

ST AUSTELL BREWERY
Proper Job

5.5% Core

St Austell, Cornwall
staustellbrewery.co.uk

A joyous and beautifully balanced IPA

In 1999 a Lancastrian brewer from Maclay's in Scotland was appointed as St Austell's new head brewer. His name was Roger Ryman and he went on to become one of the most respected and towering figures of British brewing until his sad death in May 2020. His achievements were many, and you could argue that with Proper Job he brought out one of the first mainstream US-style IPAs in the UK.

The beer was first brewed in 2004 and was directly influenced by the time Ryman spent working at Bridport Brewery in the beer-centric city of Portland, Oregon. The beer that led him to produce Proper Job was his host's own IPA, which I finally tasted on a visit in 2015 and could have sworn I was drinking Proper Job, albeit with a higher carbonation and colder temperature. However, Roger did tell me once that 'Proper Job is not a copy of their beer. The American brewers do not have access to Maris Otter of the quality we have here, so it's a more complicated malt grist. Also the hops are slightly different. I don't know how the brewmaster worked out his

hop grist, it is a bit of a hop room sweep (everything that was left chucked into one brew) with a wide range of varieties. Once again, I simplified the hop grist to just three varieties (Willamette, Chinook and Cascade), but the balance between Chinook and Cascade is critical.'

Poured into the glass it is a pale, almost wan, gold in colour, while its nose dances with a tropical and citrusy fruitiness that summons up a greengrocer's fruit aisle of pineapple, melon and grapefruit. The same fruitiness parades on the palate alongside a delectable resiny note, before a striking bitter finish, with some sweetness and dryness hanging around to keep it company. A perfect memorial to a great brewer.

Goes well with… A Cornish pasty from an independent bakery

STEWART BREWING
Radical Road

6.4% Frequently available

Loanhead, Edinburgh, Scotland
stewartbrewing.co.uk

Vivid and vibrant IPA with plenty of pine and citrus notes on both nose and palate

Here is an IPA, what we call an American-style IPA, vivid and vibrant with its rich aromatics of pine, orange liqueur and grapefruit; resinous on the palate, alongside orange marmalade, grapefruit, a pungent hoppiness, a chime of bittersweetness and a lingering dry and bitter finish. This is a beer that tingles and draws a trance on the tongue, leaving its presence behind with an almost mystic thoroughness. The resiny notes are comparable to the delicate smell of pine in a woodland after a shower of rain, while the citrus is like the scent of ripe fruit in a warm, sunny kitchen.

For Stewart Brewing this was a beer that was developed back in 2012, when the great wave of IPA was about to wash up on the shores of British brewing and claim what these days seems like an eternal sovereignty. For the brewery it was also a step in an oblique direction away from the range of traditional beers that were its daily bread and butter.

'Radical Road was one of our first ventures away from the cask beer world,' says the brewery's marketing manager Sarah Stirton. 'While hoppy IPAs are a dime a dozen now, at the time we created Radical Road it was a bit out of the box. We set out to create a beer that packed a hoppy punch but was also an easy drink. We think it embodies the second beer you have on a Friday night when you get home. You've had your first, a sessionable IPA polished off in record time to drain away the stress of the week, then you crack open a Radical Road so you can take a seat, relax and appreciate it.'

Goes well with... Closing the front door behind you and enjoying the end of the working week

THORNBRIDGE
Jaipur

5.9% Core

Bakewell, Derbyshire
thornbridgebrewery.co.uk

Game-changing IPA that still explodes on the palate with hoppy joy

This is perhaps one of the most crucial beers of the past couple of decades, a game-changer and a standard by which other brewers have measured themselves. It has also remained a vibrant part of Thornbridge's family of beers, a well-hopped, sunny-disposed, mouth-watering modern IPA that still stuns and soothes the palate with its rich explosion of hoppy joy.

It was first brewed in 2005, having being developed by a couple of young brewers, Stefano Rossi and Martin Dickie (who went on to co-found BrewDog and bring Punk IPA into the world) and quickly caught the imagination of beer drinkers. Like many a favourite beer, there is a ritual in which Jaipur is served. The sound of the ring-tab being pulled is first, a psst, the slightest resemblance to the sound of calico being torn, and if I put my nose close enough to the opened can I can identify the aromatics of ripe apricot skin, ripe mango and a suggestion of pineapple. It is not sweet though; it is slightly musky, pungent and adult.

As you pour the beer, listening to the light fizz as it bunches in the glass, its snow-white collar of foam pushing upwards, there is a gleaming, golden familiarity of the beer, the crispness and lush fruitiness, the bitterness and that feeling of satisfaction that usually elicits an 'aah', as if your soul was sitting back in a comfortable armchair. It's lush, brisk, polite, full-flavoured, chiming, delicate, and lingers long in the finish like the memory of a favourite piece of music.

Goes well with... Pork schnitzel and sautéed potatoes

UNITY BREWING
Collision

6.2% Core

Southampton, Hampshire
unitybrewingco.com

An appetising and refreshing juice-juggle of a NEIPA

It's the easiest thing in the world to ask for an IPA isn't it? All you need to know is whether the style of IPA you want is English, American (West Coast or East Coast?), session, Belgian or, naturally, New England (other styles can be found as well). When asking for Southampton-based Collision, it's a NEIPA you will get, and a very good version of the style it is, pouring a hazy amber gold with grapefruit, mandarin, pine and tropical fruit such as mango and papaya emerging out of the glass with the alacrity of a pod of exuberant dolphins.

'It was originally brewed as a collaboration with the bar our now operations manager Bolo was running at the time,' says Unity founder and head brewer Jimmy Hatherley. 'The idea was to collide ideas a little, with Columbus hops adding a more traditional dankness and a little bitterness to an otherwise juicy Mosaic-forward New England style IPA. We also decided to use flaked spelt from the guys at Craggs & Co in Country Durham. We had been using it a lot in Saisons and felt it would add a really complimentary but unique character to the style. So it really was about colliding some more unique ideas whilst keeping it balanced, juicy and really drinkable.'

It's a full-bodied beer with the collision between the dankness and tropical fruit laying down a carpet of flavour at the start of the palate, followed by a rounded, toasty sweetness and hint of honey with a dryness and unobtrusive bitterness in the finish. Maybe a Hadron Collider of a beer?

WIMBLEDON BREWERY
Quartermaine IPA

5.8–6.2%   Frequently available

Wimbledon, London
wimbledonbrewery.com

Enduring English-style IPA created by veteran brewer Derek Prentice

Derek Prentice is a legend in the British brewing industry, having started his career in the late 1960s at Truman's in East London. There then followed stints with both Young's and Fuller's, before his current berth at Wimbledon Brewery. He's also a nice chap to share a beer with. Quartermaine IPA is one of the first beers he created at Wimbledon, an English-style IPA inspired by his memory of the classic Burton-bottled IPAs that were common when he first joined the brewing industry.

'At the time this was best epitomised by Worthington White Shield,' he recalls, 'there were a few other major brewers' beers in the category, but it was really only White Shield which had retained bottle conditioning, which kept the beer vibrant in its flavour and spritziness. This style of beer was typically above 5%, pale, sparkling, clean and quite dry but combining the fruitiness of the yeast with a high loading of British bittering and aroma hops.'

When it came to producing the beer, Prentice's time at both Young's and Fuller's in producing Special London Ale and Bengal Lancer gave him vital experience in the way to proceed and when the first brew was tasted, 'they were very close to the classic IPA memory of mine'.

Amber in colour, Prentice's Proustian vision of a beer has fruity notes on the nose, reminiscent of orange marmalade as well as the pungency of fresh hops. On the palate there is a citrus sweetness (more marmalade perhaps?), hints of toffee, light pepperiness, a pithy woodiness, before it finishes dry and bitter, encouraging you to keep lifting the glass in salute to Prentice's remarkable time in brewing.

Goes well with... A chunk of ripe Stilton and fresh bread

WIPER AND TRUE
Hinterland

7.3% Occasional

Bristol
wiperandtrue.com

Mixed fermentation IPA
that reaches for the sky

As Mr Spock never said, 'it's an IPA, Jim, but not as we know it'. In fact, the words that Mr Spock never said could be applied to a lot of IPAs these days as they emerge from their boltholes blinking in the sunlight, carrying tags such as smoothie, milkshake, West Coast, cold and sour. The latter description is closest to this glorious mash-up of a bright and breezy fruitiness in collaboration with a tangy, slightly tart crispness before a bracing, dry finish. So yes, it is an IPA, and yes, it has American hops, but it is also partly fermented with Brettanomyces, the wild yeast so beloved of the Lambic producers of the Senne valley near Brussels. It's an experiment as well, but let us not begrudge Wiper and True's attempts to brew off the chosen path, for it is an exhilarating beer.

According to brewery co-founder Michael Wiper, the idea for Hinterland 'was led by our barrel store manager Will. The idea was about pairing the fruitier notes of a certain Brettanomyces yeast, the pineapple funk, with big, juicy American hops. We wanted to explore how they act together and how they both develop over time.'

It's a stunning-looking beer, translucent pale gold with a firm head of foam, and the oranges and lemons of St Clements on the nose, plus an earthiness suggestive of mature blue cheese. The Brettanomyces is integrated into the brew, producing a joyful beer that might smell reminiscent of Stilton (salt, earth, sweat), but has developed into a boldly flavoured IPA full of fruit, earth, crispness and dryness in the finish.

'The fun of this beer is that the expectations change through time,' adds Wiper. 'When it's fresh it has a vibrant, hop-forward fruitiness with a complex, estery finish. As it ages the hops fade and the yeast notes amplify, becoming more farmhouse and complex.'

Goes well with... A selection of charcuterie and olives

WYLAM BREWERY
Jakehead

6.3%   Core

Newcastle upon Tyne
wylambrewery.co.uk

A 'super-charged' IPA with a clamorous hop character

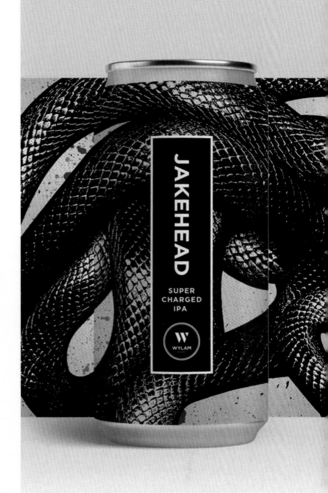

In these dizzying days of beer nirvana, we've come a long way from the Newcastle of the eponymous Brown Ale, especially as the beer is nowadays brewed far outside the city limits down in the Yorkshire town of Tadcaster. Not to worry though, just like many other major cities, Newcastle has its fair share of contemporary breweries plying their trade and Wylam is one of the shining stars of the scene.

Originally set up in 2000 at Heddon-on-the-Wall in Northumbria, and noted for cask beers such as Bitter and Red Kite, the brewery changed direction in 2015 when Dave Stone became managing director. A year later it moved to Newcastle and set up home in the stunning Palace of Arts in Exhibition Park, which was built in the 1920s for the North East Exhibition of 1929.

Jakehead, a so-called 'super-charged' IPA, was symptomatic of the brewery's new emphasis, with its vibrant and clamorous hop character, dark amber orange in colour, with the aromatics on its nose almost reminiscent of a kids'

tea party. Check out the notes of orange, passion fruit, grapefruit and mango and be prepared to be wowed from the start. There is more of this rampant fruitiness on the palate, alongside a suggestion of white pepper and a background of crisp graininess, before a dry and bitter finish that carries on with the persistence of a peal of bells. It is juicy, dry, bitter, soothing and ghostly in the way it creeps up on the palate and makes you want to drink more.

Goes well with... A plate of spicy chicken wings

THE YEASTIE BOYS
Gunnamatta Earl Grey IPA

6.5% Frequently available

UK/NewZealand
yeastieboysuk.myshopify.com

A beautifully conceived marriage of Earl Grey and beer

Cup of tea? Or maybe you'd like a beer? How about combining the two, as the Yeastie Boys did when they first produced Gunnamatta for the annual Great Australasian Beer SpecTAPular back in 2012. Every brewery at the festival was asked to release a new beer for it, and Yeastie Boy co-founder New Zealander Stu McKinlay started thinking about the things he associated with Australia.

'Surfing sat really high up the list,' he says, 'my strong surfing memories from my late teens and early twenties were camping on the beach and drinking lots of cups of tea all day and beers in the evening. The idea of tea and beer was immediately appealing.

'Every man and his dog were pumping out coffee beers back then but I was a tea drinker. I went to see a tea merchant with one idea in mind and his Earl Grey Blue Flower blew my mind. The rest is history! The beer is "dry-leafed" in the same way we'd normally dry hop a beer. We do use a little hop in the boil but all of the aromatics and those big orange, stone fruit and rose water aromatics come from the combination of malts and the bergamot-infused tea.'

The result is a gorgeous, orange-amber beer, which has a lemony, herbal note of bergamot alongside a citrusy, hoppy presence. On the palate there is Earl Grey dryness and honey-lemon flavours combining with a juicy fruitiness and a generous bittersweetness. Not a bad beer to enjoy during an afternoon break.

Goes well with... Tea-smoked salmon enjoyed in the garden on a warm and beneficent day

LAGER

Helles or Pilsner,
Bavarian or Czech,
smoked or dark, you will
find that the family of
lager has many different
members in this chapter.

71 BREWING
Outer Galactic

7.5%   Seasonal

Dundee, Scotland
71brewing.com

A handsome-looking, dry-hopped thoroughbred of a strong Pilsner

There's a restless sense of creativity about many of today's contemporary brewers. Sometimes the journeys they take don't necessarily lead to where they want to go and the end result might be what looks like a smoothie in the glass. Other times, as the team at 71 Brewing have shown with Outer Galactic, taking a sideways step with a familiar beer style works with the certainty of the written word.

'Our flagship beer is 71 Lager,' says marketing manager Victoria Scott-Lewis, 'a Czech-style Pilsner hopped solely with Saaz hops. We wanted to take this style we know so well and kind of flip it on its head a little. We increased the ABV, dosed it in the kettle and dry-hopped it with New Zealand and classic North American hops, giving it a huge, uncharacteristic tropical hoppy profile, but retaining a crisp and bitter finish. I guess it's a crossover IPL, or as we call it an Imperial Dry-Hopped Pilsner.'

It is certainly a handsome-looking beer, deep dark gold in the glass with an immediate hit of tropical fruit lushly latching itself onto the aromatics. There is more of the tropical fruitiness on the palate alongside a graininess, a crisp mouthfeel and a lingering bitterness in the finish.

'The concept of this beer was different to any other that we had brewed in terms of the end style,' says Scott-Lewis, 'so we developed the recipe and the first brew turned out pretty much where we wanted it. You're always thinking ahead to what we could do next time! So we have tweaked the hop and malt profile since the first brew, giving the beer a greater balance.'

Goes well with… A creamy risotto Milanese

AMITY BREW CO
Festoon Helles

4.6%   Core

Leeds
amitybrew.co

*A temptation of a Helles
brewed in Leeds*

Munich is one of the great European beer cities and the first thing all beer-lovers do when arriving there is hunt out a Helles, the everyday lager of Bavaria. I suggest doing the same thing when arriving in Leeds, home of Amity, who produce their own superb version of a Helles, with Amity co-founder Russ Clarke saying that inspirations for the brewery's first lager were, 'beers like Augustiner Helles and Tegernseer Helles. Our goal is not to try to "beat" these beers, but to take the elements that we love about them and construct something more modern in line with our ethos of giving a modern spin to classic styles.'

When Amity launched it at the start of 2020, just as Covid-19 was kicking off, its beers were contract brewed elsewhere while waiting for the brewery and taproom to be built. The recipe was drawn up and Amity's team took part in the brew day. However, as lockdown kicked in they had to communicate remotely to see how the fermentation behaved and the conditioning progressed, a situation

Clarke describes as 'fraught'. However, all went well and when he first tasted it, 'it was everything we wanted it to be'.

Festoon, which is named after the mill building Amity now calls home, is pale lemon-yellow in colour and has a gentle aroma of biscuity malt and floral hop. On the tongue it is crisp, clean, refreshing and bittersweet while the dryness on the finish lingers like the memory of a good night out.

'Hopefully it expresses what Amity stands for,' says Clarke, 'classic styles with a modern twist.'

Goes well with… A sunny summer's afternoon in the back garden

BEAK BREWERY
Děšt'

5%   Occasional

Lewes, East Sussex
beakbrewery.com

Luminous Czech-style Pilsner that sings in the glass

Hazy IPAs brimming with a lustrous juiciness and as golden as the hopes of a hero at the start of a fairy tale are what Beak is best known for, but when it came to creating the luminous lager Děšt' head brewer Robin Head-Fourman wanted to showcase a beer that was a little bit different.

'We wanted to produce a beer that was distinct from our core offering of hazy IPAs,' he recalls, 'and a crisp, Czech-style Pilsner seemed like the perfect vehicle for that. Something with conviction that says, "we aren't a one trick pony". So we produced a light, refreshing Pilsner that lets the ingredients do the talking. The yeast strain we use is straight from Czechia and leaves a subtle graininess, light noble hop character and refreshing finish.'

The beer when poured is a clear, burnished gold, almost like a beaming, friendly smile that has love on its side. There is a shine of sweet malt on the nose, a bright, clean aroma that reaches straight into the brewhouse.

It is full-bodied in its mouthfeel, clean but suffused with the lushness of malt and the nobleness of Saaz and Hallertau Mittlefrüh hops (a *lagering* time of 30 days also helps matters on its way); there is also a faint suggestion of vanilla mid palate before its dry and bittersweet finish.

'The first brew was great,' recalls Head-Fourman, 'and there was a long anticipation amongst the team given that it was *lagering* over the Christmas break and this meant we were eager to sample it.'

I suspect he and the team were not disappointed.

Goes well with… Roast pork knuckle, dumplings and red cabbage for that full Czechia experience

BOHEM BREWERY
Amos

4.9% Core

Tottenham, North London
bohembrewery.com

*From North London to Prague
and back again in one glass of beer*

Run and founded by a bunch of Czech guys, Bohem is a little bit of Bohemian brewing expertise based in North London. As you might guess, the brewery specialises in Czech-style lagers, which are so authentic that drinking them is like being magically transported to a Prague pub, complete with roast duck and a dreadnought of a dumpling in front of you.

Amos is a light amber-coloured delight in the glass, a beer that, according to co-founder Petr Skocek, is 'slightly more in tune with the taste of mainstream lager drinkers than other beers we brew, but it is still brewed using original Czech techniques, and I believe drinkers immediately recognise it as one of ours. When I considered what we would do in developing the beer, I sat down with co-founder Zdenek Kudr at our small taproom in North London. We agreed we wanted to make a single hop, single malt lager that would have an original taste, while beer drinkers could still immediately tell that this was a beer from Bohem Brewery – our USP is traditional Bohemian lagers, brewed by Czechs, in London, and so our "house style" is important.'

The beer has since become the brewery's bestseller, so you could say that Skocek and Kudr were successful, especially as it possesses a gorgeous, Proustian, take-me-back to Prague character. There is sweet malt and floral hop on the nose, caramel sweetness and floral and spice notes on the palate with a lingering bitterness in the finish. An ample and imperious beer that refreshes and revives and celebrates the wisdom of Anglo-Czech collaboration.

Goes well with… The masterpiece of Czech satirical literature *The Good Soldier Švejk*

BRAYBROOKE BEER CO
Keller Lager

4.8% Core

Market Harborough, Leicestershire
braybrookebeer.co

Franconian-style Kellerbier from Leicestershire

Several years ago I spent time ambling (and tasting) around Upper Franconia in Northern Bavaria, an area in which over 200 mainly small breweries produce some of the finest lagered beers in Europe. These beers are full-bodied, thanks in part to the use of the decoction mash, soft in their carbonation and bittersweet in the finish, and call out to the drinker with a sense of their own charm and uniqueness.

Keller is a Franconian-style lager that has spent the kind of time maturing that we all wish we could experience as the world races on. Instead, we drink this beer and enjoy it because it is also unfiltered and naturally carbonated, which adds to its beautiful presence on the palate. To make things even more eloquent it is brewed in that well-known sub-district of Bavaria called Leicestershire, on a farm near Market Harborough.

'Kellerbier is a style that we fell in love with on our travels to Bamberg and so we went about brewing our own,' says brewery co-founder Luke Wilson. 'We wanted to share our passion for

lager and to show that when well-made they are some of the most enjoyable beers to drink. If you go to Germany you can find all these amazing lagers made by small, local breweries with the same beer recipe that has been handed down for generations, and as the German way of brewing has always been an inspiration for us, we would like to continue to brew it in that way.'

On opening a bottle and pouring its golden delight into the glass, you will discover a gently toasted and slightly honeyed nose, followed by a crisp mouthfeel, an aromatic bready character and rounded off with a dry finish. This is a beer to be gulped in great draughts from a pint tankard in the company of friends invited over for the evening, with lederhosen, dirndls, pretzels and oompah band downloads optional.

Goes well with… Bratwurst, fried onions and sweet mustard

BRICK BREWERY
Peckham Pils

4.8%   Core

Peckham, London
brickbrewery.co.uk

A perfectly lagered Pils that is sprightly and bright-eyed on the palate

For many home-brewers (as well as smaller breweries) producing a properly lagered beer is somewhat of a challenge, mainly because of the need to keep beer in a conditioning tank for several weeks (the famous lagering part in other words). Prior to going pro with Brick Brewery, this was exactly the issue that co-founder Ian Stewart faced.

'As a home-brewer I stuck with ales owing to the lack of temperature control on my home fermentation vessels,' he recalls. 'I wanted to brew a lager both as a personal challenge but also for my wife, Sally (brewery co-founder), who at the time didn't drink ales and preferred a crisp, clean lager. So I waited until the cooler months and fermented the lager in my garden shed, which was empty then as it was too cold for an ale, but it was perfect for cold fermenting and cold conditioning a lager. I was always a fan of Pilsner Urquell and Peckham Pils is styled very much on it.'

As soon as Brick Brewery was up and running the Pils became part of its core range, even though at the time tank space for lagering was at a premium. However, Stewart's belief in the process of lagering paid off and the result is a floral, spicy and citrusy palate refresher that dances on the tongue with the carefree nature of a young fawn discovering the freedom of the outdoors for the first time. It is also a social and carefree kind of beer, which its brewer believes is 'an ideal match with short ribs and prawns on the BBQ, when the sun is out and you need a quencher with character and a balanced flavor.'

Goes well with… As well as a BBQ, this is an ideal accompaniment to Pad Thai

CAMDEN TOWN BREWERY
Hells Lager

4.6% Core

Enfield, London
camdentownbrewery.com

Refreshing, thirst-quenching Helles and Pils hybrid

Even if a beer is as ubiquitous as Hells Lager seems to be, if it still engages with the palate, still creates a rave with its aromatics and generally throws down the gauntlet to those who might ignore it, then this is a beer to be enjoyed, to be glorious about and drink deeply of and with gusto.

The central core beer of the Camden Town Brewery range is a beer that was initially designed to bridge the gap between a Helles and a Pilsner. It gleams and glitters in the glass with a pale golden sheen beneath a billowing head of foam; meanwhile bubbles rise up through the glass as if trying to escape their destiny. On the nose there's a delicate breadiness or maybe it's a graininess suggestive of breakfast cereal, alongside a light suggestion of bitter lemon. It's a shy and crystalline selection of aromatics but sometimes less is more (as the cliché goes).

You gulp this beer, for it is a refreshing thirst-quencher, a sociable beer to be enjoyed in the company of friends, especially on a sunny day in the garden when you've invited them over for a barbecue. There is more bitter lemon on the palate, a soft mouthfeel, a whoosh of dry graininess mid palate with a long and engaging bittersweet finish that encourages you to bring the glass to your mouth again. It might not be made in Camden anymore, ever since a larger and more efficient brewery was built in Enfield, but this beer still has its soul in where it first emerged.

Goes well with… A mouthwatering bowl of fritto misto

DONZOKO
Northern Helles

4.2% Core

Edinburgh, Scotland
donzoko.org

Everyday Helles with a count of
bittersweetness and brisk crispness

A Helles lager is an everyday beer,
clean and uncomplicated, but with the
kind of character that enables it to be
enjoyed glass after glass. That's the
kind of beer that inspired Donzoko's
owner and head brewer Reece Hugill
when he was at university in Munich,
and as he recalls, 'I had fond memories
of drinking cold bottles of Helles in the
English Garden, as well as unfiltered
lager from small breweries. So when it
was time for me to brew Northern Helles
I wanted to recreate not so much the
exact beer, but the feeling of easy-going
and accessible but very delicious lager.
There would be enough in the beer for
those who geek out about beer, but it
would be also perfect for a six pack, or
sharing with your friends/family.'

The beer pours a lightly hazy
gold (it is unfiltered), a brooding and
almost moody gold, but the kind of
gold that warms the soul. On the nose
there is the chime of malt sweetness,
alongside a dry graininess and ethereal
lemon and floral notes. Each swig

of the beer reveals a cascade of soft
breadiness, malt sweetness, a light
lemon smile, bittersweetness and
crispness before it finishes dry.

Donzoko is a cuckoo brewery
and at the time of writing Hugill has
moved to Edinburgh, where he will
be making his beers (which include
several intelligent and intriguing riffs
on a lager theme) at Newbarns Brewery
and then fermenting them himself, as
he did when he lived in Newcastle.

Goes well with… A prosciutto and mozzarella sandwich with a side helping of fries

DOUBLE-BARRELLED
Cagoule

6.2% Occasional

Tilehurst, Berkshire
doublebarrel.co.uk

*A crisp and brisk, bright
and joyful IPL*

Cagoule is not a regular beer, a member of the brewery's core team, but a seasonal delight, brewed in the spring, something to look forward to. It might not remain the same either, according to brewery founder and head brewer Mike Clayton-Jones: 'We don't brew an awful lot of our beers repeatedly, but when we do it will often be because we want to make a tweak to it, showcase something in a different way, or use it as an opportunity to innovate in a slightly different direction. This is ultimately the reason I got into brewing in the first place – change, innovation, learning, nuance and adaptations of styles are all huge parts of what makes me so interested in this industry and why we keep releasing new beers so regularly.'

Then there's the matter of its style. Cagoule is an India Pale Lager, in which the hoppiness of an IPA is married to the crispness and briskness of a lager, a style that makes perfect sense, but is not as popular with brewers as either an IPA or lager. Sparkling gold in colour, tropical fruit and citrus notes emerge from the glass, bright and colourful, an invitation from an old and well-loved friend. On the palate there is a joyful crispness alongside more tropical fruit and citrus before an engaging and amiable bittersweet and dry finish.

'Cagoule has a special place in my heart,' says Clayton-Jones, 'because of the role it played in introducing us to the craft beer scene when we launched it at Craft Beer Rising in 2018. Having the chance to revisit it is a lot of fun and I look forward to each brew in early spring and it is the perfect beer to spend some of the quieter months in tank through our brewing schedule.'

Goes well with... Grilled salmon with foraged samphire

DURATION BEER

Doses

5.1%   Core

King's Lynn, Norfolk
durationbeer.com

*German-style Pils from
the depths of Norfolk*

It is human nature to want to improve on an original design. In fashion a classic is brought up to date or given a modern spin; in cooking too, where the phrase 'modern twist' is as ubiquitous as well-starched chef's whites. Brewers are culpable too, taking the venerable beer styles of, say, England or Bavaria, and aiming to bring them into the 21st century.

When it came to developing Duration's German-style Pils, the brewery's co-founder and head brewer Bates was happy to leave things as they were. 'I'd say with Doses basically we're not looking to reinvent the wheel,' he says. 'I don't think much needs to be perfected in that style of beer. I don't like New World hops in Pilsners, I've tried a fair few but they just don't sit right with me on taste, aroma, or palate. Sometimes less is more in beer, in particularly this style of beer.

'Pilsner to me can be a bit of a lost in translation style of beer, and the brewer trying to be "innovative" or "improve on" the style when I just don't think it really can be improved on. I love German lagers, it was the first style of beer I learned and loved at a local brewpub I worked at.'

He has a point as Doses is a highly expressive beer that will make you yearn to sit in a Bavarian beer garden. Pale gold in colour, it has a fresh floral aroma, as if wanting to replicate the joy of sitting outside on a summer's day. It is light and lemony, slightly flowery and full-bodied on the palate, while the finish is bracingly dry with a hint of bitterness that tickles the back of the throat. An enticing and enchanting beer that, as Bates says, demonstrates less is more and all the better for it here.

Goes well with... Sitting in the garden and not doing anything at all

EKO BREWERY
Eko Gold

4.9% Core

London
ekobrewery.com

Well-rounded lager with a delicate sweetness from coconut palm sugar

Here is a lager with a difference. For Eko Gold, brewery co-founder and brewer Anthony Adedipe added coconut palm sugar. For him, with his Nigerian ethnic background, this was an attempt to create a brew that was African-inspired, not only with its ingredients but also as a reflection of its culture. However, brewing the beer wasn't without its challenges.

'There was a lot of excitement and apprehension when we were developing Eko Gold,' says Anthony. 'Excitement because this was to be the second beer in our range, but apprehension as this was the first beer to have a distinctly African influence with the addition of the coconut palm sugar. The coconut palm sugar is the sugar made from the sap of the coconut tree that is used to make the African drink palm wine, but with Gold it cuts through the bitterness that you associate with hops. In all honesty, we were blown away when we first tasted the beer as we had managed to create a beer that tasted like no other lager we had experienced before.'

Translucent gold in the glass, there are notes of citrus, light grain and a rounded, delicate sweetness, while on the palate there is more citrus alongside a light sweetness from the coconut palm sugar, which intriguingly turns around your expectations of what a lager is. The bitterness is light while the mouthfeel is soft.

'Eko Gold is so easy to drink that it is definitely a beer for social occasions,' adds Adedipe. 'It is thirst quenching and sessionable, so it is great for whether you are in the pub with friends or washing down a three-course meal.'

Goes well with... A plate of deep-fried calamari

EXALE BREWING
Der Titan

4.8% Core

Walthamstow, London
exalebrewing.com

A rare British example of the
classic Dortmunder beer style

Even though its name suggests an homage to an imperious German midfielder who has just been bought by a wealthy Premier League club for an incredible amount of money, Der Titan is actually a remarkable salute to the German beer style Dortmunder, which is rare enough in its home country never mind in the UK. If you have never heard of one, a Dortmunder is supposed to be as gold in colour as a Helles or a Pils, but is marginally stronger (and sometimes styled as an Export). It also has more of a noble hop character. It was a favourite of the city's industrial workers, but it does seem to have fallen somewhat out of favour, even though examples of the style are produced all over the world. The latest example comes from Walthamstow where Exale also has a popular taproom where its full range of beers can be sampled (including the wonderfully named Krankie, which is described as an Iron Brew Sour).

Der Titan is lemon gold in colour and sits beneath a firm head of snow-white foam; it is unfiltered so there is a slight haze. It has a fresh spritzy nose, with a suggestion of a breadiness, all of which makes it an enticing introduction. On the palate there is a trace of spicy hop, light citrus, more breadiness, all of which work together towards its dry and bittersweet finish. It is a clean beer, with each flavour standing out as if on parade. It is also a tremendous thirst-slaker and an excellent example of the reach of Exale's ambitions.

Goes well with… Watching your local football team taking on prestigious opponents in the FA Cup third round

GEIPEL BREWING
Bock

6.5% Core

Near Bala, North Wales
geipel.co.uk

*A gorgeous amber-copper Bock
with plenty of rich malt character*

Geipel is a small lager-making brewery located high in the hills between Corwen and Bala. Its Munich-made brewing kit comes from a now-closed brewpub in Japan, with founder/brewer Erik Geupel being a firm advocate of decoction mashing. He also lagers his beers for at least a month. With this sort of precision applied to brewing, it comes as no surprise to discover that his gorgeous Bock is a multi award-winner.

'I based the recipe on our Zoigl (an amber lager, now discontinued),' he says, 'along with some suggestions from a friendly German brewmaster. I turned the recipe up to 11, but I underestimated the strength of the malt flavour in the first batch; it was under-hopped and I had to dump a lot of it. Disappointing, but at the same time I knew I was on the right track precisely because of the complexity and strength brought by the Munich malt. Increasing the hop dose (including some dry-hopping) in the next batch nailed it and that second batch went on to win a national SIBA medal.'

Amber copper in colour, it has an array of floral and fruity notes on the nose alongside suggestions of chocolate, toffee and even cherry. This combination continues on the palate with a fine bitterness and plenty of rich malt character before its dry finish.

'Even I'm surprised to remember that Bock is brewed with just four ingredients, including only one hop variety, Hersbrucker,' says Geupel. 'It's bewildering the complex flavours you can coax out. Call me old-fashioned but you don't need tonka beans, Kveik yeast, Antipodean hops and sherry barrels, and, contrary to intuition, I find being constrained by rules like the Reinheitsgebot enhances creativity.'

Goes well with... Sitting in front of the fire after a glorious day walking in the Welsh mountains

HUSH HEATH ESTATE
Jake's Lager

5% Core

Staplehurst, Kent
balfourwinery.com

Crisp and bitter lager that uses both US and Kentish hops

Jake's Lager is the result of the worlds of the grain and grape coming together to produce an impressive beer that uses both Kentish and American hops. The world of the grain is provided by Cellar Head Brewing who produce the beer, and the world of the grape comes from Balfour Winery at Hush Heath in Kent. It was here that winemakers Owen and Fergus Elias came up with the idea of the beer, according to Jake Balfour-Lynn, whose parents bought the manor house in the 1980s and then set up an award-winning winery on the adjoining estate in 2001.

'Both of them had a very clear vision in their head when starting the brew,' he says. 'They wanted a clean, fresh style reflective of Kent and its brewing heritage but with a modern twist. We have a partnership with Cellar Head Brewery, investing in equipment and spending much of lockdown blending and creating together. Combining their expert brewing abilities with the drink-making knowledge of our winemakers – both also make Jake's Ciders and Owen has a

history of making beer – meant that our first rendition tasted great, which was really exciting. We didn't actually have to change much at all. It was slightly drier than we had hoped so all that was needed was a slight hop adjustment.'

The result is a yellow-gold lager that has more than a hint of the North German Pils about it. There is light lemon and sweet grain on the nose, all of which makes for a clean and aromatic profile. The bitterness and the dryness in the finish linger and are assertive in their presence; before that there are highly defined lemon and crisp grainy notes on the palate before the aforementioned bitter and dry finish.

Goes well with… Crab cakes and paprika fries

LOST AND GROUNDED
Keller Pils

4.8% Core

Bristol
lostandgrounded.co.uk

Crisp and bittersweet and a mighty quencher of parched throats

You're never far from good beer in Bristol, whether you're in need of a boisterous pint of Bitter, a slinky, asymmetrical glass of locally brewed Saison, a brooding Stout or, in the case of Lost and Grounded, this refreshing and sunny, well-hopped and sprightly lager.

This is the brewery's signature beer, its bestseller and the debut that created an instant buzz of conversation and appreciation amongst beer lovers. It's a simple beer, not overly complex, but crystalline and pure in its impact on the palate, which is what co-founder and head brewer Alex Troncoso (who left his role as Camden Town's head brewer to start Lost and Grounded in 2016) wanted when he developed the beer.

'Keller Pils was about making something really understated,' he says, 'but with a depth of character. It was something that someone could drink and think about, or just drink and enjoy without making it an intellectual exercise. The beer is about simple enjoyment in everyday life. It's also about backing yourself and having the confidence to do something on your own – just like our hippo on the label is rowing his boat across the lake on his lonesome, knowing with quiet confidence that he'll get to the other side.'

As the name suggests, it's a Pils, but far more hoppier than you would normally expect. Sparkling in the glass, with a delicate citrus lemon nose, it is bracingly crisp, appetising, bittersweet and refreshing in its mouthfeel. It's an astoundingly tasty beer and a mighty quencher of parched throats.

Goes well with... The BBQ you've finally been able to organise after days of heavy rain

LOST AND GROUNDED
Running With Sceptres

5.2% Seasonal

Bristol
lostandgrounded.co.uk

Easy-going IPL that refreshes the palate with every swig

One of the more curious beer styles that has emerged in the last few years is the India Pale Lager (IPL), which as the name suggests is a collaboration between the high-handed hoppiness of an IPA and the clean and newly starched-shirt crispness of lager. Given that Lost and Grounded co-founder Alex Troncoso was previously head brewer of Camden Town and helped develop their India Hells Lager in 2014, it comes as no surprise to see this IPL become part of the brewery's seasonal portfolio.

'This beer originally started life described as "Special Lager Beer",' says Troncoso, 'and the basis of it was to take a Vienna-style lager base and then overlay with modern hops to give an alternative to the sea of Pale Ales and IPAs on the market. The subsequent move to "India Pale Lager" was simply to make it easier for folk to understand what to expect when ordering it.'

Poured out of the can (which features the usual lovely artwork we've come to expect from Lost and Grounded), it is light amber in colour topped with a firm head of snow-white foam that is as tempting as an apple was to Eve. There are hints of biscuity malt on the nose alongside an appealing peal of citrus, peach and pine notes, while each swig reveals a crispness and a surge of refreshment alongside more citrus and peach before it finishes dry.

As for its name, here's Troncoso again: 'The basis of this beer – and in particular the artwork – is about how everyone is special, and everyone is invited to the party. This beer has inclusiveness at its core, appealing to both lager and ale drinkers alike.'

Goes well with... Friday evening's fish and chip tea

MANCHESTER UNION BREWERY
Bock

6%   Occasional

Manchester
manchesterunionbrewery.com

Gloriously rich Bock that is a showcase for malt

This is a Bock from Manchester, words I couldn't have considered writing 25 years ago when I first starting covering beer. In fact, I can't even imagine that there were any Bocks then from anywhere. It is very dark amber in colour, verging on chestnut brown, and has an off-white, firm trim of foam. On the nose there is freshly baked malt loaf, some caramel, a gentle aniseed note, liquorice and a rich, fruity sweetness that is almost like a memory of childhood. On the palate more of the malt loaf, liquorice, caramel sweetness, malt richness with a bitterness and dryness in the finish. It is a complete beer, a beer whose Bock-like attributes give it a warmth and the chance to glance back at the day as you sit there with a glass of it in your hand.

'I was originally looking at making a Doppelbock,' recalls founder and head brewer Ian Johnson, 'so that was my starting point. However, we decided to bring it back to a Bock and so I brought back the malt bill a little to adapt the recipe for a Bock. Munich and caramunich malt and decoction mashing give this beer its rich malty taste, and contributes to the rich and dark fruit flavours too. However, the malt had to be carefully used to get the colour that was required. I wanted a rich amber/red beer that was neither too light or going into brown. Cold fermentation kept the beer clean and not cloying despite the finishing gravity and ABV.'

Johnson's careful shepherding of the beer certainly worked as this is a rich and abundant beer, a beer that soothes the soul and teaches us lessons in the eternal nature of malt.

Goes well with... Pork tenderloin with a sweet glaze and served with mash and peas

NORTH BREWING
Springwell Pils

4.5% Core

Leeds
northbrewing.com

*Bright and sprightly modern Pils
brewed to celebrate North's new home*

In 2020 North Brewing moved to a new 21,000 square foot brewhouse north of Leeds city centre, in an area called Springwell. At last they had the tank capacity to help create a flagship lager, which the brewing team wanted to be a modern interpretation of a German Pils, and which would be named after the new home. However, as Sarah Hardy, head of the brewery's marketing department relates, there was the odd hiccup on the way.

'The first brew was a drainpour!' she recalls. 'We had been waiting eight weeks for it to be ready and couldn't wait to taste the first batch of it as a team. Our head brewer, Seb, had been making concerned noises that he wasn't happy with the beer's progression during fermentation, but we were all optimistic! However, he was right and the beer had a marmite-like essence to it. It was not the clean-drinking, fruity lager we were expecting. We chalked batch one up to research and development, and went back to the brewkit! Springwell Pils is a flagship beer for our new brewery so it was of paramount importance that we got it right.'

The brewing team certainly got it right and this dark-gold-coloured, sprightly little number is a palate-pleasing beer with a juicy, lightly biscuity nose and the suggestion of lemon in the background. On the palate it tingles the tongue with a delicate citrusiness alongside a light biscuitiness before it finishes with the kind of dryness that will have you taking another swig.

Or as Hardy puts it, 'this beer is easy-going, it's sociable, it's refreshing. It tastes like the first beer when you arrive at your accommodation on holiday'.

Goes well with... Grilled scallops and a big smile on the face

ORBIT BREWERY
Lentebock

6.4% Seasonal

Walworth, London
orbitbeers.com

Rapturous and joyful version of a Dutch beer usually produced for spring

I have always had a fascination with the quieter beer styles of Europe, the kind of beers that have a history but which very few brewers produce any more and when they are brewed it's usually a one-off. So when you do find one it's as if the Holy Grail has been glimpsed. I felt like that about Leipziger Gose when first reading about it in one of Michael Jackson's books around 2005. Five years later I was in Leipzig at the Bayerischer Bahnhof brewery and spent an afternoon tasting and talking Gose with the brewmaster.

Orbit Brewery share a similar interest in European beer styles with a Kölsch-style as a regular as well as occasional brews of Alt (and Sticke Alt), Lichtenhainer and Lentebock. The latter is based on a Bok traditionally produced by Dutch brewers for the autumn, though the last couple of decades has seen Dutch brewers produce them for spring. Unlike German Bocks, which are cold fermented, these Dutch examples can be either cold or warm fermented and are lighter in colour than those produced later in the year.

This golden-orange Lentebock has a sprightly, lightly spicy flurry of aromatics on the nose, some of which are reminiscent of coriander, though none is used in the mix. It is a fresh and hoppy/bittersweet nose, with sweet malt, hop fragrance, lemon zest and the weight of alcohol. It is crisp and refreshing on the palate, with the bitterness in the finish lingering like a feud that has lasted down the years but is nowhere as forbidding. This is a beer that brings together freshness, dryness, a graininess and a bittersweetness to create a joyous whole.

Goes well with… Grilled chicken with a dash of lemon

PADSTOW BREWING
Padstow Pilsner

4.4% Core

Padstow, Cornwall
padstowbrewing.co.uk

Crisp and refreshing Pilsner with a long, dry finish

'We wanted to brew a brilliant lager.' These are words of Caron and Des Archer, who set up Padstow Brewing in 2013 and together developed the recipe for this crisp and refreshing Pilsner. The couple might now have stepped back from the brewing floor to act as directors but they still have a passion and take pleasure in the way this bestselling beer has developed a loyal following.

Pale gold lemon in colour with a firm, billowing head of snow-white foam, when first poured it seems as if the beer's bubbles have a sense of urgency as they aim for the top of the glass. Sweet malt and the herbal notes of Saaz resonate on the nose, enticing and inviting, as if the aromatics could crook its finger and say, 'follow me'. There is lightly toasted grain and a hint of lemon on the palate, the richness of malt alongside the herbal and fruity notes of Saaz, while the finish is dry and bittersweet with the dryness lingering around like the memory of a day well spent.

'The thing that really stood out for us when it was first brewed was the crispness of the beer,' recall the Archers, 'certainly compared to the other beers we had drunk. We were really pleased to have achieved a crisp and refreshing beer, but also balanced that with a noticeable hop and malt character. We also didn't take any short cuts, and made sure to ferment and lager for as long as possible – patience makes a huge difference to the finished product!'

Goes well with… Sitting in the garden at your rented cottage after a day spent on the beach

REDWILLOW BREWERY
Foeder Lager V2

4.2%   Occasional

Macclesfield, Cheshire
redwillowbrewery.com

Gueuze meets cider meets lager and all get on famously

A foeder (or *foudre*) is a wooden barrel, usually ovular or cylindrical in shape, into which brewers put beer with the aim of changing its character. It can be clean oak, a freshly made container, or maybe it once held wine, with both iterations adding to the flavour and aroma of the finished beer. This is the second version of RedWillow's Foeder Lager with the first producing a clean and crisp beer with a hint of wood (this was new oak). Version two is a much more complex beer with Brettanomyces starting to make its presence, something which RedWillow's co-founder Toby McKenzie had planned from the outset.

'We wanted to keep the simplicity of a lager with an extra layer of complexity,' he says, 'something that is both refreshing on a hot day and nuanced when you take the time to examine it. The first brew was very clean and crisp, with a hint of wood, but not as much Brettanomyces character and it genuinely made us smile as we knew that this beer in this foeder had a lot of potential. The great joy of this beer is that each expression will continue to evolve as the microbiome of the foeder continues to develop.'

Poured into the glass, this deep-golden beer immediately sets the senses tingling with Champagne- and cider-like notes on the nose alongside an inviting earthiness from the Brettanomyces. It is crisp and quenching in the mouthfeel, with more cider-like notes on the palate, giving the impression of a gueuze meeting cider meeting lager. The finish is dry and bittersweet. An intriguing and very drinkable beer, with the Brettanomyces from the foeder giving it an unleashed, off-centre feeling. RedWillow also produce a Foeder Saison.

Goes well with... A chunk of artisanal Cheshire cheese, fresh bread and caramelised red onion chutney

REDWILLOW BREWERY
Smoked Lager

5.3% Occasional

Macclesfield, Cheshire
redwillowbrewery.com

A lightly smoked lager that both entertains and intrigues

Smoked beer is one of those styles that can confound beer lovers. If you're used to the juicy fruitiness of a hazy IPA then your palate might recoil in shock when confronted with the full-on smokiness of Schlenkerla's Rauchbier from Bamberg. On the other hand, RedWillow's Smoked Lager (which is part of the brewery's limited edition 'Faithless' range) is in possession of a lighter kind of smokiness, a smokiness that is gentle, and an unambiguous companion to the beer's well-rounded malt sweetness.

For brewery co-founder Toby McKenzie, the beer came about during 2020's lockdown: 'With the bars shut we had both the time and capacity to play with more beer styles than we would normally have. So this beer was in many ways opportunistic. All through the process, from the mash to packaging, the smell of the smoke was lovely, sometimes overpowering, but as the beer lagered it all came together.'

Amber gold in colour and as clear as the sound of a brand new bell, the smokiness on the nose is almost reminiscent of a wooden box that once held smoked herring, an appetising aroma that draws the drinker in. It's a refreshing beer on the palate, again with the smoked fish flavour commingling with a mid-palate bittersweetness before it finishes dry and delicately bitter with some of the smoke wafting across the palate as if it were a landscape with a bonfire in the next field. This is a beer that will entertain the palate as it is pulled and pushed between both the aridity of the smokiness and the sweetness of the malt, with both sides making a joint impression.

Goes well with… A juicy venison burger topped with redcurrant jelly

ROUND CORNER BREWING
Gunmetal

4.8% Core

Melton Mowbray, Leicestershire
roundcornerbrewing.com

Award-winning Schwarzbier from Melton Mowbray

This is a very comfortable and confident beer, happy as it sits in the glass, its edge-of-darkness colour gleaming and shining, burnished and polished, an ambassador from its home of Melton Mowbray. On first glance you might think it a Stout or a Porter, but on tasting it's definitely a lager, an English-made Schwarzbier, a style of lager that apparently emerged from the German state of Thuringia and somehow survived behind the Iron Curtain.

On the nose there are toasty notes as well as suggestions of caramel, a biscuitiness (bourbon biscuits?) and a hint of fruitiness (perhaps marmalade on toast). It is light and lithe on the palate, with some fruitiness, a graininess (breakfast cereal), a dryness, a flitter of bitterness, a crispness but also a quenching character that makes it refreshing; the dryness lingers in the finish.

Round Corner's head brewer and co-founder Colin Paige has brewed Schwarzbiers around the world and for him, when setting up the brewery, he wanted to create two core range lagers, 'but we wanted to extend the style and challenge people's prejudices about lager. A black lager does exactly this. We entered our first keg of Gunmetal into the International Brewing Awards in 2019, the "Oscars of Beer", and won the best "4.5% and above lager" category in the world. We knew then that we were on to something. We then took it to a lager festival in Manchester and it blew people's minds.'

For the moment, this is a beer that shines a light on Rounded Corner's brewing expertise. There is also a strong Gunmetal aged in a rum barrel, which, according to Paige, 'when we put it in the taproom it gets folks very excited'.

Goes well with… Duck breast, roasted skin down, with a helping of sauerkraut

TRIPLE POINT BREWING
Žatec

4.8%   Core

Sheffield
triplepointbrewing.co.uk

Classic Czech-style Pilsner with an amiable sense of drinkability

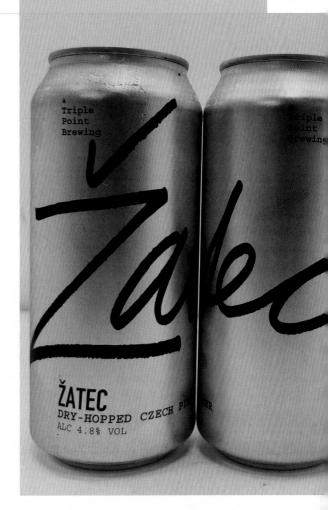

Some of the greatest beers in the world can be found in the Czech Republic, something that was not lost on Triple Point's head brewer Alex Barlow when he worked at a brewery there during the early 2000s. So when he came to produce this Czech-style Pilsner, he already knew what he wanted to achieve.

'I was lucky enough to spend a few years working with Staropramen,' he says, 'and during my time there I toured many Czech breweries drinking the beers and revelling at the depth of character, yet easy drinkability they possess.'

When it came to developing Žatec he also had an advantage in that the water in Sheffield is soft and similar in character to that of Pilsen's, while the Žatec (or Saaz) hops were sourced directly from a family farm in south-west Bohemia (some Premiant is also used alongside) and the barley was floor-malted. The only difference from a traditional Czech brewery was that Barlow dry-hopped the beer for extra aroma.

The result is a beer glimmering with a deep-golden hue, while sweet malt (almost a light caramel note) and floral hop aromatics emerge on the nose, a Pied Piper of aromatics drawing the drinker in. Each swig reveals a welcoming bittersweetness, more sweet malt and floral hop, a refreshing crispness and a dry and gently bitter finish.

'This is a beer that wants to be appreciated for its depth of character,' says Barlow, 'but it is also clean and refreshing at the same time. When we brew it it's a real staff favourite and it has become many people's go-to beer.'

Goes well with... A lively conversation with friends around the kitchen table about which is the best Czech beer

UTOPIAN BREWING
Černé Speciální

5.9% Seasonal

Bow, Devon
utopianbrewing.com

*A brooding dark lager that pulsates
with aromatics and flavour*

This is a very dark lager, the kind of
lager that broods in the glass as if it were
possessed of the thoughts of Macbeth
as he plots the murder of Duncan.

Forgetting about the lethal instinct
of Shakespeare's character, let's be more
benign and hail Utopian's tribute to the
dark lagers of Czechia, a style of beer that
might share some characteristics of the
Dunkel next door in Bavaria but which
is very much its own personage. It's also
a beer for the colder seasons, a beer to
contemplate in front of the fire, secure
in the knowledge that the cold tendrils
of ice outside cannot touch you. It is,
though, if you manage to save a couple
of cans for the warmer months (it is a
seasonal release), an ideal beer for the
BBQ or for sitting in the sun-brushed
garden. After all, we don't stop taking
the darkness of coffee in the summer
after winter has gone on its weary way.

Poured into your pint glass (for this is a
bold beer that should not be hidden away in
a tiny tumbler and sipped with the delicacy
of a gazelle) there are suggestions of

chocolate, mocha coffee, the sweetness of
berries and a soft roastiness on the nose,
an invitation to the dance. It is full-bodied
and creamy on the palate, unctuous with
more chocolate, milky coffee, soft
roastiness reminiscent of well-toasted
(but not burnt) bread before it finishes
dry and lightly bittersweet.

Brewed on a farm in Devon, and packed
with the classic English hop variety,
Fuggles, this is a rich and eloquent, creamy
and soothing beer that can demonstrate
just how complex and thrilling and
comforting a well-made lager can be.

Goes well with… Several slices of roast pork (naturally with crackling) served alongside a helping of rösti

UTOPIAN BREWING
Unfiltered British Lager

4.7%   Core

Bow, Devon
utopianbrewing.com

Lusciously lip-smacking
Bavarian-style Helles from Devon

Utopian Brewing is located on a farm in the depths of the Devon countryside, where the green, rolling hills stretch out towards the hard granite mass of Dartmoor. Founded in March 2019, the brewery's declared aim was to craft great lagers that would emulate the classics of Bavaria and Czechia, though with a slight difference – only British raw ingredients would be used. According to the brewery, this would help with cutting down food miles as well as demonstrating that English hops could have as much of a decisive effect on the beers being brewed as much as anything from Europe or across the Atlantic. A noble ambition, you might say, and from my tastings of their various beers they seem to be succeeding so well that I often feel like putting on a pair of lederhosen when I'm drinking their beers in a pub in Exeter.

This is an unfiltered version of the brewery's British Lager, a delicious riff on the Bavarian Helles style, a sign of the seriousness with which head brewer Jeremy Swainson (formerly of Camden and trained in Germany) approaches his craft. He is an ardent champion of the traditional central European brewing process of decoction mashing, which he believes gives his beers soul.

Judging by the quality of beers like this one, he is right. It gleams a gorgeous gold in the glass, with a light haze due to not being filtered. There is a soft biscuitiness and hint of lemon on the nose, while the mouthfeel is crisp and refreshing, before heading for a bittersweet and dry finish. It is one of those beers that demands to be drunk in quantity, as I know all too well.

Goes well with… A cold box containing some cans and a sunny afternoon by the river watching the world go by

WESTERHAM BREWERY
Haná

7.5%   Seasonal

Westerham, Kent
westerhambrewery.co.uk

A heady, potent lager that makes use of the heritage malt Haná

Ever since everyone and their mother decided that they were craft brewers, it is to various hops that most have looked with the aim of making their beers as cool and as swaggering as can be; think Daniel Craig in *Casino Royale*. Citra, Mosaic, Simcoe, Idaho 7, you know the names. It always makes me feel sorry for barley, famously known as the soul of beer, but sometimes more like the poor relation at the family feast that has been thrown by whatever hop variety is on-trend that week. However, barley has been biting back, as assiduous brewers plumb for Maris Otter or hunt out heritage varieties such as Chevallier.

Haná is another one of these varieties, famously used in the first brew of what would become Pilsner Urquell in 1842, and for this heady, strong, Pilsner-style beer it has been recultivated in a small batch by Crisp Maltings of Norfolk. According to the brewery's founder, Robert Wicks, 'we had access to the first harvest of Haná from Crisp in 2019. We wanted to make a Pilsner with this special malt, but not just a straight Pilsner, an imperial Pilsner or Bock to really show off the malt.'

Bruised gold in colour and sitting beneath a billowing head of fluffy white foam, the beer has a clean, bready nose with hints of floral sweetness in the background. On the palate it is clean and bittersweet with a dryness in the finish. A full-bodied mouthfeel tempts the drinker and there is also a hint of almond-like sweetness. Haná is back.

Goes well with… Friday night at home with grilled bratwurst and sweet mustard

WILD HORSE BREWING CO
Buckskin

4.5% Core

Llandudno, North Wales
wildhorsebrewing.co.uk

Crisp and refreshing Czech-style lager made in a famous Welsh seaside resort

I grew up in the jaunty seaside town of Llandudno, which is where Wild Horse make their exceptional beers. In fact, I used to live a couple of streets away from where the brewery is currently situated. This is a town that has never had a brewery. There were no aromas of brewing drifting through the air like so much spindrift, and furthermore when I first started drinking, the beers for sale included uninspiring ones from Greenall Whitley, Wrexham Lager and dear old Whitbread. That has all changed and since 2015 Wild Horse has been very much about producing vibrant and boldly flavoured beers making the best use of New World hops. Some of its beers are also members of the lager family, such as this crisp and refreshing take on Czech-style pale lager.

'As one of our core beers, Buckskin is designed to be accessible, modern and a reflection of us as a brewery,' says head brewer Chris Wilkinson, 'as well as being an invitation to try some of our other beers.'

Pale gold in colour, Buckskin chimes with fresh, sprightly mineral-like notes on the nose, alongside light hints of biscuity grain and a grassy greenness, the latter thanks to the use of the classic Czech hop Saaz. It is crisp and refreshing in the mouthfeel, with an enduring bittersweetness emerging towards the end of the palate followed by a dry and bitter finish that lingers most enjoyably. It is a clean and incredibly approachable beer, a well-defined session lager that dances on the tongue with the aplomb and lightness of a well-trained ballet dancer. Welcome to Llandudno.

Goes well with… A day at the seaside sitting in a deckchair and watching the gentle rhythms of the waves

THE YEASTIE BOYS
The Reflex

4.6% Core

UK/New Zealand
yeastieboysuk.myshopify.com

A cool mover of a golden lager that trills with the joy of New Zealand hops

Who can recall 'The Reflex', one of Duran Duran's hits during the 1980s in which they went all funky but still managed to look like a bunch of posturing posh boys in the video. This luscious New World lager from the Yeastie Boys has a much better sense of rhythm, which comes from the use of aromatic and fruity New Zealand hops such as Nelson Sauvin (New Zealand is the Yeasties' homeland though they now make their beer down under and here in the UK).

'Back in New Zealand we have a unique style of Pilsner that has become very popular over the last 20 years,' says the UK-based brewery founder Stu McKinlay. 'I've always particularly loved the beers in this rather unique style that are at the gentler end of the spectrum, and as such, always had in mind that we'd release such a beer. After a couple of years of playing with Pilsner, Helles, Dortmunder and even India Pale Lager through our single batch special release programme, we came to a place where we were happy to hang our hat on an idea.'

The result is this cool mover, a golden beer that has a fruity and citrusy aroma reminiscent of the finest of New Zealand's white wines. This wine-like fruitiness continues with the flavour, working alongside a gentle biscuit-like sweetness before a dry and appetising finish that will encourage you to reach for the glass again and again, almost as if on reflex. Or as McKinlay says, 'it's got that perfect balance of sessionability that carries it through a long afternoon with friends, alongside enough unique hop character to be the one you remember the next day.'

Goes well with... A nostalgic afternoon in the garden with friends listening to the sounds of the 1980s

LOW- and NO-ALCOHOL

Going low or no
is no longer about
choosing inferior
beer, as this chapter
demonstrates.

ADNAMS BREWERY
Ghost Ship Alcohol Free

0.5%   Core

Southwold, Suffolk
adnams.co.uk

Alcohol-free version of Adnams' best-selling Ghost Ship

Ghost Ship is Adnams' best-selling Pale Ale, but back in 2018 the brewery decided to take a tilt at the growing alcohol-free/low-alcohol market with a 0.5% version. According to Adnams production director (and former head brewer) Fergus Fitzgerald, 'we had been looking at low-alcohol beer for a long time, and we had started with Solestar, which was 2.7% back in 2011, and then we dropped that to 0.9% in 2016. We used a restricted fermentation to make it, which meant we didn't use much malt so there wasn't a lot of sugar for the yeast to ferment. We also ferment colder than normal and at lower pitching rates, essentially doing everything we can do to slow down and restrict the fermentation of the beer, then we add a lot of dry hop. The beer works really well, but we wanted to get closer to the flavour of a full strength beer.'

Pale gold in colour the beer has a lush malt character, hints of lemon and lime on the nose, a medium body and a peppery, bitter and dry finish. In other words it tastes like beer rather than a ghost of its stronger self, which is down to a unique process, as Fitzgerald explains: 'We looked at various ways and decided that if we wanted to get closer to the usual flavour of a beer we really needed to be able to ferment a beer as normal and then remove the alcohol afterwards. So for this we are using reverse osmosis, which means we can filter out alcohol and water, leaving the flavours of the beer behind, and it's all done at really cold temperatures. This was by far the best method of producing alcohol-free beers that we came across, and by best I mean best for flavour.'

Goes well with…   A round of crab sandwiches with a side helping of Caesar salad

BIG DROP BREWING
Galactic Milk Stout

0.5% Core

Ipswich, Suffolk
bigdropbrew.com

Creamy, lightly roasty and soothing on the palate

There used to be a time, maybe 15 years ago, when Mackeson was possibly the only Milk Stout being made. Then Bristol Beer Factory brewed one and the style that was usually consigned to the dusty shelf of shame in equally dusty pubs began to prick the interest of a new generation of brewers. In 2016 Big Drop went one step further and produced a low-alcohol version of this august style, which has since gone onto win many awards from competitions around the world.

According to co-founder Rob Fink, the motivation behind the beer was simple. 'It was genuinely along the lines of "why has no one made any decent AF beer?" It wasn't any more complicated than that. What I wanted was an AF beer that I would be happy to drink without feeling like I was compromising on taste and flavour.

'Johnny Clayton, now our head of production, has designed all the recipes, including the very first one of Galactic Milk Stout. When I first approached him about the project, I don't think he or I really knew what might come out of it. But I could tell from the look on his face when he handed me the very first samples that he was pretty pleased with what he'd come up with.'

Those awards, especially the ones that have won against alcoholic versions of the style, aren't a fluke. The beer is darkness visible in the glass, with light aromatics of milk chocolate, mocha coffee and a sweet creaminess. There's a creamy mouthfeel, with a light roastiness, vanilla soothingness, a nudge of nuttiness, plus chocolate and mocha on the palate before its dry finish.

Goes well with… Mary Berry's white chocolate and raspberry cheesecake

BIG DROP BREWING
Pine Trail

0.5% Core

Ipswich, Suffolk
bigdropbrew.com

A citrusy and deliciously bitter Pale Ale

Beers lacking alcohol used to be laughable and flavourless, seemingly a punishment for those poor souls who were either designated drivers on a night out with friends or just occasionally in need of an alternative to their usual pint. Without naming names, they were brands that lingered in the waiting room of undrinkable beers, in spite of well-funded TV ad campaigns that featured well-known drinkers. They were the pariahs of good beer, usually to be found in the company of canned beers, which also had a similarly poor reputation.

However, just like the new generation of canned beers, today's low- and no-alcohol beers are forthright in their attachment to flavour, as large and small brewers use a variety of ways to strip out the booze. What's more, these beers are not only winning awards in their relevant categories, but are also challenging conventionally alcoholic beers elsewhere. Big Drop is one of those breweries and has won a raft of awards for its beers, and Big Pine Pale Ale is one of those

winners. It has even taken top prize when matched against alcoholic Pale Ales.

Pouring a clear, brilliant gold, it has gorgeous notes of citrus fruit and pine on the nose, while every swig provides more of the citrus alongside a full-bodied and refreshing mouthfeel with its finish being bossed by a joint tag team of bittersweetness and a bracing dryness.

'From the very start of Big Drop,' says founder Rob Fink, 'I took the view that I didn't want to impact the flavours in any way by changing how beer is traditionally made, I just wanted to make great beer.'

There is no doubt about it that Fink achieved his aim.

Goes well with... A juicy cheeseburger grilled with finesse on a new BBQ set

BRISTOL BEER FACTORY
Clear Head

0.5% Core

Bristol
bristolbeerfactory.co.uk

Crisp and refreshing Pale Ale that just happens to be alcohol free

Philosophers and alchemists spent the Middle Ages looking to change metals into gold, while for modern brewers the Holy Grail has been to make alcohol-free beers with the same mouthfeel and body that beers with alcohol have. For Bristol Beer Factory's head brewer Tristan Hembrow, 'we wanted to test our theory that lactose was a potential answer to the eternal alcohol-free beer question: how do you reintroduce the body and mouthfeel that you lose from the alcohol.

'The first brew was nerve-wracking but tasting it at various points gave us hope we were really onto something. The big challenge of brewing our first ever alcohol-free beer combined with the critical questions of quantities of lactose and hops to use gave us some restless days, all of which combined into a feeling of monumental relief and excitement upon tasting the first finished bottle.'

The beer was brewed in collaboration with the mental health charity Talk Club, which, according to sales manager Tom Clermont, saw 'the idea of an alcohol-free beer as being a potential tool in helping them in their broader work: both as a monetary channel (the project has a profit-share element with Talk Club) and as a beer that could be consumed at their face-to-face meetings'.

Burnished gold in colour, Clear Head has ripe peach and mango notes on the nose, with hints of graininess and soft caramel in the background: crisp and refreshing on the palate, with a full mouthfeel followed by a bittersweet, dry and grainy finish which also features a peppery bitterness. This is an excellent Pale Ale that just happens to have minimal alcohol in it.

Goes well with… The company of friends putting the world to rights

GOOD KARMA BEER
Love That Feeling

0.5% Core

London
goodkarma.beer

Refreshing and endearing Hefeweizen

Hefeweizen (or Hefeweiss) is one of world's great beer styles, a thirst-quenching marvel that makes for a wonderful mid-morning libation along with a bratwurst in a sunny Munich beer garden. Hold that thought for a moment and pour yourself a glass of Good Karma's alcohol-free version of the style and take in its hazy, orange-amber gleam in the glass. There are delicate notes of banana custard on the nose with a hint of honey in the background. It's a pleasing aroma that is very much what you would expect from a Hefeweizen. On the palate there is more banana and honey, alongside suggestions of clove. The carbonation is brisk and palate-tingling, there is a rounded mouthfeel and a clean and swift finish. Refreshing and endearing, you wouldn't know that the alcohol was missing.

For Good Karma founder Steve Sailopal, Hefeweizen is his favourite German beer style, so when he began the brewery he felt it was important to produce styles that he enjoyed, hence Love That Feeling.

'It was a challenge to brew a Hefeweizen as we had never brewed an alcohol-free beer with 70% wheat in the grain bill,' he says, 'plus the yeast used in conventional Hefeweizen does add to the flavour profile, unlike the yeast we have had to use. We did have to drain pour two batches until we were satisfied with the beer and as this is a well-known beer style people know what to expect flavour wise so we had to deliver.

'With alcohol-free beer brewing we are learning with each batch and each new beer, always looking at ways to better the beer whilst challenging ourselves. Each day we hear and learn about new ideas in brewing alcohol-free beer and as brewers we want to make the best.'

Goes well with… Treating yourself to some grilled bratwurst

HARVIESTOUN BREWERY
Wheesht

0.0% Core

Alva, Clackmannanshire, Scotland
harviestoun.com

Full-flavoured, dark-ruby beer that just happens to be alcohol free

Who knows the conversations that take place in a brewery when it comes to naming a beer. Are ideas flung about with careless abandon, words dashed down on notepads like Morse code, or is it that lucky, plucking-out-of-thin-air moment when everything in the universe fits together and a new beer is named? I don't know how Harviestoun's first no-alcohol beer got its name, but it's apparently from Scots dialect for telling someone to be quiet (hence the brewery's trademark mouse holding a finger to its lips on the label).

Then there is the reason for a beer's existence. Breweries, like bakeries or bookshops, are businesses and if their beer doesn't sell then closure beckons. Hence the development of Wheesht, which was a reaction to the growing sector of no- and low-alcohol beers, though as Amy Cockburn, master brewer at Harviestoun, explains: 'We wanted to create a non-alcoholic beer that stood out in the market. We felt there was a gap there that wasn't either a light lager style or a dark Stout style.'

However, as she adds, the first brew didn't exactly get it right: 'The first trial brews didn't go to plan and it took us the best part of three years to create the finished product. We knew we could create a brilliant non-alcoholic beer, we just needed the time to refine the recipe.'

The result is a full-flavoured, dark-ruby beer that resonates with chocolate, dried fruit and sweet malt notes on the nose, followed by citrus, dried fruit and a delicate roastiness on the palate before a dry and bitter finish that will keep you quiet with satisfaction.

Goes well with… A quiet moment in a favourite armchair after the day's work is done

HEPWORTH BREWERY
Spartan

0.5% Core

Pulborough, West Sussex
hepworthbrewery.co.uk

*Low-alcohol Pale Ale that has
added agave for the body*

Until it was bought and closed by Badger
Ales in 2000, Andy Hepworth was head
brewer of the family owned King & Barnes
in Horsham, so, as many an unemployed
brewer before and since, he set forth and
opened his own. Spartan is the brewery's
first low-alcohol beer, and it has an
ingredient that you wouldn't normally
find in beer.

'Spartan is made with a restricted
fermentation rather than having alcohol
extracted,' Hepworth explains, 'and the
"filler" that provides the missing body in
most low-alcohol beers should not be an
allergen, like lactose, or entirely neutral in
character such as maltodextrin. A chance
meeting with an old acquaintance a couple
of years ago provided the answer.

'We had decided at the brewery we
needed to find something that would we
could put in beer without causing problems.
The first place to look would be those
ingredients used in other alcoholic beverages. Apples and grapes have too strong
a character, but when my acquaintance
said he was acting as an advisor to some
Mexican growers producing agave I had
a lightbulb moment. We tried some of the
different parts of the agave cactus and
found that it did not impart too strong
a character but acted like salt on food.
It enhanced the character of the other
components making the beer taste fuller.'

Spartan is gold in colour and has
hints of a clean graininess on the nose.
On the palate it is crisp and refreshing and
has suggestions of caramel and citrus
fruit, while the finish is bittersweet
and bracingly dry, or as Hepworth
suggests when discussing the beer's
name, 'strong on flavour and lean on
alcohol, hence Spartan'.

Goes well with... A tub of popcorn and *300* on the TV again

INFINITE SESSION

IPA

0.5% Core

London
infinitesession.com

*Crisp and citrusy IPA that
promises a never-ending session*

When it comes to considering a session beer, words are spilt, and split especially over the space between British vs American ideas of a session (the ABV is higher with the latter). Is it the 3.6% Bitter or the 4% session IPA or even the 4.8% golden ale that constitutes a session, or is the whole debate somewhat akin to medieval monks arguing over how many angels can be found on the head of a pin? Infinite Session's founder Chris Hannaway has perhaps added another voice to the debate with the name of his brewery and his thoughts on this crisp and citrusy IPA.

'We found too many alcohol-free beers were seen as a negative choice ("zero", "free" etc),' he says, 'whereas we wanted to celebrate the positive aspects of this beer and for it not to be seen as a compromise – it gives you an Infinite Session.'

Even though some might think that the idea of an infinite session a bit cosmic and perhaps those medieval monks might have thought it only exists in heaven, there is a grounded and down-to-earth approach to this IPA, as Hannaway explains: 'We want the whole drinking experience to be as close to drinking the favourite craft IPAs, so we naturally we looked at our favourites, like Jaipur and Neck Oil. Key issues to avoid were the ones some other no-alcohol beers seemed to have, like being too sweet, or lacking strong flavour. So it is dry yet also complex from a malt perspective, and dry-hopped to pack as much flavour in as possible.'

Sounds sessional to me.

Goes well with... A chicken burrito on a lazy Saturday afternoon

MAGIC ROCK BREWING
Freeride

0.5% Frequently available

Huddersfield, West Yorkshire
magicrockbrewing.com

Magic Rock's debut low-alcoholic beer is this fruity thirst-quencher

Hops, hops and more hops was originally the audience's expectation when Magic Rock first emerged on the brewing stage in 2011, with a kind of lupulin hush throwing its spell over the growing generation of craft beer fans. Who would have thought in those heady days that a decade on not only would the brewery be part of the Lion group, which also owns Little Creatures and Fourpure, but has also produced its first low-alcohol beer with this free-riding mango and passion fruit Pale Ale.

'We wanted to make something that was different to the other low- and no-alcohol beers on the market,' says former head brewer Stuart Ross, who is now at Kirkstall Brewery (though the recipe was developed by former head of production and operations Christa Sandquist). 'There are already plenty of lager and Pale Ale style ones available, so we had the feeling that a fruited one was probably the least explored variation available. Because of how precise we needed to be with the ABV this brew required trial brews and we eventually did three trials

before the main brew and we had settled on a process and recipe that gave plenty of residual sweetness. We were very happy with the taste of the first main batch, as it was fresh and fruity, full-bodied, thirst-quenching and quite moreish.'

Poured out of a can with trademark Magic Rock branding, there is an immediate hit of mango and passion fruit on the nose, alongside a suggestion of vanilla, which is Proustian-like in its reminder of childhood ice-cream. It is crisp and refreshing on the palate with more freshly cut mango and passion fruit before its dry finish. A summer quencher that has a clarity of fruitiness with some lightness of touch from the hop.

Goes well with... The sprightly, mouth-refreshing spritz of a lemon tart

POWDERKEG
Green Light

1.2%   Core

Woodbury Salterton, Devon
powderkegbeer.co.uk

*Bright and breezy Quarter IPA
all the way from Devon*

Like many who have spent a working life making alcoholic beer, Powderkeg's co-founder and head brewer John Magill was a little sceptical when it came to low-alcohol beers, underwhelmed by what he deemed to be their one-dimensional taste and lack of sophistication. However, as he explains, 'I never shy away from a challenge and wanted to have a crack at making one all the same. I could see their potential – mainly in increasing the number of opportunities I would have to drink beer – but it had to taste legitimately stand-alone great.'

The eventual result of his Damascene conversion was Green Light, a so-called Quarter IPA that has gathered a handful of awards since first being brewed in 2019. 'The easy way to make low- or no-alcohol beer is that used by the bigger breweries,' says Magill. 'They have big, fancy reverse osmosis machines that suck all of the alcohol and most of the flavour out of a traditionally brewed product. So our philosophy from day one was that we would only put ingredients in and layer flavour upon flavour, building up the malt and the body to provide a chunky yet nuanced base and then use four different hops across four additions to build a solid hop flavour and aroma that could provide the essential depth and intrigue.'

He evidentially got it right as this is a beer with depth and character from the moment the can is first opened and zephyrs of tropical fruit and citrus drift across the ether. It is vibrant and refreshing with a cacophony of tropical fruit and citrus also on the palate before it finishes dry and bittersweet, encouraging swig after swig after swig.

Goes well with… A homemade pizza featuring spicy cured meat, anchovies and plenty of mozzarella cheese

RAMSGATE BREWERY
Gadds' Nº 11 Ultra Light

1.2% Core

Broadstairs, Kent
ramsgatebrewery.co.uk

Zestful citrus notes on both the nose and palate lead to a dry, quenching finish

What is the appeal of a no-alcohol/low-alcohol beer? You might be out with friends, perhaps designated as the driver for the night, or there is a need to be up early the following morning. What's to drink? Fizzy water, coke, orange juice or a thin potation laughingly called beer, while all around pints are being enjoyed with gusto and palates refreshed. Let's reword that a bit. The last few years has seen a new wave of flavoursome no-alcohol beers offering the opportunity for beverages that resonate with flavour whilst dispensing with the alcohol. You could argue that these beers are the non-alcoholic cousins of the craft beer revolution that shook up British brewing in the past decade.

Ramsgate Brewery owner Eddie Gadd certainly seemed to think there was something in this temperance revolution in 2018 when he was asked if he could produce a low-alcohol beer. The result was that he tasked his then head brewer Jon Stringer with the job. 'This was in April 2018,' he recalls,

'Jon did a test batch at home and it was fantastic. I specifically asked for a Pale Ale, with none of the toasted malts that were often associated with low ABV beers at the time. He managed genius.'

Clear and golden, the beer resonates with a fresh burst of zestful citrus notes, while there is more of the citrus on the palate alongside a crisp mouthfeel and a dry and quenching finish.

'It's the best low ABV beer I've ever tasted,' says Gadd, 'however, there are no plans to make any other low-alcohol beers, but who knows, as I get older perhaps I'll drink less and seek variety.'

Goes well with... A tub of cockles on a pier of your choice

SALTAIRE BREWERY
Northern Light

0.5% Core

Shipley, West Yorkshire
saltairebrewery.com

*Prepare for a lush fruitiness
on the nose and palate*

Talk about being thrown into the deep end. Development brewer Rob Cooke had only been working at Saltaire for several weeks before he was given the challenge of coming up with the brewery's first ever alcohol-free beer. Thankfully though he had form in producing this kind of beer, having been a part of the team that had developed BrewDog's range of alcohol-free beers.

'I felt that much of what was on offer to the public in terms of alcohol-free beer was very limited,' he says, 'it was all heavily hopped IPAs or coffee Stouts from the craft breweries and de-alcoholised lagers from the big guns. I wanted something that would speak to the British ale drinker, something that was familiar and had a bit of backbone and was not just another slightly malty hop tea. With this in mind I took Saltaire Brewery's Citra (a fresh and zesty single-hopped Pale Ale) as inspiration and came up with the recipe for Northern Light.'

There is certainly a full blast of the Citra hop on the nose, which brings in a flurry of citrus and tropical fruit aromatics. This is followed by a fulsomely crisp and refreshing mouthfeel, with more lush fruitiness alongside a wilful bitterness and a long dry finish, with the fullness of the mouthfeel a real winner.

'This is a good bridge between a traditional ale and a craft beer,' says Cooke, 'the modern flavours are present, but they don't overwhelm. It is a beer that ticks many different boxes. It's a great alternative to the real thing if people are taking some time away from beer, or just want to be a bit more health-conscious. It's also a perfect fridge-filler for those that enjoy the odd beer at the weekend, but want something satisfying but alcohol-free on a school night.'

Goes well with… A special treat of a well-made and indulgently juicy meat pie

THORNBRIDGE BREWERY
Zero Five Pale Ale

0.5% Core

Bakewell, Derbyshire
thornbridgebrewery.co.uk

A deeply satisfying low-alcohol Pale Ale with citrus and stone fruit notes

The godfather of the British craft beer renaissance is better known for its muscular and ground-breaking IPA Jaipur as well as various other heady Pale Ales, soulful Sours and adamantine Imperial Stouts. However, its first foray into the world of no-alcohol beer was different, but it still works like the dream of a beer that once had an idea of scaling down its alcohol but remaining a big beer. Poured into the glass it has a lustrous, golden sheen about it, the early morning sun perhaps on a June day promising the gleam of joy. On the nose there are big and bold aromas of citrus (think of a freshly cut grapefruit, a squeeze of its juice arousing the senses) and ripe peach, its velvety skin soft to the touch, while on the palate there is an equally ripe cut-glass bowl of citrus and stone fruit before it finishes dry and bitter.

For Thornbridge's head brewer Rob Lovatt brewing a low ABV beer meant that he wanted drinkers to have something as full of character and flavour as any of the other beers he and his team produced. However, making it needed a lot of thought.

'We realised brewing a tasty low-alcohol beer was going to be no mean feat,' he recalls. 'We really thought outside the box for this one as it's very easy to make a beer which tastes like "hoppy water" if you're not careful. So we decided to take a relatively normal wort in terms of original gravity but only took the first runnings and then diluted them in the fermenting vessel. To maximise the flavour we crammed the grist with Munich malt, while the hopping rate is a relatively high for this style in terms of aroma hops but the bitterness in keeping with the ABV. We think it is pretty much perfect as it is for the style.'

Goes well with… A chunk of Sage Derby from traditional cheesemakers Fowlers of Earlswood

PALE ALE

This chapter features
a bright and
luminous array of
Pale and Golden Ales.

ALMASTY BREWING
Yellow

4_% Core

Newcastle upon Tyne
almastyshop.co.uk

*Easy-drinking and
thirst-satisfying Pale Ale*

Originally known as Simple Pleasures, but now branded with an even simpler name, Pale Ale is perhaps one of the most refreshing and thirst-satisfying beer styles within the family of ale. This is a style that should satisfy and gratify the palate rather than stretch the drinker's credibility or etch a question mark upon the mind. It is as Almasty's Pale Ale was formerly known, a simple pleasure.

'The concept behind the beer was to create a Pale Ale that was of high enough standard to be enjoyed by a seasoned IPA drinker and be drinkable enough to act as a gateway to crafted beers,' says brewery founder Mark McGarry. 'The first brew day was enjoyable as brewing a 4% Pale Ale is our staple, so you are relaxed and not pushing yourself or your kit to any limits. When we got to taste the beer I remember being pleased with the first hit of the aroma and enjoying that first sip. Although it was straight from the tank it had its flaws, which is why, like all our beers, it is continually being tweaked. Only in small amounts but I feel there is always room for improvement.'

In the glass the beer is the colour of sunshine seen through a morning mist, a haze of golden yellow that draws the eye. Breakfast grapefruit and ripe mango simmer on the nose, while there is more of this juicy fruitiness on the palate followed by a light bittersweetness and a dry finish.

Or as McGarry says, 'one of life's simple pleasures is enjoying a cold, easy-drinking, full-flavoured beer.'

Goes well with… Doing nothing and letting the day wash over you

BREW YORK
Calmer Chameleon

3.7%   Core

York
brewyork.co.uk

Jovial, well-balanced Pale Ale

They like their puns at Brew York, as their own name and that of their beer names might suggest: for starters why not have a glass of Simon le Mon, Juice Forsyth and this well-balanced Pale Ale Calmer Chameleon. Name aside, you could argue that this is a gateway beer, one of those easy-drinking versions of a style that won't be so complex that you would need to be Albert Einstein to work it out, but is still something delicious as well as being an introduction to a style that you have up until then been rather shy about.

'The beer is not intended to challenge the drinker,' says co-founder Lee Grabham. 'They should expect a beer that is balanced and most of all is super easy drinking. It's the kind of beer where you look down at your near empty glass and wonder where the beer that you had only just bought has gone already!'

This is not to say that Calmer Chameleon is a dumbed-down beer, a simplistic Pale Ale that more knowing beer-lovers would turn up their noses at. It is not. Light gold in colour, it has a sweet fruitiness of mango, pineapple,

citrus and blueberry on the nose with an underlying accompaniment of resinous, pine-like aromatics. There is an assembly of similar fruitiness on the palate, followed by a light graininess with a refreshing dryness and bitterness in the finish. It is a sessionable and thirst-making introduction to Brew York's beers.

'The mood of Calmer Chameleon, as with all our beers, is jovial,' says Grabham. 'Despite what many people may think on Twitter we don't think beer should be taken too seriously. "Calmer", as we call it, should bring you that little bit of zen as you wind down from the daily challenges of life and the never-ending cascade of negative news.'

Goes well with... Watching re-runs of Top of the Pops from the 80s

BURNT MILL
Pintle

4.3% Core

Stowmarket, Suffolk
burnt-mill-brewery.com

Exceptionally sessionable Pale Ale with a modern array of fruity and citrusy aromatics

Suffolk-based Burnt Mill, which despite the name does not brew in a mill once visited by an arsonist, is noted for pale, hoppy beers that are jammed with flavour and also act as ideal throat-refreshers. Pintle is one of these joys in a glass, an exceptionally sessionable Pale Ale with a modern array of fruity and citrusy aromatics that dance in and out of the glass like ghosts on a joyous spree.

According to Burnt Mill's award-winning head brewer Sophie de Ronde, 'we wanted this beer to be our flagship beer. So the aim was for it to be a really sessionable good Pale Ale with a modern fruitiness. We loaded up the grist with plenty of adjuncts to give a softness in the mouth and with keeping the bitterness low this makes it the kind of beer you want to keep going back to.'

The mouthfeel is soft and fruity with a gentle bitterness towards the finish alongside more of the sprightly fruitiness. This is an easy-drinking beer, complete in its holistic nature, and is wholly at home whether you are laughing and chatting around a BBQ with friends or sitting on the sofa and watching the latest cop thriller on Netflix.

'We were really impressed with the first brew,' says De Ronde, 'and didn't feel like we wanted to make any changes to the malt bill and the general profile. In the first couple of brews we just used Cascade and Citra, but there was a really gentle orange note that we felt needed a little extra oomph, so this is where the small addition of Kazbek came in and rounded the hop aromas off nicely.'

Goes well with... Some well-earned downtime

CASTLE ROCK BREWERY
Harvest Pale

4.3% Core

Nottingham
castlerockbrewery.co.uk

A zesty, tropically fruity and bittersweet Pale Ale

Cask came first for Harvest Pale, when it debuted in 2003 under the name of Trammie Dodger, apparently in honour of Nottingham's new tram system. The name thankfully changed in 2010 when bottling what was becoming an award-winning and popular beer, a deft move for Castle Rock, so that more people further afield could enjoy a beer whose mix of US hops delivers an eloquent conversation of taste and aromatics.

'On the nose Harvest Pale delivers a really fresh, zesty and floral aroma which is really robust despite not being dry hopped,' says Castle Rock's managing director Colin Wilde, 'together with a crisp and distinctive taste profile which makes the most of the US hop blend. Exceptional balance is fundamental to the beer continuing to be a stand out in many circles.'

Pale gold in colour, there is a swoon of light and ripe tropical fruit on the nose, which then reoccurs on the palate alongside a delicate but firm hint of graininess and a crisp mouthfeel before it finishes dry and refreshing.

When a brewery has a beer that is a proven winner like Harvest Pale things should remain constant in the brewing house, but, as Wilde explains, this is not always possible. 'We've had a couple of pinch points where there was an extreme shortage of the hops we used,' he says, 'so we had to change the hop mix, but we actually came out with something that proved even more popular. A good pint of Harvest Pale still stands out today, the mood for us is one of pride that we can still achieve this 18 years after its first brew.'

Goes well with… A pulled pork and crackling burrito

CHEDDAR ALES
Potholer

4.3% Core

Cheddar, Somerset
cheddarales.co.uk

Crisp and bittersweet Golden Ale

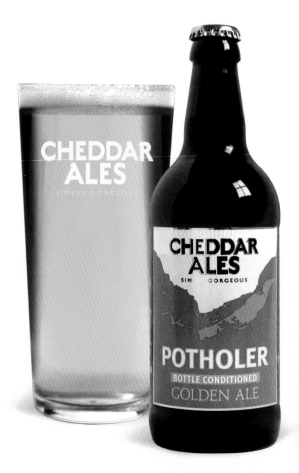

The shadow of the Mendip Hills looms large over Cheddar Ales, a long shoulder of rounded, green hills networked with caves and tunnels. This is the environment that gave its name to this sprightly Golden Ale that was first brewed in 2006 as the antithesis to the brewery's Best Bitter, Gorge Best, according to brewery founder Jem Ham. 'I wanted something lighter to tempt those customers that had "moved on a bit" from traditional Bitters,' he recalls. 'The first port of call was to omit the malts that gave Gorge Best its particular malty character and replace with lighter, more neutral malts.

'The darker kilned malts were replaced with lighter crystal malts and some wheat to aid mouthfeel. We retained the Challenger hops as a base and added some Slovenian Styrian Goldings for balance. We were aiming for a crisp, slightly more bitter but still very drinkable Golden Ale with more hop aroma. Potholer was spot on when we first tried it and it has remained true to its roots ever since. It won a silver award straight away at the 2007 SIBA Tuckers Maltings festival, narrowly missing out on gold to St Austell's Tribute so we knew we were on the right track.'

The beer is light gold in colour with a tightly laced sweetness, a fullness on the palate and a sweetshop lemon and banana note (I can almost hear the rustle of the paper bag and feel the grains of sugar being tipped into my hand for immediate consumption), plus some bitterness, but not enough to frighten the horses. The finish has a ghost of banana sweetness (again that drawing in of the laces) and a rounded hoppy bitterness before it fades away and steadies you for the next gulp.

Goes well with... A salad of smoked chicken, bacon and avocado

CLOUDWATER BREW CO
A Wave in the Marlborough Sands

5%   Annually

Manchester
cloudwaterbrew.co

DDH Pale Ale that is a showcase for New Zealand hops

A Pale Ale from 30 years ago would be totally different to the ones that are currently part of the offerings from contemporary British breweries. Modern Pale Ales fizz and pulsate with the vibrancy of American and Antipodean hops, are low in bitterness and exceptionally popular with beer lovers. Cloudwater is especially noted for its Pale Ales, which have a durable and dynamic drinkability, and this gold-flecked example is no exception.

Brewed once a year, it is double dry-hopped with the new season's New Zealand hops Rakau and Waimee, both of which impart the sweet, fruity and creamy character of mango and the juiciness of orange on the nose. There is a rawness and greenness about the nose, with the fruitiness being joined by the freshness of a foil bag of hops that have just been opened. On the palate there is more of this powerful and even primal fruitiness alongside a smooth mouthfeel while a brisk carbonation wakes up the tasting buds before a bittersweet finish that brings in more of that fresh fruitiness. This is an artful beer that when I first tasted it in the depths of winter had the ability to bring in a hint of summer.

This beer is part of a series that Cloudwater began with the aim of showcasing the best of its New Zealand hop contracts, according to founder and owner Paul Jones. 'We went back to our 2015 manifesto,' he says. 'This was when we were working with hops that weren't the headliners they are now, and so just like then we decided that when we have hops that don't hit the headlines we brew around them rather than try and squeeze them into a style. We kept looking at our New Zealand selections and we said let's make sure we are making the style fit into the hops.'

Such is the multi-verse nature of Pale Ales.

Goes well with… A creamy fish stew with mussels, prawns and scallops also in the mix

DEYA BREWING
Steady Rolling Man

5.2%   Core

Cheltenham, Gloucestershire
deyabrewing.com

Vibrant and vital Pale Ale that boldly shows off the character of US hops

Sometimes you fall head over heels in love with a beer on the first gulp, which was my heady experience with DEYA's Steady Rolling Man. A vibrant and vital Pale Ale, lemon gold in colour, its aromatics of tropical fruit (ripe mango and lychee) seemed to charge out of the glass as if to suggest this could be part of your five-a-day. There was more of this surge of tropical fruit on the palate, alongside a Riesling-like floral note followed by a Sahara-like dryness that encouraged another gulp. If we are going to talk about juicy beers that show off the bold character of American hops then this is one of them. Several years after that initial meeting I remain a big advocate of this sensuously uninhibited beer, a great tribute to the skill and dedication DEYA's founder and head brewer Theo Frayne has brought to the craft of brewing.

'Steady was the first beer we ever brewed,' he says, 'and it is very much the cornerstone of our business. I wanted to create a Pale Ale which was incredibly juicy and intense but also immensely drinkable. For us as a company it was a statement of our intent. It is still our best-selling beer and what we are best known for, and moreover, it was the jumping off point for us, style wise, to move into bigger and more intense beers.

'As for the name it comes from a Robert Johnson song. I listened to a lot of blues while home-brewing and the original versions influenced our brew sessions and the beer! The label has taken on some iterations but the feel of an old blues record remains.'

Goes well with... Pizza, especially a homemade one with plenty of spicy toppings

DURATION BEER
Turtles All The Way Down

5.5%   Core

West Acre, Norfolk
durationbeer.com

Exemplary American-style Pale Ale that is a big friendly hug of a beer

You will find Duration deep in the heart of the Norfolk countryside, south of Kings Lynn, making beer in a restored old farmhouse and flitting through a variety of styles, all of them judiciously overseen and brought into the world by head brewer Bates, who co-founded the brewery with Miranda Hudson.

When a brewery has a rural location you could argue that its relative isolation enables the brewers to engage with their own sense of creativity without the distractions of urban life. I would see this exemplary American-style Pale Ale as one of the consequences of Duration's hidden way of working. It's a common beer style yes, and made by most craft brewers, but it still has an edge and a sense of its own value when it comes to evaluating it.

The first sense to be used encompasses vision and the beer is a golden, sunflower yellow. It tilts its head to the sun and brings down joy in the glass. You think it will be a shame to disturb its beauty by drinking it but then you get the first aroma and all your aesthetics go out of the window. There are hints of blueberry, melon and passion fruit on the bright and cheerful nose, alongside a brittle lemon note and the suggestion of freshly cut grass. Then we transform ourselves to taste and it will not be a beer that you will find stays long in the glass (surely there's a magician at work here as the beer seems to vanish very quickly) as tropical fruit, passion fruit, blueberry and a counterpoint of chives and a light graininess all work together to make a friendly hug of a beer, a beer that is like the gentle nudge of a young dog eager to go for a walk on a bright sunny day. It's the kind of beer that will go all the way down very quickly.

Goes well with… Sitting around a campfire and putting the world to rights

FROME BREWING COMPANY
Riwaka Pacific Pale Ale

5.6%   Seasonal

Frome, Somerset
fromebrewingcompany.com

*Zesty Pale Ale with mandarin,
grapefruit and passion fruit notes*

Frome is not in the middle of the Pacific
Ocean, as anyone who has ever been to
the Somerset market town will tell you;
neither is the eponymous brewery for
that matter (formerly known as Milk
Street). On the other hand, the hop variety
Riwaka is a native of the Pacific, or New
Zealand to be exact, hence the name of
this bright and breezy beer. It is a popular
hop, giving colour and vitality to IPAs
and Pale Ales, which is presumably why
Frome Brewing Company used it. With
that problem solved, let's pour it into the
glass and see what it has to say to us.

The first thing to notice is that it
has the hue of a hazy sunset, the kind
of sunset that draws the curtain on a
gorgeous day that you might remember
for the rest of your life. There is more
sublimity with the notes of sweet
mandarin, zesty grapefruit and the
pulse of passion fruit emerging from
the glass, playful aromatics that draw
you in, ready to experience a similar
sort of sunshine on the palate.

Disappointment is not an option
when you taste it as there is more
mandarin sweetness, a gulp of grapefruit
and a wisp of white grape, all of which
operate in tandem with a delicate
graininess before a gentle bitterness
and appetising dryness continue to
linger in the finish, which suggests that
this perfect day is not done yet and
the sun will take its time in setting.

Goes well with... A homemade burger on a soft white bap with plenty of relish

FYNE ALES
Jarl

3.8% Core

Cairndow, Argyll and Bute, Scotland
fyneales.com

Refreshing and elegant session beer

First brewed in 2010 after the brewery's then head brewer Will Wood had become aware of the potential of the Citra hop variety thanks to ex-colleagues at his former brewery Oakham Ales, this is the flagship of Fyne Ales' magnificent selection of beers, a blonde-coloured session ale that both wins awards and quenches thirsts across the UK. If you haven't tried Fyne's beers before, it is a superb place to start before you continue on a fascinating journey through some of Britain's best beers.

Moderate in alcohol and as golden as a sunset on Fyne's part of the world (the brewery is located on a farm in the picturesque surroundings of a glen next to Loch Fyne), Jarl is a refreshing beer that bursts with juicy citrus orange and grapefruit on the nose, the kind of fruit salad that makes you think that sunlight has just entered your soul. Following this aromatic high, this scented ascent of the senses, take a gulp of the beer and you will be rewarded with that elegant citrus character alongside a zingy, bitter and dry mouthfeel. This is a beer that you can drink several pints of and still remain sharp, refreshed and focused right to the bottom of the glass.

It is available in both bottle and can with the latter featuring a slightly tweaked recipe that brings in additional oats in the grist as well as a generous Citra dry-hop infusion, both of which offer a fuller body and punchier citrus fruit flavours.

Goes well with… Loch Fyne smoked salmon

HARVIESTOUN BREWERY
The Ridge

5% Core

Alva, Clackmannanshire, Scotland
harviestoun.com

Punchy but balanced Pale Ale that spans the Atlantic

The Ridge sounds like the name of a disaster movie, maybe with an earthquake or volcano in a starring role, but in reality it's a well-balanced, palate-refreshing Pale Ale that was developed as a companion piece to the brewery's other core beers Schiehallion and Bitter & Twisted (the latter so named because the brewery's then owner Ken Brookner had just been booked for speeding and he took out his ire on the mash tun).

According to master brewer Amy Cockburn, 'we wanted to create a Pale Ale that gave a nod to the American Pale style but also kept our style and Scottish roots at heart. Hence the use of UK as well as American hops – unfortunately, hops are notoriously hard to grow in Scotland! We wanted to create a beer that held the character of a British Bitter and the tropical aromas of an American Pale all in one. The first brew was exciting! We originally bottled it into 330ml bottles, and we knew straight away we had a great beer. It was punchy but balanced – just what we wanted.'

Lustrous gold in colour, topped by a fine, firm collar of foam, The Ridge has a nose of freshly cut grass alongside hints of pine resin, while the palate has more of the pine, a beaming smile of tropical fruitiness before it descends into a dry and softly bitter finish that will leave the drinker ready for another gulp. Or as Cockburn says when asked about the mood of the beer: 'fun, interesting and a little spicy.'

Goes well with... A toasted cheese sandwich, perhaps made with Lanark Blue

HOPBACK BREWERY
Summer Lightning

5%   Core

Salisbury, Wiltshire
hopback.co.uk

Classic Golden Ale
well worth rediscovering

Sometimes it is easy to lose track of beers. One day they are the favoured flavour in your glass, something that you cannot get enough of, and the next day it's 'whatever happened to old whatsitsname?' This happened to me with Hopback's pristine Summer Lightning, one of the earliest Golden Ales that, with its appearance in the late 1980s from Hopback's first brewery in the Wyndham Arms' cellars, kicked off a beer revolution.

Throughout the 1990s and the following decade Summer Lightning was a regular presence in my beer cupboard, a dependable 5% Golden Ale that looked like Budvar or Pilsner Urquell and never disappointed, a beer that enlivened and enthralled the palate. Then somehow I lost sight of it as other beers came along, jostling for shelf space, bright, colourful and noisy in their hop character, bolder than brass.

Sometimes you have to lose track of something, whether it's a beer, book or piece of music, before you can rediscover and appreciate it again, which is what happened to me in 2018 when I reacquainted myself with Summer Lightning and found it just as compelling as it always had been. The spicy, peppery bitterness I recalled was still in place, balanced by a mid-palate sweetness and fruitiness, thanks to the use of very pale malt and East Kent Goldings with Challenger for bitterness. There remains a lucidity about the beer and a clarity in its flavour, which makes it the kind of beer that you will spend rather a lot of time with. Welcome back, old friend.

Goes well with… Chicken satay and a gorgeously golden day (which need not be in the summer)

KELHAM ISLAND BREWERY
Pale Rider

5.2% Core

Sheffield
kelhambrewery.co.uk

*Classic Pale Ale with a palate-caressing
torrent of tropical fruit notes*

Pale Rider was first brewed in 1992 and
was one of the earliest British beers to
make use of aromatic North American
hops, presumably due to the transatlantic
travels of its founder, the late Dave
Wickett, who operated a bar in upstate
New York. The brewery had only began
brewing two years earlier as well and I
recall Wickett once saying to me, 'when
we opened the brewery in 1990 there
were four big breweries in Sheffield. If
someone had told me that we would be
the biggest in the city by the end of the
decade I would have said they were mad.'
Wickett was a beer visionary in Sheffield
and even though he died 10 years ago,
in the spring of 2012, he is sadly missed
in the Steel City's beer community.

I suspect he would be happy to
note that, nearly 30 years on and after
a multitude of awards, a bottle of
this pale gold-yellow beer still has an
ability to stroke and caress the palate
with its torrent of tropical fruit notes
(I picked up passion fruit and guava),
alongside a mid-palate sherbet-like

softness and a grainy maltiness followed
by a bittersweet and dry finish.

Sometimes in the fast moving
gold-rush of contemporary beer it is
easy to lose touch with those beers
that have become milestones on the
exhilarating journey that British brewing
has taken over the last few decades.
Pale Rider is one of those milestones
and opening a bottle and pouring it
into the glass will give you a glimpse
backwards and forwards in time, for
this is also very much a beer of now.

Goes well with…   Homemade fish finger sandwiches with tartare sauce

THE KERNEL BREWERY
Pale Ale

5–5.6%   Core (with different hops)

Bermondsey, London
thekernelbrewery.com

Zingy and vibrant fruitiness balanced with a dry finish make this a joyful experience

The great joy about The Kernel's Pale Ales is that they never stay the same. There is a restlessness and relentless sense of experimentation in the way different hop varieties are used, whether the beer is single- or multi-hopped: it could be Centennial and/or Enigma, Cascade or Vic's Secret just for starters. Inevitably though, given the journey that founder Evin O'Riordan has taken the Bermondsey-based brewery on since opening in 2009, these Pale Ales will be juicy and fruity, easy to drink and packed with the sun-blessed aromatics of whatever hops are used.

'We have certain things we like to taste and feel in our beers,' O'Riordan once told me, 'a clarity of flavour, a particular intensity (especially aromatic intensity) and an articulate texture. There's also freshness for anything pale and/or hoppy. But the way we brew is not fixed on an ideal goal, or a preconceived notion of what a beer should taste like.

'When we, say, change the hops on our Pale Ale or IPA, we would like to give the beer space (or give those hops space) to express itself/themselves, rather than conform to what we want it to be. We feel that having a specific image in mind of what the flavours of this beer should be acts as a limit to the potential of that beer. So what we want with our beers is to give them a bit of freedom of expression, within the general parameters of what we like in a beer.'

With that in mind expect each Pale Ale to have a zing and a vibrant fruitiness, an exemplary balance with a dry and lasting finish.

Goes well with... Half a dozen fresh oysters with a dash of Tabasco

THE KERNEL BREWERY
Table Beer

2.7-3%   Occasional

Bermondsey, London
thekernelbrewery.com

A low-ABV beer that captures the fullness and roundness of cask

According to The Kernel's thoughtful and articulate founder Evin O'Riordan, the motivation behind the creation of the brewery's Table Beer was a desire to capture a certain essence of cask beer, its ability to deliver flavour and character at a low ABV.

'We wanted the fullness and roundness and life of a cask beer,' he says, 'which covers the absence of a certain amount of alcohol that usually provides fullness and roundness. We bottle-condition/keg-condition all our beers (excepting a few recent forays into lagered beers), but this process probably adds most to the Table Beer, though it is supremely essential across all our beers – it is what gives them life.'

Hop varieties are changed with each batch brewed, but favoured hop combinations are used fairly frequently. The Table Beer I tasted had Nelson Sauvin, Simcoe and Citra. It was pale yellow in colour beneath a firm, snowy head of foam. On the nose there was freshly cut ripe mango, a squeeze of breakfast grapefruit juice plus a hint of grainy malt. There was more of the fruitiness on the palate, plus a delicate graininess. It was quenching and lightly tart with a dryness and bittersweetness in the finish. An ethereal beer that might be light but is certainly not flimsy.

'We pushed the brewing process with this beer in a way that we were not sure would work,' says O'Riordan, 'the mash temperature is really high so as to ensure lots of residual sugars to give the body and mouthfeel of a beer with a higher alcohol level. But this temperature we felt could lead to instability/denaturing of enzymes, etc, so we were pretty concerned at the outcome. Turns out it works. We were very happy.'

Goes well with... The company of mature Cheddar

LACONS
Encore

3.8% Core

Great Yarmouth, Norfolk
lacons.co.uk

Perfectly balanced,
big-flavoured session ale

Until it was bought and then closed by the infamous Whitbread in the late 1960s, Lacons was an East Anglian brewing powerhouse, with pubs throughout the region, all of them branded with the brewery's logo of a falcon. In normal times that would be the end of Lacons, a memory becoming dimmer as its last adherents grew older, and then finally a footnote in a brewing history book. However, in 2013 Lacons was resurrected in its home town of Great Yarmouth, part of a recent trend in reviving beer names that had vanished in the last 50 years – Watneys, Trumans and Home have also had the same treatment.

Lacons uses the old brewery's original yeast strain, which had been originally deposited in the National Collection of Yeast Cultures in the late 1950s as a safeguard against infection. Will Wood was head brewer at the time of the rebirth, having spent time at Oakham and Fyne Ales. For him, his brief was to give Lacons' beers a distinctly modern face, which, as he recalls for Encore, 'the plan was to brew a modern Pale Ale using my knowledge of American hops to marry them with the recently reawakened 1959 original yeast strain. The early brews were excellent and I thought it was a winner from day one – it was a perfectly balanced, big-flavoured session ale and, as the name says, it keeps you coming back for more.'

He certainly succeeded as this Pale Ale/Amber cross-over of a thirst-quencher has light citrus and delicate biscuitiness on the nose, leading to more of the same on the sprightly palate alongside a tingle of bittersweetness before it finishes dry, encouraging the drinker to have more of the same. Sometimes the dead return in a perfectly respectable fashion.

Goes well with… All the fun of the seaside and enjoying fish and chips on the promenade

NEWBARNS BREWERY
Table Beer

3% Frequently available

Leith, Edinburgh, Scotland
newbarnsbrewery.com

Refreshing and juicy beer with plenty of hop character

Each brew of Table Beer features a different hop variety and with that in mind it's not too fanciful to claim that the brewing team at Leith-based Newbarns approach every individual brew as if it was a blank canvas, an empty space ready to be daubed and splashed with the bright colours of whatever hop variety is chosen. It could be Mosaic (as you can see in the photograph) or Idaho 7, or, in the case of the can I tasted, it was Callista, a variety that was originally developed in Germany and pulsates with an intense fruitiness.

Newbarns was founded in 2020, which was not the most auspicious year to begin any sort of new business, but the hard work and energy the owners Gordon McKenzie and Emma Mcintosh and their team have put in since has paid off handsomely, not only with Table Beer but also with beers such as Oat Lager.

Time for a beer. First of all, the eyes have it as it has the look of a sunny day, as sunflower yellow meets gold, a gleaming day full of good intentions and even better beer. On the nose there are suggestions of apricot, passion fruit and blueberry with the latter definitely at the forefront. With that in mind, I'm almost tempted to say it is reminiscent of the aroma of a blueberry muffin, with no chocolate thankfully added. There is the same chime of fruitiness on the palate, making for a classy, easy-drinking and refreshing beer that is packed with plenty of flavour for its strength. The addition of oats also gives it a rounded mouthfeel and the gentle bitterness in the finish is an added boon. A gorgeous beer, juicy and judicious and ideal for that first swig of the day as you settle yourself at the table.

Goes well with… A bag of artisanal salt and balsamic vinegar crisps

NORTH BREWING
Sputnik

5% Core

Leeds
northbrewing.com

Pale Ale with bold, juicy flavours and an empirical sense of drinkability

First of all there was North Bar, the pioneering Leeds craft beer bar opened in 1997 by John Gyngell and Christian Townsley. Other bars followed and then in 2015 along came the companion piece North Brewing, also in Leeds. Sputnik was one of its earliest beers, a rumbustious hazy Pale Ale that is packed with citrusy hops and soothes and swipes right so that you know your palate is going to be just fine. This is the brewery's signature beer, the one that the brewers drink when the day is done and the time for just being is now, and has a zen-like balance between bold, juicy flavours and an empirical sense of drinkability.

The aromatics of this amber-orange joy in a glass are all about ripe tropical fruit that might have been sitting in a bowl in a well-maintained kitchen into which the sun has been streaming throughout a gorgeous summer's day. The palate keeps the juiciness of these fruits, a result of the wisdom of the hopping rate, and then races onto a dryness and soft bittersweetness that lingers at the back of the throat, as if emulating the not-there, but-there echoes of the cheering crowd after their team has scored a spectacular goal.

'Sputnik is by far the beer that we brew the most of at North,' says head brewer Seb Brink, 'so it continues to evolve as we strive for continuous improvement. In the early days of Sputnik we leaned a little more towards using lots of Columbus, meaning that the beer was grassier and more herbal. As we've developed the recipe Ekuanot and Citra have come to the forefront, enabling us to aim for a fruitier Pale Ale.'

Goes well with… Calling out for a sunny pint on a hot day

OAKHAM ALES
Citra

4.6%   Core

Peterborough, Cambridgeshire
oakhamales.com

*The first British beer
to use the Citra hop*

Given its current ubiquity in the hop-flecked ranks of craft brewers, it's hard to believe there was a time when Citra was, well, not there. At the end of the 00s, American hops were common visitors in British beer, with Cascade in the lead, but of Citra there was nothing. Until, that is, Oakham's then head brewer (and now brewing director) John Bryan was on his annual trip to the hop-growing region of the Yakima Valley in Washington State during the 2009 harvest.

As he once told me when we shared pints of Citra in a Cambridge pub, 'this hop (Citra) was thrown on the table and I was told they had 1500 kilos of it if I was interested. It was full of lychee, gooseberry, tropical fruit aromas and I was rubbing this hop and getting goosebumps and a shiver up my back. I wanted it big time and it was agreed that some would be pulled back for me. I was so confident that I said I wanted my section flown back rather than brought on a boat.'

The result of this serendipitous moment was the first brew of Citra at the end of November 2009. It is still a beer that charms with its friendly, chatty, colourful aromatics of lychee, grapefruit and ripe gooseberry notes. On the palate, the tropical fruit savours of grapefruit, lychee, papaya and pineapple run riot on the palate before being reined in by a dry, bitter finish that lingers in the air like the echo of applause in a hall at the end of a storming rendition of Mahler's 2nd Symphony.

Goes well with... A cross-cultural mix of breaded pork schnitzel and sautéed potatoes

ORBIT BREWERY
Nico

4.8%   Core

Walworth, London
orbitbeers.com

Kölsch-style beer that hosts a delicate and gentle interplay between malt and hops

Nico, initially of the Velvet Underground and then a solo artist who sang along to a harmonium, made one of the most depressing albums I've ever heard. This was *The End*, which was released in 1974. Listening to it was like being subjected to 40 minutes or so of darkness, even though it did have some sort of perverse appeal, especially in her maudlin, slit-your-wrists version of the Doors' *The End*. Thankfully, there is nothing but sweetness and light about Orbit's tribute to the German-born singer.

Nico is described by Orbit as a Köln lager (the singer was born in Cologne), which is another way of saying that it is inspired by the Kölsch beers that are brewed and fermented in the same way as an ale then matured like a lager, emerging as delicious, gold-coloured thirst-quenchers served in the German city's taverns by waiters nicknamed *'Kobes'*.

Orbit's version is dark gold in colour and has a light breadiness and hint of fruit on the nose, with each swig revealing more of this attractive breadiness alongside suggestions of pear and wild strawberry, all of which give it an appealing elegance. Don't be deceived by this lightness of touch though, the grip of dryness in the finish lets you know that this is a beer with muscles.

The skill in making a Kölsch is to keep a delicate and gentle interplay between malt and hops to create a beer that is light on the tongue but still thirst-quenching enough to warrant several glasses throughout a session. The brewers at Orbit have certainly succeeded here.

Goes well with… Listening to the Velvet Underground's first LP

THE PARK BREWERY
Gallows Pale Ale

4.5% Core

Kingston upon Thames, London
theparkbrewery.com

Well-balanced Pale Ale that has tropical fruit, citrus and a brisk bitterness in the finish

This shimmeringly golden Pale Ale is powered by Mosaic and Simcoe, well-established superstar personalities on the fruity hop scene, a holy alliance of two varieties that swirl with the ringing, chiming, almost musical notes of tropical fruit, stone fruit, blueberry, citrus and pine. The soft aromatic of peach first of all pokes its way out of the glass, followed by the assurance of ripe mango and a Riesling-like sweetness. A well-balanced basket of tropical fruit emerges on the palate followed by a svelte dryness and brisk bitterness in the finish, which makes me think that, because of its bitterness that anchors it from being too sweet and juicy, this could perhaps be a new style of beast, an Anglo-American Pale Ale.

For head brewer Josh Kearns, who founded Park with his wife, Frankie, in 2014, 'Gallows is extremely close to my heart, it's our original and first commercial beer release, so it is the main core of all the core beers and really was the starting block for starting Park

Brewery. Back in 2013 when I was home brewing, I was trying out different grains, hops and yeasts, and the recipe for Gallows was the eighth all-grain recipe that I did. The inspirational beers at the time that were blowing me away were Goose Island IPA (not a beer I'd choose now though), Odell 5 Barrel IPA, any Kernel Pale or IPA and Punk IPA (when it *was* good).The recipe has had a couple of tweaks along the way but is essentially the same beer scaled up, with the dry hop having increased a bit over time.'

Goes well with... Chilli con carne with plenty of tortilla chips

POMONA ISLAND
Phaedra

5.3% Core

Salford, Greater Manchester
pomonaislandbrew.co.uk

*A perceptive and appealing
Pale Ale from Salford*

Sometimes all we want from a beer is a simplicity of flavour and aroma, the certainty that whatever we have just opened a can of will satisfy and enrich our senses and make the world seem a much better place than it actually is. Imperial Stouts, mixed fermentations and beers that resemble fruit salads all have their place but sometimes all we want is a Pale Ale. Pomona Island Phaedra is that kind of beer, a stalwart of this Salford-based brewery, which demonstrates that you don't need too much to make a beer that goes down the throat with the same breathable ease that oxygen demonstrates.

Along with Factotum, this is the brewery's only other core beer (as I have written elsewhere in the book, the idea of regular beers is not to every modern brewery's taste these days) and it is rather delicious. Pale orange in colour and cast with a light haze, this has a juicy, luscious nose of citrus, tropical fruit and stone fruit (think ripe peach); the aromatics are almost fragrant as they drift their way out of the glass. On the palate there is more of this lush fruitiness – mango, grapefruit, peach – plus a mouth-watering juiciness and the tang of refreshment. The finish is dry and bittersweet and it is time for you to take another gulp. For even though its ABV is 5.3%, this is a beer that you will devour as if you were a wolf coming down on the fold. My advice: buy more than one and prepare to have this beer cast its spell on you.

Goes well with… Playful, celebratory, friendly and conversational moments with friends

RAMSGATE BREWERY
Gadds' Nº3

5%   Core

Broadstairs, Kent
ramsgatebrewery.co.uk

*Dry-hopped Pale Ale that shows off
the sensuality of East Kent Goldings*

Many beers have a sense of place as well as the ability to transport the drinker to their source. That is certainly the case with this classic English-style Pale Ale, which is produced in Kent, on the edge of one of the great hop-growing areas of Europe and home to the East Kent Goldings variety. This is a beer that has the power to transport you to harvest time with the aromatics and spices of the hop bines wafting across the fields. There is time travel too as a sip of the beer will bring to life images of the Londoners who once made their way down to Kent for working holidays.

This was the first beer that founder Eddie Gadd brewed at Ramsgate Brewery back in 2002, with his intention being 'to create a dry-hopped Pale Ale much like Sierra Nevada Pale Ale but I wanted it to be a Kent version. With the first brew I was really pleased with it and had a pint of it in the back garden. It was everything I hoped it would be.'

Burnished gold in colour the beer has a deep, sensual hop character, allowing a citrusy marmalade orange to combine with grainy malt on the nose, while it is bittersweet, biscuity and blossoming with more hop spirituality (spice and pepperiness) on the palate.

This is a beer that is an adventure in the glass, and when you pour it be prepared for it to magically transport you to the great hop gardens of Kent as if it were a magic carpet of flavour and aroma.

Goes well with… Taking Eddie's advice and take a bottle (and a glass obviously) into the garden

ROOSTER'S BREWING
Yankee

4.3% Core

Harrogate, North Yorkshire
roosters.co.uk

One of the first American-style Pale Ales to be made in the UK

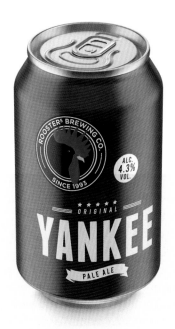

Yankee was first brewed in the mid-90s when the US hop variety Cascade was a rare beast. It was also one of the first American-style Pale Ales and it swerved through the British brewing scene like George Best in his pomp. Even though the originator of Yankee, Sean Franklin, sold the brewery to Ian Fozard and his two sons, Oliver, now head brewer, and Tom, whose role is commercial director, it is a tribute to Franklin's legacy that the beer has remained the same, being still brewed with just four ingredients – soft Yorkshire water, pale malt, Cascade hops and Rooster's house yeast strain.

'The perception of the beer has shifted over the past decade or so,' says Tom Fozard, 'as more aggressively hopped beers formed a larger part of the mainstream beer market and sub-styles of beers have been created, resulting in a shift in consumer expectations. With this in mind, Yankee, in the 21st Century, offers the drinker an easy-going experience and acts as a gateway beer for those who are setting out on their craft beer journey and making the switch from mass-produced lagers and the like, while also holding true to how it was when it was first brewed all those years ago.'

Pale gold in colour, it has a shopping basket full of tropical fruit aromatics on the nose, while each gulp (for this is a beer to be gulped) has more of the tropical fruit, and a light, malt-led sweetness before finishing dry and issuing invitations to drink more of the same. Or as Tom Fozard says: 'the mood of this beer is football in the mid-90s before the Premier League and Sky Sports took hold of it and created a caricatured version of the beautiful game.'

Goes well with... Grilled chicken and a sunny afternoon in the garden

SOLVAY SOCIETY
Halmos

4.2%   Core

Leytonstone, London
solvaysociety.com

*Brussels-style Pale Ale with a subtle
fruitiness and elegant bittersweetness*

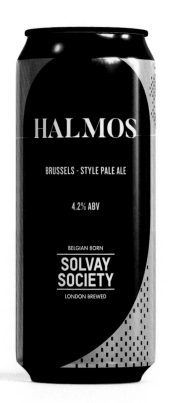

Belgian beer is a major influence on
Solvay Society, though don't expect
carbon copies of the likes of Trappist
ales, Witbiers or Lambics. Under the
direction of its Brussels-born founder
Roman Hochuli, Belgian beer is used as
a guide for the beers he brews, a beacon
perhaps to light the way. Take Halmos,
which he describes as a Brussels-style
Pale Ale, which in his words, 'means
nothing but it does indicate how the beer
might taste'. The two beers that came
to his mind when he was developing
Halmos was Brasserie de la Senne's
Taras Bulba and De Ranke's XXX,
both of them beers that fly a flag for
hops and bitterness, with a stated aim
of taking elements from this brace of
beers, including the dry finish and the
hop aroma that runs through them.

'These are things that work well in
a 4.2% beer,' he says, 'Halmos was very
much designed with the drinker in
mind, and with NEIPAs doing so well
at the moment I use characteristics
from them in Halmos. For instance,
I used a decent amount of oats, and the
addition of Pilsner malt, which helps
to create a nutty background that runs
through the beer. The hops rotate a
little, but I always use Tettnang, though
later versions have used Saphir, whose
aromatics I liken to Alpine meadows.'

Pale gold in colour, there are light
aromas of apricot and strawberry
with a hint of lemon curd in the
background. This subtle fruitiness is
repeated with each swig, but there is
also a bittersweetness to remind you
it's a beer not a fruit tart. The finish
is dry and refreshing with the earlier
fruitiness making a brief reappearance.

Goes well with... Reclining in a meadow, Alpine or not

STANNARY BREWING
Verde

4.6%   Seasonal

Tavistock, Devon
stannarybrewing.shop

*An assured and confident
green-hop Pale Ale from Devon*

Though they have been made since the 1990s, the last few years have seen green-hopped beers become an essential part of many breweries' seasonal selections, a nod and a wink to the change of taste a fresh hop can bring to a beer. A small explanation: fresh hops are not dried in the traditional manner but usually shipped straight from farm to brewery, to be used as soon as possible. Some liken the effect of green hops in a beer as similar to the transformation fresh herbs give to a dish in comparison to dry ones. Tavistock-based Stannary has gone one hop-step further in that their 2021 vintage of this annual release uses hops that have been grown by one of the brewers and Dartmoor is hardly a place known for hop cultivation.

According to Garry White, 'Verde was dreamt up by Chris John (Stannary co-founder with White) who had started growing his own hops after going on a foraging course. For the first couple of years the beer was brewed on our pilot kit but for the past two years it has been brewed on our commercial kit.

We've always loved the way the green hops showcase a different side to hop flavours and essential oils with the more grassy, herbal flavours coming to the fore and it has become a permanent fixture in our seasonal range of beers.'

Orange amber in colour, Verde resonates with a pungent hoppy nose, incorporating a grassy-like freshness alongside a sweet citrusiness and an undercurrent of spiciness. There is more of the same on the palate, with a generous bittersweetness before finishing with an assured bitterness and dryness. Think of it as the summer that has just gone in the glass.

Goes well with... A pasty, and ponder on some Devonians' claim that the Cornish stole the idea from them

TRACK BREWING
Sonoma

3.8%   Core

Manchester
trackbrewing.co

A sparklingly lucent dry-hopped Pale Ale

You just know that a beer named after Sonoma County in California is going to have a big burst of hoppiness when poured into the glass, especially as the county, which is well-known for wine, also has plenty of hops grown there. In fact, it was Track's founder Sam Tyson's visit to Sonoma County whilst on a cycling trip around the USA that inspired him to produce this sparklingly lucent dry-hopped Pale Ale when it came to opening Track in Manchester.

'I had been cycling across the US and coming across all these new beers – big, hoppy, full-bodied IPAs and Pale Ales,' he says. 'These were something of a revelation – bright, citrusy, full-bodied and totally infused with hop character. This stayed with me the rest of the journey all over the world. With the UK market in mind I wanted to develop a lower ABV version of these beers that kept that body and didn't sacrifice on the hop character.'

A pale yellow gold and hazy in appearance, there is a judicious juiciness of tropical fruit on nose as its aromatics emerge from the glass with the freshness of a bright, new morning. There is more juice on the palate, tropical fruit perhaps, followed by a mouth-watering bittersweetness which leads to a dry finish. A well-made Pale Ale with an arc of flavour that crosses the palate with the certainty of a rainbow.

'Its mood is relaxation, groups of people winding down, conversation and good times,' says Tyson. 'A sunny afternoon in a beer garden with a gentle breeze and a cold pint in hand. Sometimes hard to imagine in Manchester, but that is the genesis of the beer, and when my mind drifts back to being on my bike in Sonoma County in California over a decade ago.'

Goes well with…   Homemade crab cakes with a sprinkle of chilli flakes

VERDANT BREWING
Headband

5.5%   Frequently available

Penrhyn, Cornwall
verdantbrewing.co

A vivid and vivacious Pale Ale that characterises Verdant beers

Swirling colours and a typeface last seen in San Francisco in the 1960s – there's a definite psychedelic vibe about the branding of Headband, which makes the beer's name all the more appropriate. The coolness continues when it's poured into the glass, an orange-gold colour that acts as a beacon to draw you into the vivid aromatics of freshly cut chives, sweet orange, pineapple and ripe mango, all thanks to the use of Citra, Mosaic, Chinook and Columbus hops. This is a beer that represents the desire of Cornwall's Verdant to make the best Pale Ales they can.

'Headband started life back in late 2014 whilst I was brewing loads of single-hop Pale Ales in a shipping container in a quarry in Cornwall,' recalls head brewer and co-founder James Heffron. 'It was just a bunch of thoughts and ideas until early 2015 when I started to brew a few batches of it. I was looking to build a Pale Ale that had layers of flavour and complexity, but remained easy drinking. The first brew was excellent. Very West Coast – it has since become a juicier affair ... but we're slowly moving it slightly back towards California. It was one of the first brews that really made me sit up and realise we're onto something.'

That 'something' continues its journey on the palate with peach, mango and chives, a smooth but impressive mouthfeel and a sandpaper-like dryness in the finish. A beer with character, like the sort of person who saunters into the bar and before long everyone is talking to them and making friends.

'The beer never remains the same!' adds Heffron. 'There are too many variables at play. As a brewery we're still trying to decide what is "The Headband". Once we've figured that out we'll let you know!'

Goes well with... Chilling on a Cornish beach in the evening sun after a day in the surf

PORTER and STOUT

In this chapter darkness is your friend as a wholesome collection of Stouts and Porters is featured.

ACORN BREWERY
Gorlovka Imperial Stout

6% Core

Barnsley, South Yorkshire
acornbreweryonline.co.uk

An Imperial Stout packed with layers of flavour and aroma

So you're happy with the new beer that you have just brewed but there's one issue still to be resolved: what to call it. That's the issue that Acorn Brewery's founder Dave Hughes had in 2005 when he decided to brew a strong Stout after the success the brewery's Old Moor Porter had experienced in beer competitions run by both CAMRA and the Society of Independent Brewers (SIBA).

'Finding a name for a core beer is never easy,' he recalls, 'but having passed many signs welcoming you to Barnsley and listing its twin town the name was decided. Gorlovka is the name of a mining town in the Ukraine and is also Barnsley's twin town. The mayor of Gorlovka on a town-twinning visit pulled the first pint of it at a local pub in Barnsley.'

As an Imperial Stout Gorlovka is very much towards the lower scale of alcoholic strength of the style, and you could even call it old school, but that doesn't mean it lacks character or bite. Exceptionally dark in colour with mahogany tints, it has an assertive and rich array of dark

stone fruit, fruit cake, mocha coffee and liquorice notes on the nose, while there is more of this darkness on the palate with fruit cake, treacle, roastiness, chocolate, dark stone fruit and a glimmer of citrus before it finishes peppery, bitter and dry.

This is a presumptive and gorgeous Imperial Stout which consults the palate with the poise and ease of an artist who knows with a serendipitous certainty that they are about to create a masterpiece.

Goes well with... A spicy chimichanga made with cooked and shredded beef short ribs

ANSPACH & HOBDAY
The Sea Salt & Chilli Stout

7.4% Seasonal

Croydon, Greater London
anspachandhobday.com

*Complex, multi-layered Stout
with chilli and salt in the mix*

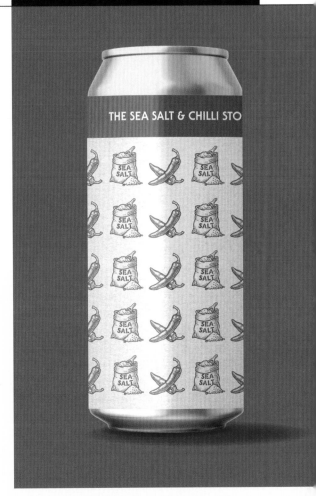

There is a right way of putting chilli in beer and a wrong way. The latter often involves slipping a whole chilli into the bottle and woe betide the drinker. Thankfully for the fine-tuned palates of those who enjoy the beers of Anspach and Hobday, the brewery has gone for the right way with this earthy, rooted, well-dug in strong Stout which has cacao nibs, sea salt and Scotch bonnet chillies added to give it an extra oratorical blast when it comes to addressing the palate. It is a fine beer of consequence, with roastiness, chocolate, mocha coffee, the smoke of the Industrial Revolution, vanilla and a suggestion of Demerara sugar to lasso in any tendency to overheating.

Originally planned as a beer to accompany oysters, it initially featured just salt and the chillies, but tasting during maturation convinced the brewing team that cacao nibs would add a slightly oily mouthfeel that would mellow out the heat.

For the brewery's Jack Anspach, 'this beer is a great example of how flavours and experiences from the culinary world can cross over into beer. Most people are pretty familiar with salt and heat when it comes to food, but perhaps not so much when it comes to drinks – this is also true of smoke, which is another flavour we play with a lot. Whilst salt and chilli are pretty unusual ingredients in beer, the Sea Salt Chilli Stout is by no means a novelty drink. The salt balances the sweetness of the malt, and the heat brings a gentle warmth. Everything is in balance and playing a meaningful role, resulting in a very drinkable Stout.'

Goes well with… Laying out half a dozen oysters and letting rip with the shucking

BOUNDARY BREWING
Export Stout

7% Core

Belfast, Northern Ireland
boundarybrewing.coop

An exemplary example of a strong Stout

Boundary is a cooperative brewery owned by its members, and given that it is based in Belfast, its name could be seen as an acknowledgement of a city whose history has seemed to be full of boundaries. Brewery co-founder Matthew Dick, however, has said that Gustave Flaubert's quote, 'Be regular and orderly in your life, so that you might be violent and original in your work' was the inspiration for the brewery's name. Flaubert aside, though, it is to be hoped that these city boundaries are easing and the cooperative nature of the brewery, which opened in 2014, is perhaps a sign of this.

This is a classic strong Stout roaring with a furnace of flavours and aromatics that emerge from the glass with an ease and elegance and a certainty of their righteousness. Dark brown verging on black in colour, this is a beer whose nose resonates with suggestions of chocolate liqueur, vanilla, dark ripe plums, booze-soaked dry fruit, butter toffee and mocha coffee. It is a complex and almost decadent nose, a soothing collection of aromatics that draws you further into the beer. The mouthfeel is smooth and creamy with more of the dried fruit, plus mocha coffee, vanilla, the smooth words of chocolate and a light roastiness that translates into a creamy, bittersweet and dry finish.

This is a beer of length, of strength, a beer that makes an impression and acts as a gracious ambassador for the exemplary brewing skills of Boundary. Gustave Flaubert would have been impressed.

Goes well with… Seafood chowder, cooked and enjoyed on the beach as the sun sets

BURNING SKY
Robust Porter

5.8% Seasonal

Firle, East Sussex
burningskybeer.com

*A boldly flavoured Porter
from an inspirational brewery*

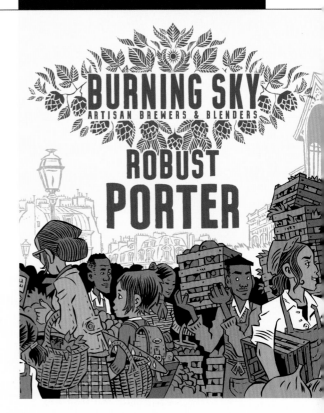

What can be seen in this glass of Burning Sky's pristine Porter? For starters, a thick collar of tan-coloured foam, undulating in its surface, collapsing slowly, like the Roman Empire, one province at a time. We can also see a dark, inky blackness, a night in which the old moon is dead and the new is waiting to be birthed.

So what can we taste? Burnt toast with a thin layer of butter and marmalade that suggests acridity, fruitiness and sweetness, and then within nanoseconds there is a dryness that crackles and cackles like a coven of witches rehearsing for *Macbeth*. There's a chewiness and a creaminess suggestive of softness and childhood; there is also mocha coffee, chocolate, toast and fruit (the aroma of marmalade if caught from the other end of the breakfast table).

For Burning Sky's founder and head brewer Mark Tranter, the motivation for Robust Porter was his desire to produce a Porter for keg and can, especially as he had already produced one in cask. 'I wanted something balanced with good malt complexity and not too astringent,' he says. 'I wanted the coffee and caramel notes, something that had a good mouthfeel. I wanted something that would work at a lower temperature and higher carbonation but without losing those lovely malt flavours.

'I first brewed it in 2018 after spending a lot of time thinking about the recipe and I was really happy with it on first tasting it. It's a contemplative beer, it's not a dissimilar strength to Easy Answers, but a different style of drinking. Easy Answers can be quite quick to drink, the Porter is more of a slower approach. It is the double album of beer.'

Goes well with... Several skewers of chicken satay and a good drama on Netflix

BURNT MILL
Big Sur Moon Cocoa Porter

4.2% Occasional

Stowmarket, Suffolk
burnt-mill-brewery.myshopify.com

*Luscious cocoa Porter that leads the
palate on a journey of discovery*

A nice cup of cocoa, just before you head
off to bed, tranquil and warming, a hug in a
cup. It's a journey back to childhood, a story
at bedtime. Let's turn this innocent image
around and look at Burnt Mill's cocoa Porter
instead. Big Sur Moon brings together two
soothing beverages to create something
that is obviously a bit more grown-up
than the archetypal cup of cocoa, but you
could argue that it is just as comforting.

For Burnt Mill's head brewer Sophie
de Ronde, the aim of Big Sur was to make a
drinkable Porter that would be accessible
to a wide audience. 'After using cocoa husks
in a few dark beers we thought it would
be a really positive addition to this beer,'
she says. 'We use the husks from a local
chocolatier, Deanna Tosier, who roasts her
own cocoa beans. We find that cocoa adds
a distinct silkiness and mouthfeel to a beer
with hints of chocolate aromas, while the
husk still carries a lot of oils from the bean
so we get a lot out of them for our beer.'

The result is a glorious beer that sits
in the glass as dark and impenetrable as
a voice heard on a misty, moonless night,
mysterious but still worthy of investigation.
There is the warmth of cocoa on the nose,
alongside a creamy chocolate sweetness
and a hint of roast coffee beans. On the
palate it is luscious and smooth, featuring
both cocoa and chocolate notes, while a
light roastiness and a chewy mouthfeel
add to the attraction. The finish features
bittersweet chocolate notes alongside a
dryness and growing bitterness, and as
the beer warms up more cocoa comes
through. Who would have thought such an
innocent drink as cocoa would work well
with the scoundrel-like nature of beer?

Goes well with… Being poured over a generous scoop of high-quality vanilla ice cream

BUXTON BREWERY
Rain Shadow

10% Annual

Buxton, Derbyshire
buxtonbrewery.co.uk

A deeply dark Imperial Stout that crackles and fizzes with character

The darkness that surrounds this sombrely dressed Imperial Stout is the vast darkness of interstellar space, where no stars or suns or supernovas glimmer. In the glass it is a darkness that echoes T S Eliot's words 'they all go into the dark', an impenetrable, unseeable dark, dark mahogany that broods beneath a crema-coloured head of foam. If a beer held mystery in the glass, then Rain Shadow is that beer.

Let us calm down a bit and actually see what the beer has to offer. On the nose there are draughts of treacle, toffee, leather, old books and vanilla, as well as a ghost-like tremor of creaminess. These are the aromatics of an Imperial Stout that knows how perfect it is, that knows there is no need to include adjuncts or fruits or spices or whatever else is in the kitchen cupboard.

It is a chewy, leathery beer, with coffee, toffee, the lightness of chocolate and vanilla, a soft roastiness and a bittersweetness all leading in one way towards a dry and bitter finish with a creaminess on the mouthfeel that possible suggests burnt cream, the cousin of a crème brûlée perhaps? It is a beer that crackles with character and swells with the flavours of what an Imperial Stout should be. It is a beer that should have been brewed in a remote castle while the storm rages outside, but instead it comes from lovely old Buxton, the cultural centre of the Peak District as well as a place where those who fancy a bit of health and beauty can take the waters. Such is the flight of fantasy that beer can take you on.

Goes well with… A resolution to watch the entire series of *Game of Thrones* again

CAMPERVAN BREWERY
Leith Porter

5%   Core

Leith, Edinburgh, Scotland
campervanbrewery.com

*An easy-drinking and
harmonious Porter*

Dark beers are not just for winter. After all, no one stops drinking coffee when the summer comes along. But there still exists amongst some beer drinkers the common misconception that a good Porter or Stout is only for when the nights draw in. That's the kind of mistaken thinking that Campervan founder Paul Gibson was aiming to overturn when he developed his brewery's easy-drinking and harmonious Porter.

'When we decided to create Leith Porter,' he recalls, 'we were thinking about brewing a balanced Porter people could drink all year long and never get bored with. A classic Porter, close to the traditional British style, that would remind people of something they know and maybe are used to drinking on cask at the pub, but something that could also seduce the craft beer drinker too.'

The result was a beer that is impenetrably dark in the glass, but lightened by a firm head of tan-tinged foam. There are creamy aromatics of toffee, mocha coffee and chocolate, which are repeated on the palate alongside a delicate roastiness, and a rich and soothing mouthfeel. The finish is dry and melodic.

'We were very pleased with the first batch we brewed,' says Gibson. 'We have brewed a lot of Stouts and Porters here, including our fan-favourite Mutiny on the Bounty, so we had a good starting point. By only using chocolate malt in the mash for our roasted grains we are able to stay clear of any burnt or harsh roasted flavours and instead focusing on the smooth chocolate and cold press espresso flavours.'

Goes well with... A sun-blessed garden or a comfortable armchair in front of a blazing fire

DURATION BEER
Fortitude

8.5% Seasonal

King's Lynn, Norfolk
durationbeer.com

A rich and potent Imperial Stout ideal for the wildest of nights

Fortitude is the ideal name for an Imperial Stout, suggestive of the beer style's potency and its intensity of flavour. According to Duration co-founder Miranda Hudson, 'we designed this in the depths of lockdown as a big beer to have, much like you would a bourbon as a post-meal drink. Fortitude seemed a fitting name for the occasion. We felt inspired from a windy day walks' soul searching to blow the cobwebs away on the north Norfolk coast. The kind of walk you take wrapped up warm and looking out to the sea for answers.'

On the technical side of things, brewery co-founder Bates recalls that he was looking for a beer that was balanced between malt, hops, yeast and alcohol, a harmonic beer that would be stealthy in its impact on the senses. 'I also like the character our Belgian yeast blend brings to the party,' he adds, 'it's like something you can't quite put your finger on when tasting but gives it another layer of complexity. Also this is a beer that we split half the batch off, which goes to foeder to age for a year or more so it had to be able to play both sides of the field, clean and sour without being a half-ass version of either.'

Darker than the soul of a tyrant and topped with a rocky, crema-coloured head of foam, this is a beer that immediately impresses with elegant aromatics of caramel, milk chocolate, light coffee and Demerara sugar rising into the air with the certainty of smoke on a still winter's day. The mouthfeel is silky and smooth, allowing the richness of caramel, chocolate, mocha coffee, a light roastiness and the merest hint of vanilla to enrich the palate before a dry finish that lasts like the wind in the chimney on a wild night. A beer that fortifies the soul.

Goes well with… A rich, meaty stew such as the Polish classic bigos

DURHAM BREWERY
Temptation Russian Stout

10% Core

Bowburn, County Durham
durhambrewery.com

A marvellously complex Imperial Stout brimming with character

We live in a beer world where Imperial Stouts and Porters are part of the common currency of many independent breweries, up there with DIPAs, double dry-hopped sours, etc. However, if you cast your mind back 40 years, Courage's Imperial Russian Stout would have been the only example of this style available, sold in 'nip' bottles and known only to the connoisseur. It was this beer that Durham Brewery's co-founder Steve Gibbs recalled from his time as a passionate home brewer in the late 1970s/early 80s, and which at the start of the 21st century he would be inspired by to produce Temptation, Durham's own Imperial Russian Stout.

'I wanted to call my new beer after the original,' he says, 'but Scottish & Newcastle had the trademark for "Imperial Russian Stout". They had bought Courage and then stopped making the beer, but retained the name. Not wishing a lawsuit, I looked for a new name. One of my favourite beers is Hoegaarden's Verboden Vrucht (Forbidden Fruit) and the name Temptation seemed obvious. We had already aligned the beer names with Durham and its cathedral, so

this seemed appropriate. A trademark search showed the name to be owned by Marston's, who sold it to us.'

The beer is now a regular part of Durham's portfolio, a big bruiser of a beer, brimming with aromatics of caramel, vanilla, berries, mocha coffee, and chocolate liqueur, all held together by a bracing roastiness. On the palate the chocolate character is rich and luxurious, working alongside a citrus fruitiness, more roastiness and a boozy pepperiness before it descends to a long exclamation of dryness, bitterness and more of that velvety smoothness. This is a beer that lends itself to barrel ageing, and whisky, rum and bourbon barrel-aged versions have been produced, alongside one with Brettanomyces. A tremendously complex beer with the hops, malt, yeast and time all doing the heavy lifting.

Goes well with… A pungent, creamy, salty and well-aged Stilton, from either Colston Bassett or Cropwell Bishop

ELLAND BREWERY
1872 Porter

6.5% Seasonal

Elland, West Yorkshire
ellandbrewery.co.uk

A smoothing and soothing Porter that dedicates itself to pleasing the palate

Let's start with the beer, gently poured out of the bottle into the glass, darkness on the edge of town. One sip and you will know that this is a perspicacious kind of Porter, offering all kinds of insights to the palate. There is treacle, but not the thick stuff that you often think might be good to lay a road, but a lighter, featherweight kind of treacle, which is joined by coffee, chocolate, vanilla and the memory of leather as well as a soothing creaminess, a friendly dryness and bitterness in the finish. All is well with the world and this Porter is now your friend and you think that you might have another bottle. This is the kind of effect this judicious and award-winning Porter has on drinkers.

Looking for its origin story, I turn to brewery manager Ryan Truswell for some history. 'The intention behind it was to create an old English Porter, he says, 'and we got the recipe from an old Tetley's head brewer who had formulated it in the late 1990s/early 00s, and then our head brewer Michael Wynnczuk tweaked it and added the finishing touches before it was launched.

'When we first tasted the beer it was very strange as you felt you were drinking something that doesn't taste 6.5%. It is very drinkable, which means that as soon as someone finishes one they want another. It is also very smooth and there is a little bit of chocolate. It felt like something that we could put to the trade and it would sell. I see it as a great finisher to a session, your last drink when you want something lovely and smooth. It is also the one you recall the next day.'

Goes well with… Those quiet and reflective meditative moments that we all need now and again

EXMOOR ALES
Beast

6.6% Core

Wiveliscombe, Somerset
exmoorales.co.uk

*A full-bodied and
lusciously rich Porter*

Back in the late 1990s when I was living in Somerset and starting to write about beer, Exmoor Beast was a bit of an enigma. In those days 6.6% was seen as a strong beer and I would shun it at the bar, especially if I had a long walk home. However, as soon as it was bottled it felt a lot safer, because you could drink it at home and not worry about falling in a river on the Somerset Levels or walk in front of a tractor (mind you it didn't stop my late mother-in-law from drinking two bottles of it one lunchtime and having to retire to bed for the rest of the day). Times and fashions in dark beers might have changed, but Exmoor Beast still remains a dark… er… beast of a beer that always satisfies.

In the glass, it broods like Arthur having discovered Lancelot's treason, while its nose has roast coffee beans, dried fruit, and even a suggestion of a brandy-like spirituousness. I get fruit cake, mocha, a hint of citrus, milk chocolate and a bittersweetness on the palate before it finishes dry and bitter. It is full-bodied but luscious in its richness, and a great contemplative beer.

In 2020 Exmoor released a one-off 10.2% Megabeast, an elegant and finessed Imperial Porter that was incredibly complex and which I hope will be brewed again one day. I thought this expression of Beast was a one-off but in late 2021 as I was finishing this book, Exmoor's head brewer Tom Davis brewed a limited run of Bumblebeest, a 9% version of the beer with organic honey added. Clearly there is life in this beast yet.

Goes well with… A plate of seafood so fresh you'd swear you could hear the sea

FALLEN BREWING
Chew Chew

6_%   Core

Stirling, Scotland
fallenbrewing.co.uk

A smooth and creamy Milk Stout

When Paul Fallen set up his eponymous brewery in 2014 he was adamant that he would not go down the modern route of producing multiple versions of the same style of beer, and so was always in search of new styles he could brew. One of these was a sweet Stout, which then became a caramel Milk Stout. Early brews were tested out on friends, but, as he recalls, 'the real eureka moment was at Christmas when one of my older uncles asked me for something to go with his Christmas cake. He honestly thought I was kidding when I gave him a trial bottle of an early version. "Stout … with cake?", but he absolutely loved it and the beer evolved from there.'

Salt was then added to the beer, making it a salted caramel Milk Stout, which, as Fallen explains, 'the subsequent brews with the salt addition were a different level. Almost like seasoning a steak, the salt addition lifted all the flavours and gave it a lovely, briny savouriness that was missing from the original.'

Smooth and creamy in its mouthfeel, the beer pours a very dark mahogany verging on black. On the nose there is plenty of chocolate, milky coffee and a hint of hazelnut, with more chocolate, caramel and a light toastiness on the palate alongside the suggestion of salinity which gives a balance to the sweetness. The finish has a gentle bittersweetness with more chocolate and a suggestion of salinity once more.

According to Fallen, there have been some subtle recipe tweaks with 'Salted Caramel' being removed from the style description, but for him it remains a beer to savour: 'It's rich and satisfying without being cloying and artificial. One for savouring in front of the fire with your whisky, or with your dessert at the end of a nice meal.'

Goes well with… A sense of experimentation especially if there is cheese and especially if there is aged Dutch Gouda

FIERCE BEER
Very Big Moose Imperial Stout

12%   Core

Aberdeen, Scotland
fiercebeer.com

*A lush and imperiously
delicious Stout*

Sometimes you need to take your time with a strong, imperious beer, linger over the glass as if you were debating whether to fall in love or not, sit back in your favourite armchair and hold the beer up to the light and express wonder at the gleaming, well-burnished, impenetrable and dangerously silent darkness that you have in front of you. Fierce's Very Big Moose Imperial Stout is that kind of beer, an elegant and eloquent expression of dark malts and the additions of cacao nibs, vanilla and cinnamon.

'The beer started life as our entry into the annual Brewdog Collabfest event in 2017,' recalls co-founder Dave Grant, 'when we were paired with their original bar in Aberdeen. The rules were strict on ABV, style and price, but we saw this as a great marketing opportunity and wanted to produce a big, memorable beer that would win. We all love beers like Alesmith's Speedway Stout and so set out to make a 12% chocolate and vanilla Stout.'

The hard work paid off and the beer won the competition, with BrewDog co-founder James Watt declaring (with his usual lack of humility) that the beer 'was the best non-BrewDog beer ever produced in Scotland'. Since then it has become available all year round, with seasonal variations including additions of maple syrup, coconut or tonka beans as well as subjecting it to barrel-ageing.

It is a smooth beer and you need to be back in that favourite armchair again, if only to enjoy the lush notes of chocolate, mocha coffee, the merest hint of cinnamon and vanilla on the nose, all of which continue onto the palate alongside a creamy, velvety mouthfeel and a soothing, luxurious finish.

Goes well with... A gorgeous sense of contentment and humility

FIVE POINTS BREWING
Railway Porter

4.8%   Core

Hackney, London
fivepointsbrewing.co.uk

Rich and luscious modern Porter with a bittersweet, dry finish

What is the soundtrack of a brewery? For starters there is the clang of the cleaning of metal kegs and casks, the sibilant hiss of compressors and the shouts of the staff as they go about their work, sometimes with heavy metal in the background. At Five Points there's an extra dimension of sound, as their beers are made adjoining a railway line in Hackney, with the thunder of the trains providing the soundtrack to the day's work. Railway Porter is a very apt name for the brewery's gorgeous riff on the style.

This was Five Points' third brew when they started in 2013, as head brewer Greg Hobbs explains: 'We felt strongly that as a London brewer we should have a Porter as part of our core range as a nod to the brewing heritage and traditions of the city. We wanted to create this historical style but with our modern twist on the recipe using today's availability of ingredients and techniques. On first taste, I was impressed by just how much roast malt character was in the glass whilst still remaining balanced. We use seven different barley malts in the beer but the one that shines for me is the "brown malt" which, along with being traditionally used, also gives a unique coffee character.'

Full-bodied, it is dark brown in colour, and is a rich and luscious beer with a creamy mouthfeel, suggestions of mocha, chocolate and vanilla and a bittersweet, dry finish. The kind of beer that you definitely drink while watching the trains go by.

Goes well with... Beef brisket cooked in coffee – honest

HARVEY'S BREWERY
Imperial Extra Double Stout

9% Core

Lewes, East Sussex
harveys.org.uk

A classic, world-renowned Imperial Stout that resonates on the palate

This dark-as-a-moonless-night beer was first brewed by Harvey's in 1999 after being commissioned by an American importer who wanted the brewery to recreate the Imperial Extra Double Stout last brewed in 1921 by the Estonian brewery A. Le Coq. According to Harvey's head brewer Miles Jenner, 'as far as the recipe was concerned, the Tartu Brewery were as helpful as they could be but not exactly precise. We all researched and I relied heavily on the recollections of the generation of brewers who had produced Barclay Perkins Russian Stout in the 1950s.'

When the brewery started on its Imperial adventure, the beer was bottled with a cork in the neck, but disaster seemed to be on the cards because some weeks after bottling Jenner spotted that the corks in some of the bottles he'd kept back in the UK were gently easing themselves upwards and were only held in place by the metal Champagne-style closures. After a few of these corks dangerously popped out of the bottles, he feared the brewery was doomed as he imagined American beer drinkers suing Harvey's for eye injuries or worse.

Thankfully, such a fate was avoided and it was subsequently decided to leave the beer longer in tanks for future brews and to use metal bottle tops instead of corks.

Whether cork or cap, this remains a remarkable beer which still stuns with its depth of character. Just think and savour coffee, chocolate, dark fruit, orange, figs and Demerara sugar pulsating on the nose and palate alongside an appetising roastiness and bitterness, with a subtle hint of Brettanomyces funkiness. This is a beautiful beer that deserves long and fruitful study.

Goes well with... The company of an old friend alongside a ripe slice of Shropshire Blue

HEANEY FARMHOUSE BREWERY
Irish Stout

4.3%   Core

Bellaghy, County Derry, Northern Ireland
heaney.ie

*A complex Stout that
thrills the palate*

So you start up a brewery in Northern Ireland and one of your core beers has to be a Stout, for after all there is a certain beer of that ilk well-known the length and breadth of the island of Ireland. Naturally, a Stout was one of the first beers Heaney founder Mal McCay produced when opening the brewery in 2019 on the working farm once home to Seamus Heaney, an uncle to McCay's wife, Suzanne. However, there were certain challenges to overcome before the beer was ready to go out into the market.

'It's a tricky market to introduce a Stout into Ireland as everyone expects a creamy mouthfeel like a certain macro Stout,' he says. 'Our first challenge was to give "weight" to the beer and to achieve the correct carbonation so as not to have it too "prickly" on the tongue. We also wanted a roundness to the flavour with the usual dry finish of an Irish Stout attained from the astringency of the roasted barley and not the actual final level of sugars left after fermentation.'

On first tasting it, he recalls being 90% satisfied, with everything you expect from a Stout all in place, though he felt that the hop profile was slightly muted. With the addition of more late boil hops and a hint of liquorice in the finish he now declares himself 97% happy.

In the glass, this sensual Stout is impenetrable in its darkness, its soul and heartbeat a pulse of coffee, chocolate, liquorice, ripe and dark stone fruit and roastiness on the nose and palate, while the deeply satisfying finish has a bitterness and dryness that stimulates the appetite to return to the glass.

'Of all our beers this one is the true reflection of our brewery and values,' says McCay. 'It's modest, yet complex and always interesting.'

Goes well with… A quiet reflective hour reading Seamus Heaney's *The Haw Lantern*

HOOK NORTON BREWERY
Double Stout

4.8% Core

Hook Norton, Oxfordshire
hooky.co.uk

Resurrected from brewery archives, this is a rich and roasty Stout

We all have archives and memories of those members of our family who went before us, faded photographs, tattered letters and the odd medal won on a foreign battlefield, where maybe some of them still sleep. Imagine, though, if you were in charge of a brewery a great-great-great grandfather might have set up when Victoria was on the throne. As well as the mementoes mentioned above, your archives would hopefully include the recipes of beers that were brewed and drunk before the First World War and changed the British brewing industry, sweeping away some of the varieties that existed at the time, such as stock ale, Imperial Stout and dinner ale.

Hook Norton was founded in the 1850s and has remained in the same family since. Records show that the first brew was a Mild XXX, and sometime during the latter years of the 19th century Double Stout became a brewery regular, until its demise during the Great War when supplies of dark malt became difficult to get hold of. That was it until 2005, when managing director and head brewer James Clarke decided to resurrect the beer, brewing it where possible following the original recipe. The result is a rich and roasty dark-shaded Stout from which aromas of roasted coffee beans, liquorice, vanilla, chocolate and treacle emerge to draw the drinker in. There is more roastiness and mocha coffee on the palate alongside a wisp of smokiness and a dry, bitter and roasty finish. To drink this beer is to drink history.

Goes well with… A rapturously juicy burger with thick cut chips on the side

HOPHURST BREWERY
Porteresque Irish Cream

5.5%   Frequently available

Wigan, Greater Manchester
hophurstbrewery.co.uk

Lush and luscious milkshake Porter with Irish cream added

A beer is a canvas upon which the brewery splashes and daubs the colours and shapes of malt, hops, water and yeast and, depending upon the style of beer, we could be either looking at a Constable, a Picasso or even something that Tracy Emin used to dash off in her spare time. However, some beer styles are more responsive to certain colours and shapes than others. Take this so-called milkshake Porter, which has had Irish cream added to it – the creamy, chocolate and vanilla notes of the liqueur work well in conjunction with the smooth, unctuous character of a Porter, but it would be a car crash of a flavour matching with an IPA or a Bitter, so this is a piece of work that would hang well on the wall of your front room, if it was a painting of course.

Hophurst was set up by Stuart Hurst in Wigan in 2014 and it is a social enterprise brewery that re-skills and employs people over the age of 50 through its own training programme. Hurst's ambition with the Irish cream version of Portersque (there has also been a salted caramel expression) was to create a 'milkshake Porter that was like drinking an Irish Cream coffee. The

first brew was great and it was very close to what we wanted, all we needed to do was a slight adjustment to the amount of Irish cream. I felt excited about how good the beer could be, it ticked all the boxes of what we wanted it to be.'

The beer is unyielding in its darkness, with a sweet, creamy, vanilla-like nose, leading to a palate with chocolate, mocha coffee and Irish cream before a dry, slightly roasty finish. It is an excellent example of a Porter that has been enhanced by the Irish cream flavouring, which is integrated and integral to the beer.

Goes well with… An afternoon break and a chocolate brownie (homemade of course)

THE KERNEL BREWERY
Imperial Brown Stout

9.5% Occasional

Bermondsey, London
thekernelbrewery.com

A soothing sipper of a strong Stout

When you walk amongst the hubbub of Borough Market in south London, try and cast your mind back to the 19th century, for on Park Road, just off the market, stood Barclay Perkins' Anchor Brewery, one of the largest, if not *the* largest, breweries in Britain at the time. Meditation over, let's return to the present and think about The Kernel, which makes its exceptional beers a couple of miles eastwards in Bermondsey in a railway arch. Two different breweries, two different times, but its Imperial Brown Stout provides an organic connection with Barclay Perkins in that this rich and spirituous beer is brewed to an 1856 recipe from the Anchor Brewhouse.

This is an exceptionally contemplative beer, the kind of beer you take your time with in studying and enjoying and working out the various journeys on which it takes you. It has a dark chocolate sweetness on the nose, alongside a creamy, soothing nature; there is delicacy as well with suggestions of vanilla also emerging to create an assemblage of aromatics that draws you in, but also tames your anticipation, which is why you take your time. This is a sipping beer, with each sip revealing layers of chocolate-coated nuts, milky coffee, espresso bitterness and roastiness, a creaminess in the mouthfeel and also a hint of coconut (or is that vanilla?). The finish is long and dry with the creaminess adding a soothing counterpoint. A well-integrated beer that is both historic and modern and a symbol of London and of The Kernel's holistic approach to making their excellent beers.

Goes well with… Your own company whilst leafing through the classic history of London, *The London Encyclopaedia*

LOCH LOMOND BREWERY
Lost Monster

10% Occasional

Dumbarton, West Dunbartonshire, Scotland
lochlomondbrewery.com

A monster of a Milk Stout brimming with flavour and character

Milk Stout was always the unfashionable beer style, the ancient uncle in the corner, socially awkward, boring everyone else with memories of smog-filled London, rickety Hansom cabs and ancient, stewed pubs with equally ancient, stewed clientele. Not the kind of beer (or uncle) you would want to be seen in public with. However, times are changing for this venerable beer style as it keeps being revitalised and brewed by all kinds of breweries, and Loch Lomond has imperialised this meekest of beer styles with Lost Monster.

'We decided that the one thing Loch Lomond was missing that the other famous Loch had was its own monster,' says George Wotherspoon, the brewery's sales and development manager, 'so we decided to give it one. We decided it had to be a big beer and that's what we aimed for. We were blown away when we first tasted it. It was the biggest beer we had created and we were delighted with the results. We have tweaked the production process since first brewing this in 2018 to get more coffee and chocolate flavours from the recipe and love the present results.'

This monster is sleek, dark mahogany in colour, warm and all-embracing, a hug of a colour, a friendly monster. There are chocolate, toffee, milky coffee and cocoa notes on both the nose and palate, with the latter accompanied by an oat-like silkiness and a bittersweet finish. Ideal for a quiet, thoughtful glass or, as Wotherspoon recommends, 'an end-of-dinner beer so best served with cheese board or a rich chocolate pudding for a total chocolate overload'.

Goes well with... Wotherspoon's suggestion of a rich chocolate pudding

McCOLL'S BREWERY
Bloom Coffee Stout

7.4% Seasonal

Bishop Auckland, County Durham
mccollsbrewery.co.uk

A lush and luxurious coffee Porter

At the end of an indulgent meal, you might fancy a cup of coffee, but hold that thought and turn your internal spotlight on this gorgeous coffee Stout instead (you might sleep better as well if the meal is in the evening). Bloom is a relatively recent addition to McColl's range of beers, motivated by the need, according to brewery founder Danny McColl, to reinstate a dark beer into the company's portfolio.

'Plus our head brewer has a massive love for ultra-fresh roast coffee and we were desperate to brew a big, flavoursome beer,' he says. 'The coffee used was single origin Sumatra from a local Teesdale roaster called Lonton Coffee Company. The whole (uncrushed) coffee beans were added loose to the fermenting vessel only three days before packaging to achieve the freshest, aromatic coffee effect. We absolutely loved it as soon as we tasted it and were genuinely over the moon with its balance, depth of flavour, body and the coffee aroma and flavours. It wasn't lacking anything.'

When the can is popped and the beer poured it is darkness visible in the glass,

a darkness suggestive of the bottom of the deepest part of the ocean perhaps. On the mellow and enticing nose there is a lithe fruitiness from the coffee beans, a wisp of roastiness, plus a suggestion of milk chocolate and even the delicacy of vanilla/coconut in the background. The palate has a display of more of the coffee fruitiness, alongside chocolate, dark fruits and a light roastiness followed by a dryness and bitterness pulsating away in the finish. With an ABV of 7.4% this is a heady beer that swaggers on the tongue and proclaims its dominion over the senses.

Goes well with... Roast pork and apple sauce

MOONWAKE BEER
Milk Stout

4.5% Core

Leith, Edinburgh, Scotland
moonwakebeer.com

Smooth and roasty-sweet Milk Stout

Along with Double Diamond, Mackeson's Milk Stout was one of the first beers that I tasted. It was a favourite of my paternal Liverpool-Irish grandmother who would have it with her Sunday lunch, but at the age of 12, when I was offered a taste, I thought it terrible, all burnt toast and just undrinkable (I didn't like Guinness either, which she also enjoyed). However, times and tastes change and I rather enjoy a Milk Stout these days, with its smoothness interposed with a light roastiness, all of which brings a general well-being to the palate.

Based in Leith, near Edinburgh, Moonwake is a relatively young brewery, having being founded in 2021, and Milk Stout is one of their core beers, with head brewer Vinny Rosario explaining that, 'we wanted to create an easy-drinking Milk Stout that could be enjoyed regardless of the season. We did not want to make it too sweet as if you were drinking a dessert, nor did we want to make it too astringent, so as not to turn away people unused to dark beer.'

Mahogany brown in the glass, there are notes of vanilla, roast grains and the lightest of mocha coffee on the nose, while the palate is smooth and roasty-sweet, brushed with a vanilla soothingness, plus herbal menthol (think mint humbugs) notes. The finish is dry and grainy, a finish that lingers like the memory of the smile of a loved one.

I think Rosario might have succeeded in his aim.

Goes well with... Roast beef and Yorkshire pudding (with a drop of the beer in the batter mix)

NEPTUNE BREWERY
On The Bounty

5.8%   Seasonal

Liverpool
neptunebrewery.com

Smooth and soothing chocolate and coconut Stout

Back in the 18th century a life on the ocean wave was all very well until either a pirate ship came along or the crew mutinied, as happened with *HMS Bounty*. Thankfully, there is little cause for concern with Neptune's On The Bounty, a rich and elegant chocolate and coconut Stout that was originally brewed as a one-off for the Liverpool Beer Festival in the summer of 2018. 'We wanted to brew a lighter, easy-drinking Stout,' says Julie O'Grady, who co-founded Liverpool-based Neptune with husband Les. 'Something different to the Stouts that were currently on the market, and also to say Stout isn't just for the colder winter months. To us On the Bounty brings a taste of summer with its rich chocolate and hit of coconut. A beer that can transport your mind to somewhere you can relax in warmer climates no matter the season.

'The love for the beer took us by surprise, and once canned it sold well over the spring and summer months.'

Since then the beer has become a Neptune regular and as soon as you pour this mahogany-brown, luscious-flavoured Stout and take a deep sniff you can see why as it takes you straight to the sweetshop counter and a certain chocolate bar. It is a luxurious beer, with rich and smooth aromas of chocolate and coconut emerging out of the glass with the finesse of spindrift. There is a similar mellowness with each taste, as chocolate, coconut and vanilla notes work hand-in-hand with the gentle roastiness of a classic Stout, before it finishes dry and bittersweet. As O'Grady says, Stout is not just for the colder months.

Goes well with… A delicious bowl of Kung Lao chicken

NORTH BREWING
Full Fathom Five

6.5% Core

Leeds
northbrewing.com

Lush and luxurious collaboration between coconut, coffee and Porter

You would have to be very unlucky to suffer death by coconut, even though standing beneath the *cocos nucifera* tree is not to be recommended. Apparently it happens now and again, though the old story that you are more likely to be killed by a falling coconut than eaten by a shark is an urban myth (unless you go swimming off Amity Island of *Jaws* fame). With all this in mind, it would be far safer to engage with North's Full Fathom Five, a luscious beer in which the soft, fruity and almost milky character of the coconut is an ideal partner to the roastiness of coffee, alongside the smoothness of the Porter.

'The idea with the beer,' says the brewery's brand ambassador Alex Millhouse-Smith, 'was to brew a core range Porter with a difference, that wasn't a sweet or dessert inspired. Something with added ingredients that would complement the beer rather than overpower it. North Star Coffee Roasters power the staff every morning here at the brewery so they were an obvious choice for us, while for head brewer Seb adding coconut in the mix

was just a whim, a flare, a creative spark that not even he could fully explain.'

Naturally, it is dark in the glass while there are soft and creamy notes on the nose, reminiscent of a mocha coffee with perhaps a dash of coconut. On the palate there are light coconut notes, hints of chocolate and the roastiness of coffee wrapped around a soothing mouthfeel before a bittersweet and dry finish featuring more coconut and coffee.

'The mood for the beer is comfort,' adds Millhouse-Smith, 'it's the perfect balance between a sweet treat and a robust and nourishing Stout.'

Goes well with... A cold winter's day and jugged hare for lunch followed by plenty of relaxation

ORA BEER
Balsamic

6% Core

Tottenham, London
orabeer.com/en

Milk Stout meets balsamic vinegar and all get on famously

As I have written elsewhere in the book, my paternal grandmother liked Milk Stout with her Sunday lunch but heaven knows what her traditional beer-drinking soul would have made of ORA's exceptional and individual version of the style. As the name might suggest, the beer is brewed with an infusion of balsamic vinegar that has been aged for 10 years in a wooden barrel; vanilla is also added.

'This was the very first innovative beer we brewed at ORA,' says Daniele Zaccarelli, who originally co-founded ORA back home in Modena with two home-brewing friends before coming to London, 'and when we used the balsamic this is where we started to match Italian ingredients with British beer styles. Since we are all from Modena where balsamic is produced that was the way forward. Balsamic is sweet and sour at the same time, but it has not been easy to find the right mix for our Milk Stout and balsamic. Sometimes it was too sour, other times too sweet. When we finally matched the recipe we got a beer that has a very consistent mouthfeel backed with balsamic flavour without the sourness of vinegar.'

There is a fascinating sense of yin and yang about this beer, as the smooth creaminess of a Milk Stout comes up against the almost fruity-sweet and gentle sourness of the balsamic. It could so easily have been a disastrous crash of waves against a rocky shore as the two opposites met, but instead it is a creative and characterful collaboration as sweet and sour combine to produce a memorable beer.

Goes well with… The kind of Sunday roast lunch my grandmother used to make

ORBIT BREWERY
Dead Wax London Porter

5.5% Core

Walworth, London
orbitbeers.com

*A creamy, smooth, toasty
and bitter Porter*

There is a romance about Porter, especially when we think of its connections with London, of how it became the beer of the capital city during the 18th and 19th centuries. Even the first President of the USA, George Washington, had his own recipe for it. That was then though, and contemporary Porter is probably a different beast, but for Orbit's head brewer Paul Spraget, London was still at the forefront of his mind when he developed Dead Wax in 2018.

'I wanted to pay tribute to Porter, the beer that built London, the city in which I live,' he says. 'I wanted to take inspiration from historical brewing recipes, ingredients and techniques used by London brewers in the 1800s, and then give it a modern sheen to reflect the 21st-century London that I know and love.'

The result is a dark, burnished, chestnut-coloured beer that is creamy, smooth, toasty, bitter and herbal all at once. There are suggestions of vanilla, mocha coffee, chocolate and a light toastiness on the nose alongside hints of liquorice and treacle. This all continues on the palate in conjunction with a brief flash of mid-palate berry-like fruitiness before it tumbles into an elegant and rough/smooth finish of dryness and bitterness.

Asked about the mood of the beer, Spraget becomes poetical: 'Past, present and future. Standing on Waterloo Bridge, the mighty Thames churning below your feet, watching the sunset over St Paul's Cathedral, behind it the gleaming hi-rise skyscrapers of the City reaching up into the vibrant, purple hues of the London night sky. History and tradition colliding with the infinite potential of The New.'

Goes well with… A whitebait supper and a perusal of *Little Dorrit*

PRESSURE DROP BREWING
Choice of Dessert

10% Occasional

Tottenham Hale, London
pressuredropbrewing.co.uk

Banana and chocolate collide within the confines of an Imperial Stout

I once sat in a Mikkeller bar in Copenhagen and I fancied an Imperial Stout. There were three choices, but all of them were flavoured in one way or another. One had cake mix in it, another was fermented with a Sahti yeast strain and the other had been boosted with coffee. This was my first encounter with what we now call a pastry Stout. Several years on, however, I have changed my mind. Providing they are well made and not just some concoction of ultra sweetness, I enjoy the luxury and elegance of an Imperial Stout that has had various flavours judiciously added.

Pressure Drop's Choco-Banana Imperial Stout is one of these kinds of beers, where, yes, there is a sweetness amongst the aromatics and flavours of light roasted malt, chocolate, banana, vanilla and Demerara sugar, but everything is highly defined and well-integrated, making for a lush and languorous experience in the glass.

'This is one of a series of luxury Imperial Stouts we developed in 2020,' says sales and marketing manager Sienna O'Rourke. 'The aim was to present real banana and chocolate flavours into our Imperial Stout base recipe to provide a beer full of fun. It's all natural, no flavourings, real bananas and loads of cocoa nibs.

'The first brew of any new beer is always nerve-wracking as a brewer, especially a full-length run of a beer that is chock-full of expensive natural ingredients. There is a lot to go wrong. However, on sipping from the tank, we were delighted to find it had all the flavours we were hoping for and things were nicely balanced. This is a beer that makes you smile.'

Goes well with... A gorgeous helping of banoffee pie

QUANTOCK BREWERY
Late Night Breakfast

9%   Occasional

Bishops Lydeard, Somerset
quantockbrewery.co.uk

Bourbon barrel-aged Imperial Stout with unfathomable depths of flavour

Here is an Imperial Stout, a beer style name that some would say has a certain gravitas to it (while others might flinch at the use of 'Imperial'). It is a beer that perhaps summons up the image of a calm, tranquil man or woman sitting in a chair while lifting a glass of a beer that resembles the colour of deep space to whatever cause they fancy, whether it is the revolution, the reigning monarch or just the success of their horse in a forthcoming big race. This is the type of beer that has a profound depth of flavour, whose colour has a crumpled sense of darkness that flings a challenge in the face of Pale Ales and golden-hued lagered beers. This is also a modern Imperial Stout whose presence flies in the face of tradition even though the style is tradition itself, but for now let us leave all debate behind and consider this beer with its fulcrum of dark malts and the time it has spent in the depths of a bourbon barrel and let it swoop on the palate.

This is a beer that makes an instant impression as soon as it swirls out of the bottle into the glass, its creamy, crema-coloured head a temptation in itself. There is a flurry of vanilla, soft coffee (chocolate-coated coffee beans perhaps?), a gentle dab of roastiness and luscious creaminess on the nose, whilst each sip reveals layers of creaminess, vanilla, mocha coffee, chocolate and a general sense of luxurious and elegance and late-night contemplation. The finish is dry and bittersweet and mysteriously dark, which suggests nooks and crannies in which we can hide and plot the downfall of something or other.

Goes well with... The sound of silence

REDCHURCH
Old Ford Export Stout

7.5%   Core

Harlow, Essex
redchurch.beer

A roasty, chocolatey, smooth-drinking strong Export Stout

This is a big and bold Export Stout, coming from a brewery that was founded in East London in 2011 (the name paying tribute to its original railway arch home in Bethnal Green close to Old Ford Road), but is now based in the Essex town of Harlow. Originally a seasonal winter special but now available all year, it is a rich and roasty strong Stout that is an ideal companion when the January weather does its worst. On the other hand, I would drink it any time of the year.

When poured, it's as dark as the kind of night when even the shadows have gone to roost, with a potent waft of roast coffee beans and dark chocolate emerging out of the glass. The roastiness is assertive, muscular, as if saying take note of me – and you will. The dark chocolate is a smoother counterpoint to the roastiness, the other side of the mirror. On the palate, each sip, each contemplative sip, reveals layers of fruit cake, marzipan, espresso, chocolate, cherry, a smokiness and an earthiness and something that I can only describe as the memory or suggestion of old books in a well-furnished library. Alongside this there is a creamy mouthfeel, all of these constituent parts producing a gorgeous beer that will deserve your full attention when studying it. This is also a beer that tells tales, that perks up the imagination, and if you listen to it quietly enough you will hear the story of about the time this Export Stout went to Harlow by way of Bethnal Green.

Goes well with… Bangers and mash and don't forget to add some of the beer to the gravy

RIDGEWAY BREWING
Imperial Russian Stout

10% Seasonal

Reading, Berkshire
ridgewaybrewery.co.uk

A masterpiece of an Imperial Stout

Once a year Ridgeway's founder and head brewer Peter Scholey produces this rich and unctuous Imperial Stout, which is a masterpiece of his experience in the industry (he was Brakspear's last head brewer) and time. The first beer was brewed in 2011 and then warm conditioned in a tank for five months, but subsequent releases have needed less time and typically take three months. For Scholey, if asked about the time the beer spends, he replies, 'it's a classic case of "it is ready when it is ready", in much the same way as Harvey's head brewer Miles Jenner does with his wonderful Imperial Extra Double Stout'.

It is stygian in its darkness, brooding beneath a firm crema-coloured head of foam. Depending on how long the bottle has been aged, you can expect aromatics of coffee beans, stewed plums (plum crumble anyone?), some chocolate and a hint of your grandmother's toffee pudding (once sampled, never forgotten). It's a complexity of flavours on the palate with chocolate, mocha coffee, dried fruit, a curlew's song of roastiness and a bitterness and dryness in the finish that will make you think about buying a case for each year.

Mind you, it's no accident that Scholey is a wizard with this style of brewing given that in the early 1990s he worked at John Smith's in Tadcaster where the final versions of Courage's momentous Imperial Russian Stout were brewed. 'The Courage beer was held in tank for up to two years before bottling,' he says, 'so when it came time to bottle, filtrating it was a total nightmare because of the amount of sediment it threw.'

Goes well with... The pungent saltiness and creaminess of an aged Gorgonzola

SALCOMBE BREWERY
Island Street Porter

5.9% Frequently available

Ledstone, Devon
salcombebrewery.com

*Creamy, smooth and
bittersweet Porter*

Porter was a child of the 18th century, which fell ill in the 19th and 20th centuries and then was declared deceased in the 1970s. At the same time, however, its slow but sure resurrection began when a small 'craft' brewery in San Francisco called Anchor made one. Times change and Porter is one of the most popular beer styles that any brewery of consequence (usually indie or self-declared 'craft') has to have in their portfolio. On the subject of dark beers, though, it seems that there are still some people out there who drink with their eyes and who consider dark beers to be too mind-numbingly strong or too consistent in their closeness to a well-known dark beer produced in Dublin to be a beer they would choose.

Such an erroneous view would deprive them of tasting the joys of Salcombe's ravishingly full-bodied Porter, a modern take on the style with a creaminess and a bitterness, coffee, chocolate and a carnation cream-like smoothness before it finishes dry and bittersweet. According to Salcombe head brewer Sam Beaman, 'we set out with a relatively broad goal of creating a malt driven beer and settled on a Porter with eight different malts. Every malt that was selected was done so for a specific purpose and without giving too much away, the key to Island Street Porter's flavour is the balance between the chocolate malt and the roast barley.'

Two barrel-aged versions of the Porter have also been released, one having held bourbon and the other Speyside whisky. Meanwhile, for those who still view dark beers with suspicion, Beaman has a message: 'Don't let your eyes deceive you as this beer will not disappoint.'

Goes well with... Not very Devonian, but a Texas beef chilli would be an ideal match

SIREN CRAFT BREW
Broken Dream

6.5% Core

Finchampstead, Berkshire
sirencraftbrew.com

An unctuous, soothing and luscious coffee Stout

I was at a beer dinner back in 2005 and the final beer was brought to the table: Meantime's Coffee Porter. Alastair Hook, brewery founder, was there to talk to us about what he had done, which was to add real coffee to the beer, something that was rare on the British brewing scene then (Dark Star's Espresso was perhaps one of the first several years earlier). Naturally, I didn't sleep too well that night, but it was still a beautiful beer, using Arabica coffee beans grown by a co-operative in Rwanda and hand roasted in London.

Now we're all used to coffee beers, and perhaps have them earlier in the day, which is perhaps why this award-winning coffee-flavoured beauty from Siren is sub-titled a 'breakfast Stout', though I think I would wait until the sun is well past the yardarm before cracking open a can.

'The first brew hit the mark,' says brewery founder Darron Anley. 'Instead of going for something rich and chocolatey we went with a coffee that had fruit and acidity and it worked really well, delicious, rich, but with balance.'

Sleek and gleaming in the glass, this is an unctuous, soothing and luscious coffee Stout, which has espresso coffee beans in the mix from renowned East London roasters Climpson & Sons. Naturally, the nose resonates with the aromatics of freshly ground coffee, with added hints of treacle, chocolate and a caramel sweetness, all of which create a gently enticing stroke of the senses. There is more cold coffee, mocha creaminess, roast bean dryness, smokiness and graininess, a dab of soft vanilla and chocolate on the palate before it finishes with a light roastiness alongside a pleasing bittersweetness.

An indulgent pleasure that Siren has produced in several expressions including the Hard Pour Broken Dream Nitro.

Goes well with... A chocolate mousse and then contemplatively finishing off another can on the sofa afterwards

TEMPEST BREWING CO
Mexicake Imperial Stout

11% Core

Galashiels, Borders, Scotland
tempestbrewco.com

Indulgent Imperial Stout with added chillies

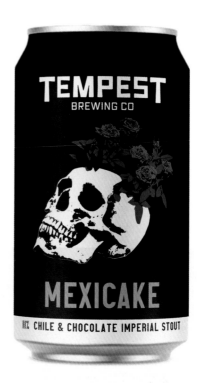

Sometimes when a brewery produces a certain style of beer it doesn't always go to plan. Take Tempest's Mexicake Imperial Stout for instance, as marketing manager Neil Blackburn explains: 'It was conceived on a trip to Barcelona while getting on the wrong side of too many Imperial Stouts. Once back, we were hellbent on making a big and sticky dessert Stout. The idea was to make a caramel in the kettle, which didn't quite work; having already mashed in the malt we had to think on our feet to salvage the beer.

'Thankfully our well-stocked pantry came to the rescue – we've always got an unhealthy amount of chillies to hand and the idea of bringing sweet and heat together seemed obvious. Next thing, we'd added cocoa nibs, cinnamon and vanilla to the mulato and chipotle chillies and we'd made a cakey, Mexican Stout.

'It tasted similar to how it tastes now... sweet, chocolatey with a bit of heat with the quality of the vanilla shining through. The quality of the ingredients was high then and that's never changed.'

This glorious accident has become one of Tempest's most followed beers, which, if it is out of stock for too long, Blackburn notes 'it's always flaming pitchforks at the door'. This recourse to acting like something out of an old Frankenstein movie is entirely reasonable once the beer is tasted. On the nose there is chocolate, caramel, vanilla, spice and sweetness, all of which swirl out of the glass like an enticement. The palate is bewitched by the spice of the chillies alongside a hint of smoke, the soothing nature of the vanilla, the rich creaminess of the chocolate and caramel, all combining to create a whirl of sweetness and heat in the finish. Oh, and watch out for barrel-aged versions.

'When we first tasted it, we knew it was good,' says Blackburn, 'but not for a minute did we expect it to go on to become a semi-core Imperial Stout for the next five years with such a devoted, cult following.'

Goes well with... Definitely dessert or to meditate on as it slowly emerges from the glass

THORNBRIDGE BREWERY
Necessary Evil

13%   Occasional

Bakewell, Derbyshire
thornbridgebrewery.co.uk

A big, luscious hug of a bourbon barrel-aged Imperial Stout

Here is a mighty potentate of a bourbon barrel-aged Imperial Stout that both glowers and glows in the glass, the colour of a dark star, the absence of light noted, with a firm, crema-coloured head of foam inviting and encouraging contemplation. It is lush and ambitious in the sway of aromatics that sashay out of the glass: vanilla, the sweet butteriness of bourbon, the charred complexity of the oak as well as a treasure chest of chocolate, roastiness and caramel. There are more of these layers of flavour and lusciousness on the palate, creating a beer that you must spend time in studying and contemplating.

First produced in 2019 after the beer had spent eight months in wood, this was the brainchild of Thornbridge's head brewer Rob Lovatt after a conversation he'd had with co-founder and owner Simon Webster. 'He mentioned how the one thing I'd never brewed was a special strong, dark beer,' recalls Lovatt. 'In the past, Thornbridge has produced some very famous examples, such as Saint Petersburg, Heather Honey Stout and Bracia so Simon threw down the gauntlet and said it was about time I came up with my own.'

Generous liquid research on the nature of big, dark beers took place in the USA and once back home Lovatt and the team tasted a series of more big beers before deciding on a course of action. 'Soft and silky, this full-flavoured Stout has layers of complexity and flavour unlike any other beer we brew,' says Lovatt, 'and it has a lot of potential for various iterations. We currently have it ageing away in rum, madeira and sherry barrels.'

Gauntlet picked up and thoroughly taken.

Goes well with… Meditative moments of contemplation as you sink into the sofa

TITANIC BREWERY
Stout

4.5% Core

Burslem, Staffordshire
titanicbrewery.co.uk

A rich and roasty Stout

When Titanic first produced this beer at the start of the 1990s, brewery owner Keith Bott recalled that there was very little choice in the UK when it came to dark beers, apart from the obvious one from Dublin. 'Back then the only thing you had as your friend was a bottle of bottle-conditioned Guinness,' he recalled in an interview about Titanic's Stout. 'Then Guinness stopped doing it, which was a real shame as it had more complexity than the draught version, and at the time it was also bottled by almost every regional brewery in the country. You would try some from one brewery and it would be different from another who had bottled it.

'It was that go-to drink if you wanted a flavoursome dark beer. So this was my attempt at recreating those flavours from bottle-conditioned Guinness. Hence that's why it is still bottle-conditioned, I think it develops in the bottle and gives a third dimension in flavour to the beer.'

Part of the distinctive taste of the beer is the roastiness which comes from the use of roast barley, which Bott has always been insistent that the brewery use. The result is a classic, full-bodied Stout, whose nose is a celebration of roast and toasted notes. In the mouth it is full-bodied, rounded and creamy, with hints of treacle. It is also bittersweet and roasty, before saying goodbye with a lingering dryness and appetising bitterness. According to Bott, 'this is one of our beers that I am most proud of'.

Goes well with… A homemade steak and kidney pie

TORRSIDE BREWING
Fire Damage

5% Occasional

New Mills, Derbyshire
torrside.co.uk

A smooth and silky smoked Stout

Smoke is very much part of Torrside's brewing philosophy, with many of its beers utilising smoked malts, which help to create a multi-layered complexity, whether it makes drinkers think of the lightness of smoky bacon or the more intense nature of sitting around a camp fire. 'Smoke gives you an extra dimension,' says co-founder Chris Clough. 'All beer has a basic balance of malt sweetness and hop bitterness, and adding smoke brings in a distinctly different savoury element.'

Fire Damage is a smoked Stout, and was only the second beer to be brewed by Torrside. 'One key thing we wanted was to make sure it was a really solid, proper Stout,' adds Clough's brewing partner Pete Sidwell (the third member of the team is Nick Rothko-Wright), 'so it needed to be pitch black and have lots of roasted malt flavours. Then we just had to decide how much of the pale malt base to switch to smoked malt. Smoke impact gets softened by two things – sweetness and roastiness – so to get the distinct smoke character in

a full-on Stout, around 60% of the total grain bill was rauchmalt. The balance we aimed at was to have a beer smoky enough for our tastes, and stouty enough for the stoutest of Stout fans.'

This vision of the trio certainly worked as Fire Damage is a smooth, silky and smoky Stout, with hints of smoked bacon alongside mocha coffee on the nose. The smokiness comes through on the palate and is well balanced by malt sweetness and hints of chocolate, followed by an accompanying roastiness before it finishes dry and smoky. Mission accomplished, indeed.

Goes well with… A plate of Bratwurst and sauerkraut

TRING BREWERY
Tea Kettle Stout

4.7% Core

Tring, Hertfordshire
tringbrewery.co.uk

An intensely flavoured,
robustly inclined Stout

It's tea kettle because the town of Tring is in Hertfordshire, which some wits used to say resembled a tea kettle. It's Stout because Tring Brewery was well-known for its copper-coloured Bitters, sparkling gold beers and ruby-hued strong ales, so a drop of the dark stuff was in order. According to the brewery director, Andrew Jackson, 'the first brew was a great success. Soon after trial tastings the branding was complete, and barrels were being sent out to pubs. Though we had planned for a sweet Stout, the impressive abundance of chocolate and caramel notes in Tea Kettle were most satisfying, we had distilled a chocolate box into a pint glass!'

As well as chocolate there is also an abundance of treacle and coffee notes in the beer, all of which create an intensely flavoured, robustly inclined Stout that is strangely reminiscent of the Yorkshire delicacy Parkin. There are also plenty of roast notes, a delicious chewy mouthfeel with bittersweetness, dryness and a bracing roastiness in the finish.

'As this was our first Stout,' says Jackson, 'we have drawn inspiration from Tea Kettle's award-winning brewsheet as we look to produce other iterations of the style. Since our first brew of Tea Kettle, we have brewed India Stouts, coffee Stouts, chocolate Stouts and even a coconut Stout, each woven with a little Tea Kettle DNA! Though Stouts can be complex, we like to think this beer evokes the pleasures of the little things in life, such as good beer and great company.'

Goes well with… Roast pheasant and all the trimmings

VIBRANT FOREST
Black Forest

4.9% Core

Hardley, Hampshire
vibrantforest.co.uk

An expressive Porter that simmers with chocolate richness and espresso roastiness

A forest is not a silent place. Birds sing as they flit from tree to tree; the wind rustles the leaves, a divine musical concerto that all too often also features the pattering and delicate handclaps of falling rain. Meanwhile, occasionally, out of the sight and sound of anyone living, a tree crashes to the ground and the question is asked if it actually did make a sound when it fell as no one was around.

All of these sensations would constitute a vibrant forest, which perhaps is why this New Forest-based brewery chose their name. Vibrancy is also present in the range of beers they produce, especially with Black Forest, a tactile and expressive Porter that shimmers and simmers with dark chocolate richness, espresso coffee roastiness, the laidback sweetness of autumnal berries and a crooner's worth of smoothness in the bitter finish.

'I was very much inspired by Fuller's London Porter back in 2012 when I first made this beer in my small garage at home,' says brewery founder Kevin Robinson. 'I wanted to match the smooth chocolate and coffee notes of this beer but add a little more body and roast character. The first commercial brew turned out really well. Our brewery was just a part-time, one-barrel operation back then and I was absolutely chuffed when I first tasted it and thought it a triumph.

'The recipe has barely changed since then and today we are packaging this beer to keg, can and cask and it is a great no-nonsense example of the style without being over the top in the current times of many adjuncts being used in Porters.'

Goes well with... Time well spent relaxing after a long dog walk in the winter woods

WIPER AND TRUE
Milk Shake

5.6% Core

Bristol
wiperandtrue.com

A creamy, vanilla-led, soothing Milk Stout

Sometimes the idea for a beer emerges from the most surprising of experiences. Take Wiper and True's luscious Milk Shake Milk Stout. 'This one was not at all highbrow,' recalls co-founder Michael Wiper. 'It was whilst drinking a milkshake and thinking about how the vanilla and thickness would work really well paired with roasted barley. There's a very strong tradition of Milk Stouts from Bristol and it felt like something fun to explore. The original concept was for a very light ABV (3%), really thick, dark roast, but very soft, vanilla-infused Stout. Drunk ice cold with a big, thick, pillowy head.'

At the time Wiper thought that the beer would be a one-off, especially as he thought it tasted fine but hadn't got the milkshake-like thickness and vanilla-ness. Bristol's drinkers begged to differ and wanted more of it, a response that took the brewery by surprise, so the recipe was tweaked and demand soared.

'The breakthrough moment was when we made a double strength version of it for a beer festival,' he says, 'a 6% beer we called Hard Shake. We were so happy with it and realised that was actually what Milk Shake should become. So now the beer is 5.6%, and we are really happy with it. And Hard Shake? That became an 11% bourbon barrel-aged version.'

It took 27 recipe tweaks for the brewery to get Milk Shake to where they were happy with it and in its current incarnation it's a creamy, vanilla-led, soothing, chocolatey, liqueur-like beer that you would be as happy drinking on its own or with a dessert. Sometimes, as Robert the Bruce once observed whilst sharing a cave with a spider, you have to try, try and try again before you get it right.

Goes well with… A large dollop of good quality vanilla ice cream (or even better make an ice cream float with it)

SPECIALITY

This chapter celebrates
the imagination of the
brewer with beers that
include ones that are
smoked, barrel-aged
and flavoured.

ANSPACH & HOBDAY
The Rauchbier

5.6%   Seasonal

Croydon, Greater London
anspachandhobday.com

A delightful smoked beer that pays homage to Bamberg

The Franconian town of Bamberg is one of the most vital and vibrant pilgrimages for all beer lovers. It is not only stunningly beautiful with its baroque-style architecture and old buildings, it is also home to Rauchbier, a gorgeously lagered beer style that is made with smoked malt. When you visit Bamberg and drink a large glass of Schlenkerla's Märzen Rauchbier, smoke gets in your glass in the most delightful way.

It might not have the architectural beauty of Bamberg but Bermondsey is another essential stop on any beer-loving pilgrim's travels, with its taprooms and breweries, many of them housed in railway arches. Even though they now brew in Croydon, Anspach & Hobday still maintain a taproom in Bermondsey, at the site of where they began brewing.

'When it comes to our yearly Rauchbier, it's all about trying to pay homage to Schlenkerla,' says co-founder and head brewer Paul Anspach. 'I don't think we ever get quite the intensity, largely because we have to rely on the smoked malts that are available to us to purchase, rather than smoking our own. I don't necessarily think that is to the detriment of the beer though.'

Dark chestnut in colour, the beer has the suggestion of smoked ham lingering on the nose along with bonfire toffee. The smokiness continues in the flavour, with more smoked ham balanced by a toffee/treacle-like sweetness followed by an appetising dry and bitter finish. A wonderful beer, just right for an autumn evening when the smell of woodsmoke hangs in the air like a spell cast by a benign magician.

Goes well with… A smoked pulled pork baguette alongside gherkins and a lot of friends

BRASS CASTLE BREWERY
Wallop Yorkshire 'Stingo' Strong Ale

7.5-8.4% Seasonal
ABV varies

Malton, North Yorkshire
brasscastle.co.uk

A dark and soulful barrel-aged beer that is released every year

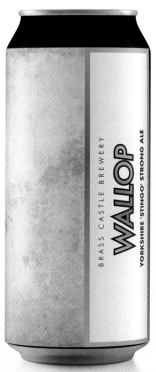

Once a year the team at Brass Castle produce this hearty strong ale and decide what kind of wooden cask it should be aged in. Various expressions have slept the sleep of the just for at least six months within casks that formerly held brandy, rum or bourbon, while other brews, as brewery founder Phil Saltonstall explains, have been 'packaged into wooden firkins, which have been broken down from madeira and port barrels. We have them sent them to selected bars for direct dispense, so the base beer is unchanging – but the modification possibilities to packaging/handling are endless.'

Given the annual variation, this is a dark and inviting, soulful and suggestively comforting beer that drops the drinker into a delicious maze of aromas and flavours, depending on what kind of vessel it has been matured in. Is that a hint of smooth rum or the fiery vinousness of brandy you can taste? However, whatever it has been aged in you can also expect a rich and smooth mouthfeel that has suggestions of toffee, dried fruit, liquorice, chocolate, molasses (black treacle is used in the brew) and a massive presence on the palate.

'As far as we can tell,' Saltonstall has written on the brewery's blog, '"Yorkshire Stingo" is a beer style rather than a brand. Indeed, it is the only beer style that is indigenous to Yorkshire. But we have to be careful using that phrase, because Samuel Smith's Brewery have trademarked those words. Given that brewery's history for litigation, we are therefore circumspect about bringing the words "Yorkshire" and "Stingo" together… As a result, we usually refer to our Wallop brew as a Yorkshire "Stingo" Strong Ale.'

Goes well with… Wallace and Gromit and a chunk of Wensleydale cheese

BURNING SKY
Saison Provision

6.7% Occasional

Firle, East Sussex
burningsky.com

*A pale gold-coloured Saison
of incredible complexity*

This is one of Burning Sky's special
releases, not always available, but
well worth the wait when you can get
hold of it. It's a beer that you take your
time over, consider and contemplate,
don't rush and instead savour; it is a
beer that you study as if it was a poem
whose words contained basic truths
and lessons on how to live life. And as
you study it, you can think of how time
is the extra ingredient, time well spent
ageing in oak barrels (otherwise known
as *foudres*), after the initial brewing
process that sees the use of a Saison yeast
during fermentation and the addition of
lactobacillus and Brettanomyces during
the time the beer sits within its wooden
womb. The result, as you might expect,
given the care and attention that Burning
Sky's founder Mark Tranter takes, is a
pale-gold beer of incredible complexity
that reaches out from the green and
pleasant Sussex rural surroundings
of the brewery across the Channel to
the Saisons of Hainault in Belgium.
    Given the use of Brettanomyces,
the nose has funky aromatics of aged

leather, farmyard earthiness, grapefruit
and an ineffable sense of mystery. It is
tart and sharp on the palate, bringing
in grapefruit citrusiness, a delicate
sourness, a soft carbonation, a zesty
and quenching spiciness and the kind
of refreshing mouthfeel that brings
a smile to the face with every sip. If
you cannot wait for the release of this
monumental English Saison, then
Burning Sky's dry-hopped Petite Saison
will provide a supportive shoulder
upon which you can rely until then.

Goes well with... Grilled paprika-coated chicken and charred red peppers

CAMPERVAN BREWERY
Salted Speyside Wee Heavy

8% One-off

Leith, Edinburgh, Scotland
campervanbrewery.com

A thoroughly demonstrative representative of Campervan's Lost in Leith barrel-aged project

This is not a beer that you will easily find. In fact, you probably won't be able to find it at all, because it is a one-off. However, the reason it is in this book is that it is a thoroughly demonstrative representative of Campervan Brewery's Lost in Leith barrel-aged project (in this case a barrel that once held Speyside whisky), in which the brewing team aim to bring a different drinking experience with every release.

According to Patrick Smith, brewer and in charge of the barrel-ageing project, 'the idea of this particular beer was to pay tribute to the traditional Scotch Ale style. We had been talking about brewing a Wee Heavy for quite a long time and including it in our barrel-aged project was a way to play with the style and add complexity and uniqueness to it. This is the only batch. What's interesting is how different the Salted Speyside version of this base beer is to our Old Fashioned inspired version (whilst ignoring the orange zest). The salt really brings out the esters in this beer and adds a slight minerality.'

Ruby red in colour, it has impressive notes of sweet caramel, a hint of cherry (maraschino?), marzipan, shortbread, vanilla and a boozy fruitiness, like a bowl of canned fruit doused in whisky. It is soft, smooth and creamy on the palate, with vanilla, caramel and cherries (canned maraschino again), marzipan, orange marmalade and even sherry-like notes before its long, dry and fruity finish. It might not be available by the time you read this, but if this beer is any indication, the Lost in Leith barrel-aged project will be well worth investigating.

Goes well with... Remembering that beer can be as fine as the finest of wines

ELGOOD'S BREWERY
Coolship Sour Ale

6%   Core

Wisbech, Cambridgeshire
elgoods-brewery.co.uk

A tart and softly acidic beer from one of England's most venerable family breweries

Elgood's head brewer Alan Pateman was showing an American beer importer around the brewery and upon seeing a handsome set of double coolers used for cooling hopped wort until sometime in the late 1990s, the guest exclaimed, 'you've got a coolship, why not produce a Lambic?'. This was 2013 and these words set off a train of thought for this venerable family brewery that would eventually result in the enigmatic Coolship, a Lambic-style beer that had more in common with the Senne valley outside Brussels than Elgood's home territory of the Fens.

'The recipe is 50/50 malt and raw wheat and we use aged hops,' Pateman once told me, 'and to ensure we build up the correct micro flora we have installed plain wood planks over the coolers to give the correct environment for the wild yeast and bacteria to develop. Only we could install planks of oak from a 225-year-old tree that we just happened to have air drying in our gardens! Due to our location we are able to take advantage of being surrounded by fruit orchards and soft fruit fields, which helps to give the beer its fruity notes.'

The result is a tart and softly acidic beer, grapefruit-like in its embrace, daubed with a soft sweetness and gifted with hints of sherry. It is a brilliant companion to Stilton, with the sharpness of the beer muting into a fruitiness when meeting the salty creaminess of the cheese. Both cheese and beer grow in stature as they greet each other, like two great titans of art meeting for the very first time.

Goes well with... Sweet and sour pork, believe it or not

HAMMERTON BREWERY
Crunch

5.3%   Core

Islington, London
hammertonbrewery.co.uk

Chocolate and peanut butter
and Stout harmonise together

Peanut butter Stout? Why ever not? After all, a similar combination works well with peanut butter cups, where the flavours of the chocolate and the peanut butter dovetail to create a sticky, unctuous confection that can be rather tempting in the right circumstances.

However, that's the vibe of the sweetshop counter, surely peanut butter and beer is the end of the world for craft beer, the sign that everything that is good and natural about beer has crumbled and we can no longer be sure about this world. Those kind of thoughts would have flitted through my mind several years ago when brought face to face with Hammerton's Peanut Butter Stout at the Craft Beer Rising festival in London. However, I tasted the beer and immediately got the symmetry between the creamy, light roastiness of the beer style and the richness of the peanut butter flavouring.

The beer is a very dark and impenetrable chestnut brown in colour, with aromatics that suggest peanut butter ice cream, which immediately makes me think that this is the kind of beer

you would like to take into the cinema to watch the latest Batman movie. It has a soft and soothing aroma, elegant and elongated in the way it lasts. On the palate it is peanut butter ice cream with mocha coffee and light chocolate alongside a delicate roastiness and a chiming fruity finish, which then makes you want to spread this beer on toast, but you drink it instead. There is a dry, bittersweet finish with suggestions towards more peanut butter. This is an incredibly well-made beer with all the flavours working together as if they'd known each other for years.

Goes well with… Either chicken satay or pecan pie

HARVIESTOUN BREWERY
Ola Dubh

8% Core

Alva, Clackmannanshire, Scotland
harviestoun.com

A rich and brooding Stout that has been married with Highland Park whisky barrels

Venice has an ancient ceremony in which it is married to the sea, an annual event that goes back centuries and is symbolic of the ancient city's link with the cold, blue waters of the Adriatic. At Harviestoun you could say that something similar happens with Ola Dubh, with the nuptials this time taking place between beer and single malt barrels that once held Highland Park, an event that has been happening regularly since 2006.

Poured into the glass it is a rich and brooding ale that originally began life as the brewery's Old Engine Oil before going on to spend at least six months in barrel. To make things even more interesting and compulsively collectable, Harviestoun has produced several expressions of Ola Dubh featuring barrels in which the whisky has spent 12, 16, 30 and 40 years, all of which can tell tales of how complex the beer becomes.

For Ola Dubh 12, the beer is as dark as a night in which no shadows are cast, though there is a slight tint of dark chestnut red at the edge, a glow in the sky that might suggest dawn is slowly stirring. The nose is a suggestion of leather saddle, whisky marmalade, dark chocolate and the faintest hint of smoke, while the palate is woody, whisky-like, stern and Presbyterian in the initial pass, with time and warmth softening its iron rod of certainty and allowing flavours of vanilla, bonfire toffee and chocolate to emerge and soften up the tongue before a bittersweet, dry-roasted finish that makes the drinker want another sip. This is a contemplative and dramatic dram of ale that can't help but create a sense of anticipation for trying the next expression in the series, which is strongly recommended.

Goes well with... Putting the port to one side for once and contemplating the glory of flavour

JW LEES
Vintage Harvest Ale

11.5% Seasonal

Middleton, Greater Manchester
jwlees.co.uk

A symphonic display of beer's capacity to improve as it ages

Once a year, J W Lees produces a Vintage Harvest Ale, a potent and muscular Barley Wine that is meant to age, and as the years pass it will change and develop and grow and turn itself into something extra special. It is the Manchester-based brewery's chance to use the new season's hops and barley, and not just create a talking point amongst beer fans but also demonstrate the potential for beer's aptitude for time. Every vintage will show a difference in its character, though the unifying factor will be that it is a Barley Wine, one of the great beer styles of Britain, though taproom jokers used to say it was a 'sitting down beer' because you didn't have far to fall when you drank too much of it.

I have tried many vintages down through the years and if there is going to be some common thread that unites them all it will be that the beer is warming due to its high alcohol. Various vintages will range in colour from deep to light amber and when young the nose will have rich aromatics of bready biscuit malt and a chime of orange citrus, but as it ages

you will pick up hints of a sherry-like nuttiness. The palate will be resoundingly complex, symphonic almost in the flurry of flavours that emerge, such as sweet toffee, dried fruit, earthy hoppiness and more of that sheer sherriness. The finish will be bittersweet and tantalisingly dry and it will be the kind of beer that you save for your favourite armchair on a dark, windy night where you can toast your good fortune to be safe and snug with this grandee of a beer.

Goes well with… The ripest chunk of Stilton you can find

LITTLE EARTH PROJECT
Stupid Sexy Suffolk Blend IV

5.4% Seasonal

Edwardstone, Suffolk
littleearthproject.com

*A refreshing and exuberant
Flemish-style Red Ale*

Back in the 1830s a member of the Rodenbach brewing family came to England to investigate the practice of making Porter, especially the blending and ageing process that would become such a vital part of the Flemish brewery's soul. Rumour has it that East Anglian breweries were visited, which is a neat symmetry given that Little Earth are based in Suffolk and this is their Flemish-style Red Ale.

'Flanders Red was a style of beer that I really got into when I first discovered sour beer,' says Little Earth brewer and co-founder Tom Norton. 'It's got a sweetness that is reminiscent of a traditional English Bitter and a lovely acidic tang that brought back memories of childhood salads dressed with malt vinegar and sugar.'

Based in a sleepy backwater of sturdy barns converted into rustic hideaways outside Ipswich, Little Earth Project uses time as an added ingredient for an intriguing portfolio of barrel-aged beers. Stupid Sexy is produced every year and is a blend of several differently aged beers.

'Our first batch was a single barrel so it was a little different to later ones that are several barrels blended together,' says Norton. 'Tasting the first one was strange, as it often is when you make mixed fermentation beers. There are always going to be flavours that are unwanted in normal beers. In this case we wanted some acidic (vinegar) characteristics but needed them to be subtle. I think we managed that and have made something pretty unique.'

The resulting crimson-amber beer is refreshing and exuberant, with hints of wood, balsamic vinegar and soft vanilla on the nose, while it is sharp, brisk and quenching on the palate, bringing in suggestions of cherry and vanilla, plus a soft acidity that intermingles with an equally relaxed fruitiness.

Goes well with… A wild rabbit stew simmered in Kriek

LOST AND GROUNDED
Saison D'Avon

6.5% Seasonal

Bristol
lostandgrounded.co.uk

A complex Belgian-Style Saison that ambles along like a river

The Bristol Avon ambles along, sinous and slow to start, sleepily drifting through Wiltshire but then becoming more wakeful amid the honey-hued stone of Bath and finally, as it broadens and becomes navigable, arrives at Bristol, cutting through the Avon Gorge before it reaches the open sea. Despite its apparent ordinariness this is a river of contrasts and quiet mystery, a river that has a sense of its own presence as it flows implacably towards the Severn Estuary. For me the river's qualities are mirrored in this Saison, as I imagine sunlight glinting on its pale-gold surface, and an imponderable flurry of spice and floral notes that keeps keen students of the Wallonian style fascinated and transfixed whenever a glass has been poured.

Lost and Grounded make their beers close to the Bristol Avon, and this softly spoken Saison is one of several Belgian-style beers in their portfolio. Lost and Grounded co-founder Alex Troncoso explains the motives in making the beer: 'We wanted to brew a version of a Saison that was soft and fruity, and whilst being complex would be a great introduction to the style which can at times be confronting to drinkers unfamiliar with it.'

Saison D'Avon is golden amber in colour and blessed by a billowing, cotton-wool white head of lip-enticing foam. A curveball of fruit (peach perhaps, alongside lemon and grapefruit) emerges on the nose, alongside a peppery spiciness (thanks to the use of grains of paradise in the mix). The off-centred fruitiness and spiciness also dance on the tongue before a bow of dryness in the finish, similar to the bow that Avon makes as it says farewell to the land.

Goes well with… A selection of charcuterie

LOVIBONDS
Sour Grapes

6%   Seasonal

Henley-on-Thames, Berkshire
lovibonds.com

A 'mistake' that underwent barrel-ageing and came out a champion

This was one of the first British sour beers to be released (circa 2012) and apparently came about through a mistake during fermentation with the brewery's flagship beer Henley Gold. However, serendipity took a hand and when brewery founder Jeff Rosenmeier tasted the 'mistake' he realised it was too good to let go. After barrel-ageing it in French pinor noir barrels, out into the world it went – and it won a gold at the World Beer Cup in the same year.

It's a beautiful beer, bruised gold in colour and pulsating with barnyard-like earthy aromatics reminiscent of a Belgian Gueuze, alongside a muscular accompaniment of grapefruit notes. This is a beer whose nose sets you up for the delights on the palate, where it is tart and slightly acidic with a sharpness of citrus, including more grapefruit, and finishing dry and citrusy. There's a juiciness about the beer, alongside a tartness that really sparks the appetite. The palate is sharpened and prepped up, just like a chef getting ready for lunchtime service, while a pepperiness

also makes an appearance in the finish, not big and overwhelming but on the edge of the palate, whispering 'I am here'.

This is one of those beers that is just meant to accompany food. Perhaps you'll fancy a glass with salted almonds, slices of chorizo, olives, even some anchovies – you will find the explosive effects in the mouth worth it. Or maybe try it with a bowl of shrimps where the natural sweetness and a twist of lemon sharpness will clasp hands with the beer's unique sweet-sour flavour. Whatever you do, embrace this beer with the fervour of a fanatic.

Goes well with… Gastronomic experimentation

M^CCOLL'S BREWERY
Beet de Garde

7%   Seasonal

Bishop Auckland, County Durham
mccollsbrewery.co.uk

A robust Bière de Garde with added beetroot

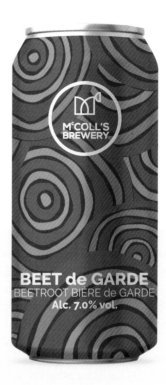

Even though most things get thrown into beer these days, the idea of beetroot being added often seems rather peculiar to me (I always blame primary school where I carefully hand-wrote a 'doctor's note' excusing me from eating beetroot). On a more positive note, I do recall the now closed Otley Brewery's Beetroot Stout being rather good. Thankfully, McColl's look certain to make me reconsider my views on beetroot even further with this superlative beer.

Beet de Garde is McColl's annual springtime sipper, a Bière de Garde with beetroot, a beer which, according to brewery founder Danny McColl, is 'where we celebrate two unsung heroes, and the perfect pairing that they make. Both are modest, yet full of depth and strength, sweetness and freshness. Bière de Garde is ultimately the style of beer that led to McColl's being founded, a style we are very fond of, and the addition of beetroot was very much to entice drinkers to enjoy the style as much as we do. This is why it had to be the correct modern twist to this traditional style.'

It is amber in colour with a spicy nose, alongside a sweet and funky earthiness and a Champagne-like spritziness. The palate is also earthy with the beetroot coming through to give a good counterpoint of earthiness to the spice and sweetness, plus a flinty dryness in the finish that is suggestive of Saison — which is not such a big surprise when you consider Bière de Garde and Saison share similar characteristics. A triumph of a beer, which is stretched even further with an annual release of Beets Rouge, a Rioja barrel-aged version that according to Danny McColl always sells out before Christmas, so keeping a careful watch of the brewery's social media is definitely recommended.

Goes well with... Chocolate, it really does

MILLS BREWING
Running Beer

5% Occasional

Berkeley, Gloucestershire
millsbrewing.com

Hazy, golden-lemon beer that is very much an English-style Gueuze

Mills Brewing specialises in making beers that experiment with mixed fermentation and barrel-ageing, with the latter bringing in time as an extra ingredient. Blending is important as well, as brews of different ages are brought together, and, returning to the use of time, the finished item is conditioned in bottle for several more months. This is brewing as a risk, as an adventure, as Johnny Mills explains: 'A key element of our approach to making beers is letting the fermentations do their thing, then blending the best beers we can from the finished barrels. We work on the understanding that mixed fermentations can make more interesting flavours than we could have conceived, so let them lead. We never make a wort intending for it to be one defined/finished beer. I just make sure I brew a range of worts every year and we go from there.'

This is the seventh version of Running Beer that Mills has produced, with an average blending time of 18 months followed by conditioning in bottle for a further six months. It brings forth a hazy, golden-lemon beer with a nose that tingles with grapefruit, hints of vanilla and an earthiness reminiscent of a farmer's barn in which cider is resting. The palate is tart and quenching with a moussec-like soft carbonation, blending in grapefruit, the ghost of cider apples and a peppery spiciness at the back of the palate before its swift finish. It is refreshing and magical and very much an English Gueuze-style beer, if you can imagine such a thing.

'It is the purest expression of the way we brew,' says Mills, 'and the beer we originally set out to make when we were dreaming up Mills Brewing. Turbid mash, wild culture, slow barrel ferment, long bottle conditioning.'

Goes well with… A toasted cheese sandwich made with Yarg

ORKNEY BREWERY
Dark Island Reserve

10% Frequently available

Quoyloo, Orkney Islands, Scotland
orkneybrewery.co.uk

Barrel-aged dark ale that pulsates with flavour

Dark Island has been one of Orkney's flagship beers since its foundation in the late 1980s, but in the mid 2000s the new owners of the brewery built on the original brand and developed this whisky barrel-aged beer (probably Orkney's Highland Park though the brewery just says Orkney whisky barrels), which, at the time, was a rare occurrence amongst breweries in the British Isles.

'We wished to bring something different to the market for drinkers,' says managing director Norman Sinclair, 'with a beer that was not just oak aged, but actually matured in casks, picking up and developing flavours from the whisky they had once stored. The first hint that we had that it could be special was when we filled the first cask; the aroma of the beer and whisky combined was incredible. After two months maturation we sampled it and the flavours of the beer itself now had whisky notes, which all combined beautifully.'

Dark mahogany brown in colour, almost verging on black, the beer has a richness of chocolate and milky coffee notes on the nose, alongside dried fruits, hazelnut and an oaky vanilla from the barrel. This lush parade of aromatics is replicated on the palate with an elegance and smoothness that makes it an easy beer to drink despite its alcoholic strength. It is a well-valued companion at the end of a dinner, a cherished accompaniment instead of an evening dram and an eloquent example of what beer and whisky can emerge with once they decide to link arms like allies in the great fight for flavour.

Goes well with… A slab of homemade duck and orange paté with oatcakes

QUEER BREWING
Flowers

4% Core

London
thequeerbrewingproject.com

*Complex, refreshing and
easy-drinking Witbier*

The Queer Brewing Project was set up by
award-winning beer writer, photographer
and ceramist Lily Waite with the aim of
empowering and improving the visibility
and presence of LBQT+ people within
the beer industry. Collaborations have
taken place with various breweries in
different countries, but there is a core
range of beers brewed by Waite with the
help of Cloudwater and this blissful and
winsome Witbier Flowers is one of them.

According to Waite it began life as
a 3.5% table beer-strength, homage to
one of her favourite beers, Allagash's
White. 'That beer is so complex, so
refreshing, so well-balanced and
easy-drinking,' she says, 'and I wanted
to brew something similar at a much
more sessionable strength – I generally
prefer lower-ABV beers for their ease
of consumption and lower inebriation
than stronger counterparts.'

Statement of Intent was the first
attempt to bring to life Waite's vision,
followed by various tweaks on the spice
and fruit peel additions, before the first
tasting of Flowers as a finished product.

'The first time I tasted this beer, I literally
jumped for joy,' she says, 'I was overjoyed
to taste something I'd invested so much
care and energy into, and that it had
tasted just how I had imagined it initially.'

Bright gold and sparkling in the
glass, Flowers blossoms with hints
of delicate orange and coriander
spice on the nose, with the aromatics
continuing onto the palate alongside
citrus juiciness and a light, fruity
sweetness that brings a smile to the face
and a chime of delight on the tongue.

Goes well with... Mussels that have been cooked in a glass of Flowers

SAINT MARS OF THE DESERT
Jack D'Or

5.8%   Seasonal

Sheffield
beerofsmod.co.uk

*The perfect beer: simple, hoppy,
bitter, complex, but very drinkable*

Ask Saint Mars of the Desert co-founder and brewer Martha Simpson-Holley about what motivated the creation of Jack D'Or and you will get a simple answer: 'It was an attempt to make the perfect beer: simple, hoppy, bitter, complex, but very drinkable. We were inspired by Belgian Saisons, definitely something like Dupont but also XX Bitter (Brouwerij De Ranke) and Taras Boulba (Brasserie de la Senne). We wanted to make an American version, inspired by New England, which is why Jack D'Or stands amongst white birch trees. So we started with American hops but everything else as close to a Belgian Saison as we imagined at that time.'

The beer, subtitled 'Saison Americaine', was first brewed in 2008, when Simpson-Holley and husband Dann Paquette had set up the Pretty Things Beer and Ale Project as a cuckoo brewery in Massachusetts. This operation came to an end in 2015 and after a stint of travelling the couple turned up in Sheffield in 2018 and Saint Mars of the Desert was the result.

Deep gold in colour, Jack D'Or has characteristically Saison-style notes of flinty sharp lemon and spice on the nose, alongside a lean and yet muscular flurry of aromatics. There is citrus lemon on the palate, alongside more of the ascetic spiciness, hints of clove and banana, a tartness and pepperiness before a dry and lingering finish. It is a very complete beer, which, as Simpson-Holley explains, has gone through several changes over the years, though the initial motivation has remained the same.

'Our old tagline was "good time artisanal beers" and for Jack it was "golden, bitter and contrary",' she explains. 'At the time we first brewed Jack in the USA, it was certainly a contrary beer because other than Jack every beer was an IPA. Now over here we find ourselves back in a very similar environment!'

Goes well with… Turbot in a shrimp sauce, with the beer bossing the dish

SALTAIRE BREWERY
Triple Choc

4.8% Core

Shipley, West Yorkshire
saltairebrewery.com

*An indolent and indulgent
chocolate Stout*

How would you describe a Yorkshire beer? For those of us who think and drink deeply of beer, the use of a sparkler immediately springs to mind like a silver bullet and creating that tight head of foam; but then you might think of an uncompromising bitterness balanced by a spine of malt and a Sahara-like dry finish perhaps? Or maybe your thoughts about Yorkshire beer turn to one where the malt character mutters away like the invocation of a prayer and flurries of dark fruit, caramel and chocolate emerge from the glass as if a magician was at work. Of course, let's not forget the use of that most traditional of fermentation vessels, the Yorkshire Square, as to be found at Theakston's and Black Sheep.

Hold these thoughts though. Times have changed and though both these types of beer would have been the correct answer a few years ago nowadays there is a multitude of styles that you could call Yorkshire, such has been the change in our vibrant brewing industry.

Take this indulgent Yorkshire beer, a luxurious, so-laidback-it's-horizontal

Stout that uses chocolate malt, real chocolate and chocolate syrups, a combination giving it an especially sensuous silkiness that wouldn't be out of place in a cup of hot chocolate. However, it still remains a beer and despite the introduction of all things chocolate any tendency to over-sweetness is halted by the use of the English Fuggle hop that brings in a balancing bitterness and earthiness. Lightly roasted coffee beans, liquorice, vanilla and hints of digestive biscuit also appear on the palate, a combination that makes this beer an exceptionally complex joy in the glass.

Goes well with… The brewery suggestion that it is an ace accompaniment to chilli con carne

SIREN CRAFT BREW
Calypso Dry-Hopped Sour

4%   Core

Finchampstead, Berkshire
sirencraftbrew.com

*Juicy, bright and bubbly
dry-hopped sour*

This is a sour beer (as in refreshingly sour and sprightly on the tongue rather than pulling a funny face). Pale lemon in colour, and luminous in the glass, it has the regulation haze of many intriguing indie brews, while the nose is juicy, lemony, citrusy, bright and bubbly. There's a lightness of touch on the palate, with lemon, a suggestion of salt (think tequila slammers and salt) and a tartness that refreshes and rejuvenates.

According to Siren's founder Darron Anley, 'Ryan Witter-Merithew, our first head brewer, pretty much brought to the UK the initial skills for kettle sours with Limoncello IPA, a ridiculous 9.1% of a beer that had been soured and brewed with lactose, lemon zest and juice and all the lemony hops. Calypso was to be the first ever flagship sour beer in the UK. We wanted a full-on, mouth-puckering sessionable beer that was refreshing, balanced and tasty. So we took our soured wort, after it had been boiled and fermented, and added dry hops to give it a fruity aroma. As we had brewed a number of kettle sour beers already, the

first beer hit the mark. It was refreshing, puckering and a fantastic palate cleanser.'

Another unique aspect of the beer is that each brew is dry-hopped with a rotating selection of hops, all of which makes for a fresh and frisky beer that dances on the taste buds.

Siren was founded in 2013 in the Berkshire town of Finchampstead, which up until then was hardly a place known for brewing innovation. Now as well as Siren, it is also home to Elusive Brewery and keen beer-lovers are apt to spend their Saturdays flitting between the two breweries' taprooms.

Goes well with… Being served on its own or with a BBQ

SIX° NORTH
Wanderlust

4.6% Core

Laurencekirk, Aberdeenshire, Scotland
sixdnorth.co.uk

Complex and refreshing Witbier influenced by the work of Pierre Celis

Back in the 1960s/70s, milkman Pierre Celis was the hero of the Witbier renaissance, bringing back to life a beer style that had died out some years before. The beer he brewed went onto become known as Hoegaarden, after Celis' hometown. For Six° North's founder, Robert Lindsay, Celis' work was the guiding light behind Wanderlust.

'Belgian brewing has always been an inspiration for us,' he says. 'For Wanderlust we looked at the original work of Pierre Celis and how his recipes live on through the current classic range of Belgian Witbiers, such as the one produced by St Bernardus. We wanted to create something complex yet eminently refreshing so we dialled the citrus levels up a little by using fresh orange, lemon and grapefruit alongside the balancing spice of the coriander seeds. This was one of the first beers we brewed so there was a lot of emotion in the first brew as the recipe had been in my head for a number of years. The first taste was relief as much as anything!'

In the glass, Wanderlust is pale lemon yellow in colour and there are scents of dried coriander spice and orange peel on the nose that straight away transported me back to a Belgian brewery on a hot day a few years ago when its Witbier was being poured. It is crisp and refreshing on the palate, with more spice, a juicy sweetness and fruitiness followed by a dryness in the finish that is the calling card of a classic Witbier. A perfect beer to remind you that the sun is always shining somewhere in the world even though it might be raining outside.

Goes well with… Fish and chips or a plate of fried seafood (with a squeeze of lemon on top)

SOLVAY SOCIETY
Superposition

3.7%   Core

Leytonstone, London
solvaysociety.com

*Session IPA meets Witbier
and the result is joy in a glass*

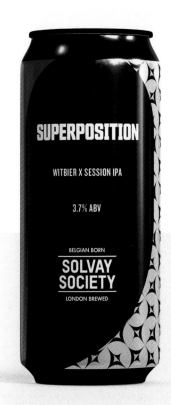

Let's get the intellectual stuff over with first. This is a Janus of a beer, which looks two ways, one in the direction of session IPA and other towards the Belgian Witbier. However, if you're going to get scientific, it is on a par with the thought experiment of Schrodinger's cat, which is both alive and dead, in other words a superposition of states, hence the beer's name (brewery founder Roman Hochuli has a background in physics, you won't be surprised to hear).

According to Hochuli, 'when session IPAs emerged about eight years ago or so I thought about how Witbiers would be very good to showcase citrusy aromas. I would call Superposition a dry-hopped Witbier and to brew it I stole some of the elements of making a New England IPA, such as using oats and dry hopping during fermentation. I use Centennial, which gives an intense lemoniness to the beer, and it was easily the recipe that took the longest to create. There were certain challenges in getting the water chemistry right and also with the use of acidulated malt, which gives it some acidity that compliments the citrus, but I recall when I got it right it felt like a bit of a eureka moment.'

The result of this eureka is an incredibly fresh tasting beer that does manage to weld together the character of a session IPA and a Witbier. It is refreshing, citrusy and jingle-jangles in the glass as if it didn't have a care in the world. It is a beer that is celebratory in its mood, a cheers, a lifted glass, a smile to the world. And maybe the cat is alive after all.

Goes well with… Offering your guests as an aperitif before dinner

ST AUSTELL
Bad Habit

7.4% Seasonal

St Austell, Cornwall
staustellbrewery.co.uk

A Belgian-style Tripel from Cornwall

Bad Habit is a Belgian-style Tripel and a luminous and luscious beer that was initially brewed in 2012 especially for the brewery's annual one-day Celtic Beer Festival. This is an event for which the brewing team has always been encouraged to consider supplying with unique beers, with some of them, such as Bad Habit, then becoming part of the brewery's bottled beer portfolio. Bad Habit can also be seen as a reflection of the late head brewer Roger Ryman's love of Belgian beers, something which he had in common with many of his brewing colleagues. Roger was a good brewing friend to beer writers and I, along with many of my colleagues, had countless discussions with him on the glories of Belgian beer. He is sadly missed.

It is a sleek, gold-amber-copper beer with a generous head of snow-white foam. The nose is sweet and honeyed, spicy even, and with the slightest suggestions of both banana and a muscat orange-like fruitiness. The palate is lightly fruity, suggestive of a dessert wine, with a medium sweetness, spice and pepperiness and a long dry finish.

Until recently Bad Habit was produced at an ABV of 8.2%, which is closer to the traditional strength of a Tripel in Belgium, but it is now 7.4%, presumably so as to come in below the 7.5% tax threshold for strong beers that was introduced in 2011. Drink in a wide-brimmed chalice glass but robes and habits are optional.

Goes well with… Cornwall's famous Yarg cheese

UNBARRED
Tropic Soda

5.8% Frequently available

Brighton, East Sussex
unbarredbrewery.com

Gloriously fruity Pale Ale with added passion fruit, mango and pineapple

Talk about the wheel of life, how the most innocent can find themselves thrown to the four corners of the earth without realising it. Take the individual passion fruits, pineapples and mangoes that at one stage in their short, sunny lives would have been picked and then transformed into pulp. Little did they know that some of them would end up in a gloriously fruity Pale Ale made by UnBarred Brewery in Sussex.

According to UnBarred's marketing manager, Brett Preston, 'the concept for Tropic Soda was to create a hybrid beer based on a popular soft drink. From the fruit and well-paired hops, Tropic Soda gives passion fruit, mango and pineapple. The malts have been layered to give a full mouthful without an opaque haze and we use citric acid in our water treatment to help create the zingy character you get with a soda and some lactose for a cream soda accent.'

According to a mindset I might have harboured several years ago, this beer is stark raving bonkers, but times change and it is perfectly acceptable now. On pouring it there is the immediacy of mango and pineapple, sweaty, ripe, chopped-up fruit pulp on the nose (maybe carried out with a well-sharpened cleaver). I take a few gulps and get the vibe of a fruit juice that has gone rogue, fruit juice with added weight and heft, mid-palate sweetness and flurries of pineapple, mango and blueberry; it has a slight creaminess in the mouthfeel and there is even a light bitterness in the finish. It's not the style of beer I often like, but somehow UnBarred have made a style of beer I like.

Goes well with… A plate of a tangy, aged goat's cheese

VAULT CITY BREWING
Strawberry Skies

8% Annual

Edinburgh, Scotland
vaultcity.co.uk

Strawberries-and-cream-inspired sour beer

Sometimes it often feels as if sours are beer's last frontier, a mark made in the sand across which the brewer does not cross – until another brewer dashes forward and a new frontier is formed. Just as Bitter is positive and appealing when it applies to a pint, the exploration of what is sour is just as palate pleasing when it comes to beer. Edinburgh-based Vault City is seen as one of the most practised makers of sour beers, something they have tried to get across in part of what seems like their mission statement: 'Committed to making delicious fruit-forward Modern Sour Beers.'

Strawberry Skies is a strawberry, hibiscus and vanilla sour beer, whose initial thought process for the recipe was strawberries and cream, according to the brewery's marketing manager, Andy Gibson: 'We wanted to present sour beer in a whole new light,' he says. 'Vault City Brewing is inspired by traditional and historical sour beers but not beholden to their practices. With a residual sweetness and big body this mixed fermentation sour beer was meant to be and is balanced, sour with sweet.'

Using Scottish barley, and matured on Scottish strawberry puree, hibiscus flowers and Madagascan vanilla beans, the beer begins with thorough aromatics of strawberry followed by a hint of vanilla in the background. The mouthfeel is quenching and tart before diffusing into a full-bodied strut down a smooth boardwalk. The finish has the sweetness of strawberry and creaminess of vanilla alongside a pinch of tartness.

It is brewed once a year and part of a 'Skies Trio', which also includes raspberry and cherry. 'Strawberry Skies is all about breaking down barriers and having fun with flavour,' adds Gibson, 'at the higher end in strength of our beers it is our prototypical Modern Sour Beer.'

Goes well with… A summer's day and a bowl of Eton mess

WILD BEER CO
Coolship

ABV
varies   Annual

Westcombe, Somerset
wildbeerco.com

*An annual treat of funkiness
and barrel-ageing*

Back at the start of 2020 I interviewed James Bardgett, Wild Beer Co's master blender. I asked him his thoughts on what the latest trend in British barrel-ageing beer could be and he said coolships, long, shallow, metal trays into which beer was introduced in order to harness whatever yeast was floating in the air to kick-start fermentation. Those who know anything about the Lambic beers of Belgium will recognise the process. Wild Beer had already released their first Coolship beer in 2019 and at the time of writing, the third has just emerged.

For co-founder Andrew Cooper, using a coolship to create a Gueuze-style beer 'is the final frontier of brewing to us. The combination of nature and nurture is the most natural way to brew a beer, to create the most complex, compelling and contemplative drink. We have gradually refined our coolship processes over the last few years. The barrels, the seasons, and the cultures will dictate if it remains the same. Our job is to blend the barrels to create the best expression of this year.

It will be similar, but it's an annual vintage, so will have slight differences every year.'

Coolship 2021 (5.9%) is an elegant and expressive beer with tranquil zephyrs of ripe apricot on the nose, interlinked with an underlying earthiness. There is more of the ripe apricot on the palate, a genial fruitiness that is also suggestive of peach, balanced by an earthiness, tartness, woodiness and a moussec-like mouthfeel before it finishes dry. This is a beer of many talents.

Goes well with… Being drunk on its own as a toast to life or as an accompaniment to the freshest seafood you can find

WILD BEER CO
Modus Operandi

7% Frequently available

Westcombe, Somerset
wildbeerco.com

*One of Wild Beer's earliest —
a barrel-aged lush and generous beer*

When Wild Beer opened in 2012 Modus Operandi was its calling card and declaration of intent, an Old Ale put into oak barrels that had either held red wine or bourbon; oh, and Brettanomyces was invited to the party. After 90 days the beers were blended together and the result has always been a lush and generous beer with a stunningly complex nose that ranges from earthy to milk chocolate to vinous to cherry and balsamic vinegar. On the palate there's a wild chocolate note accompanied by a sexy earthiness, chocolate, cherry, soft vanilla and a generous bitter finish.

'We brew into a *foudre* for initial ageing,' Wild's master blender James Bardget says, 'and then we transfer it into a steel tank to remove the dead yeast. After this the beer is racked into a variety of red wine, bourbon and sour culture barrels, with some beer also being returned back into the *foudre*. The beer is then brought back together once aged and it's blended into life!

'Barrel-ageing can bring totally different dimensions to flavour and extra levels of depth to beers. The drinks we produce pay homage to classic beers styles whilst using modern techniques that put our twist on the way they are created. The beers are heavily influenced by wine- and spirit-makers in the way in which we produce vintages and use a huge variety of barrels. The culmination of this can blur the line between what people think a beer can and can't be, and it is this variety that can make this style of beer so desirable.'

Every year Wild also produces Beyond Modus, a version of Modus Operandi that might be aged within different barrels or even have added fruit.

Goes well with... Roast duck with a honey glaze, as Wild's Andrew Cooper once recommended to me

WILD BEER CO
Ninkasi

9% Seasonal

Westcombe, Somerset
wildbeerco.com

Belgian Saison-style with Brett, apple juice and Champagne yeast joining in the fun

Home for Wild Beer is a small village in rural Somerset, surrounded by green fields and rich swathes of woodland. Westcombe cheesemakers are also next door. Ever since their foundation in 2012, the brewery's aim has been to produce beers with time as the extra ingredient, alongside various different yeasts including Brettanomyces.

'Historically we looked to Belgian breweries such as Cantillon and Rodenbach,' co-founder Andrew Cooper once told me, 'while more modern influences came from the likes of Russian River and Lost Abbey, but when we first started the idea of a modern British brewery, barrel-ageing with wild yeast seemed fresh and different, but also to us, incredibly exciting and challenging.'

Ninkasi was one of the earliest beers produced, a strong Belgian Saison style with a cascade of New Zealand hops, Brettanomyces and – for refermentation in the bottle – Champagne yeast. As well as time, the other extra ingredient is apple juice gather from fruit picked in the local area. All of this creates a sprightly and incredibly complex beer where every sip tells a different story. The nose has notes of apricot, cherry, tropical fruit, a funky earthiness and the lightest suggestions of cider-like apple juice; there is also a vinous, white wine hint, which presumably comes from the use of the Nelson Sauvin hop.

The story told with each sip is one of stone fruit, tropical fruit, elderflower, Brettanomyces' earthiness, a delicate suggestion of apple and a smooth and well-modified finish. Give a glass of Ninkasi to a Champagne drinker who says they don't like beer and watch the alchemical transformation of their palate.

Goes well with... A slab of fabulous Westcombe Cheddar

WILD HORSE BREWING CO
The Serpent and the Worm

5% Seasonal

Llandudno, North Wales
wildhorsebrewing.co.uk

*A highly accomplished Saison
from beside the seaside*

The serpent is what the Vikings called the Great Orme, an imposing headland overlooking Wild Horse's home town, Llandudno, while the worm refers to Wormhout in French Flanders, which happens to be the seaside resort's twin town. There is a further connection, as lead brewer Chris Wilkinson explains about this spritzy Saison.

'Saison Dupont is a key reference point,' he says, 'but I also looked for other clues in terms of the style. Despite having never tried his beer, I was inspired after reading about Daniel Thiriez at Brasserie Thiriez, Esquelbecq, in French Flanders. Wormhout is actually just a few miles from Brasserie Thiriez and the brewery is also reportedly the origin for the yeast strain that kicked off interest in the style in the USA.'

It took Wilkinson three brews before he was happy with this Saison, having initially used a Belgian ale yeast strain, which made it too sweet. For the third version, with a blend of a Belgian ale and a clean American ale yeast strain, he was much happier:

'On first tasting this version, I was thrilled at the balance. The yeast, hops and malt were all there and working together, with no element dominating.'

The beer is lemon gold in colour and topped by a firm head of snow-white foam. The aroma is an elemental spiciness plus sweet lemon, a hint of pineapple, and a suggestion of white pepper. A fruitiness and spiciness resonate on the palate alongside more pepperiness, followed by a lasting dryness and satisfying bitterness in the finish. A highly accomplished Saison that the brewery intends to release every spring.

Goes well with… What else but fish and chips

WIPER AND TRUE
Old Twelfth Night Orchard Ale Vintage 2018

6% Occasional

Bristol
wiperandtrue.com

A unique adventure of barrel-ageing and apple juice

When is a beer not a beer? Twenty years ago you could have answered that question with authoritative ease, but it is much harder to provide a definitive reply for contemporary beer with its milkshakes, smoothies, sours and pastry Stouts. Old Twelfth Night would have probably had drinkers scratching their collective heads in the early noughties as well, as it sees a freshly brewed wort pumped straight into red and white wine barrels and then newly pressed apple juice and pulp added for fermentation. Even now it might sound rather hazardous, but the Wiper and True brewing team are nothing if not adventurous rather than hazardous.

'Three of us were journeying back from Amsterdam's Carnivale Brettanomyces in 2017 and digesting everything we had learned,' recalls Michael Wiper. 'A lot of the discussion was around how we could bring our own unique "thing" to wild fermentation, and the beauty of the beers we tried that were so unique to their specific heritage and story. Our conversation quickly found its way to the small cider apple orchard that my wife, Francesca, and I planted before we even thought about starting a brewery.'

The first vintage wasn't immediately a success with Wiper saying that it tasted 'unpleasant' after a few months in barrel. However, time persevered and after two years they had hit the jackpot. This is the fourth vintage.

Bruised gold in colour and shimmering with a light carbonation, the enticing nose evokes old barns, straw, sweet apple cores, Demerara sugar and the earthiness of an orchard. It is dry and still on the palate, medium bodied, refreshing, with a residual sweetness stopping any drift to oversweetness. It has a hint of cider but there is a depth and a body to it that you don't get in even the best ciders. Is it a beer? Maybe you should just enjoy.

Goes well with... A pasty and chips and hang the consequences

STRONG

This is the muscular chapter,
which features beers that
accelerate above 7% ABV,
including Barley Wines
and Double IPAs.

ABBEYDALE BREWERY
Black Mass

6.66% Core

Sheffield
abbeydalebrewery.co.uk

A devilishly handsome dark beer pulsating with flavour

There's nothing Satanic about this beer, though you'd have a devil of a hangover if you drank too much of it. When held up to the light, it is as dark as a demon's thoughts and as impenetrable as the Riddle of the Sphinx. This is a beer with a swirling carousel of flavours including chocolate (both milk and dark, as if it wants to shimmer between those two worlds), mocha coffee, grilled brioche, roast espresso coffee beans and the brief daybreak of light citrus before it finishes with a roastiness that lasts with the vigour of belief.

According to brewery founder and owner Patrick Morton, Black Mass was partly a development of the Stout he had previously brewed at Kelham Island Brewery, and also partly inspired by the Guinness he used to drink in his early twenties in Irish pubs.

'I was aiming for a very dark ruby colour, along with which came strong roasty, toasty flavours and good head retention,' he recalls, 'and there would have to be a very significant mash tun contribution from roasted, unmalted barley. In terms of hopping, the emphasis was on a good depth of bitterness – more akin to Foreign Export Stout than to draught Guinness – and a lot of assertive late hops to cut through the flavours from the roasted grains. It was an expensive beer to make!'

It was first brewed in 1996 and for Morton it remains somewhere between a Stout and a well-hopped dark beer, which certainly chimes with the words I wrote down when tasting the beer: 'A modern Old Peculier perhaps?'

Goes well with...   A well-aged, well-matured chunk of Cheddar accompanied by homemade onion chutney

ABBEYDALE BREWERY
Last Rites

11%   Occasional

Sheffield
abbeydalebrewery.co.uk

*A potent Barley Wine
with plenty of character*

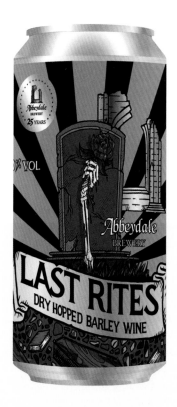

Over 40 years ago Gold Label was one of the few visible Barley Wines, and in comparison to others was unusual in being pale. It was first developed at Sheffield's Tennents Exchange Brewery in the 1950s, but that closed in the early 1990s and it is now brewed at AB-InBev's Samlesbury plant in Lancashire.

According to Abbeydale's Pat Morton, this beer was the main inspiration for the brewery's equally pale Barley Wine, Last Rites. 'I became very familiar with it in the 1970s when it was common practice to top up one's last pint of the night with a Gold Label,' he says. 'Two or three years after the brewery closed I am at Abbeydale brewing mainly Moonshine and it occurs to me that the first runnings of Moonshine's wort with the addition of white sugar in the copper would enable me to produce a strong, pale Barley Wine. There were a few failures and some judicious blending but we had again a Sheffield-originated pale Barley Wine.'

The beer gleams gold amber in the glass with aromatics of citrus, caramel, tangy orange marmalade and the well-integrated heft and weight of alcohol. On the palate there is the richness of malt, more orange marmalade, a peppery spiciness, bittersweetness, some caramel-like nuttiness before it finishes dry and bitter alongside a delicate suggestion of pepperiness, all of which demonstrates that all is well with the world.

The beer is only brewed occasionally, which underlines Morton's vision of it as constantly evolving: 'We will always consider using different hops, malts, sugars, yeasts and maturation techniques in order to maintain Last Rites as an exemplar of a pale Barley Wine. You stand still, you die.'

Goes well with… Showing off to foodie friends with roast duck breast and plum sauce

ADNAMS
Tally-Ho

7.2% Seasonal

Southwold, Suffolk
adnams.co.uk

A rich and lusty dark ale
ideal for the cold months

Here comes autumn and in Adnams' brewhouse it is time once more to engage in the annual brew of Tally-Ho, rich and fruity in its spread of flavour, the promise of its warmth a delicious reward for the winter months ahead, which can be especially bracing and iron-like in the brewery's home on the Suffolk coast.

When you pour this beer you are brought face to face with one of those rare survivors of British brewing that have their roots in the 19th century, though doubtless its recipe has changed over the years (and according to the brewing historian Ron Pattinson on his blog barclayperkins.blogspot.com it might not even have been brewed for several decades following the First World War). There has also been a change of nomenclature when it comes to its style. For many years it was referred to as a Barley Wine, but now the label says, 'Traditional Dark Ale', though it has remained bottle-conditioned, which suggests it will change and deepen its flavours with time.

It's definitely dark in colour, though not infernally dark, being more of a deep

mahogany brown. The nose is nutty, earthy, bittersweet, some suggestions of marshmallow sweetness and a hint of Christmas cake. On the palate there is more of that Christmas cake and marshmallow sweetness (though any tendency to over sweetness is reined in by the earthy hop character), plus a whisper of citrus fruit, bitterness, a nuttiness and a bittersweet finish that lingers like the wind in the chimney on a raw, sleep-broken night. Whether it is a Barley Wine or Traditional Dark Ale, this is a beer of consequence.

Goes well with… Thoughtful sipping on a windy night with the coals glowing red in the grate

BLACK ISLE BREWING
Colonel Custard's Christmas Ale

ABV
varies Seasonal

Munlochy, Ross and Cromarty, Scotland
blackislebrewery.com

*An annual, big-tasting beer produced in
memory of an extra-special brewery dog*

Every year Black Isle brews a strong
seasonal beer in fond memory of brewery
founder David Gladwin's dog, Tusker,
whose nickname was Colonel Custard.
'He was with us for 14 years, and had
many adventures,' he says. 'When he sadly
passed we wanted to immortalise him. I
mean, I have a five-foot high photo of him
over my desk. It felt right to create a place
in history for him, and the best way to do
that was in a beer series. Each year we
brew a big beer, age it in wood and release
it for Christmas under the moniker
"Colonel Custard's Christmas Ale",
always with a hand-drawn caricature of
Tusker front and centre.'

The first expression was an Imperial
Milk Stout, followed by a bourbon barrel-
aged Scotch Ale, while future ones will
be equally fulsome and potent on the
palate. 'The intention each year is to make
something extra special, like Tusker was,'
says Gladwin. 'Not just a beer, in the same
way he wasn't just a dog. The first taste is
always the same, a sense of excitement.
The water here is perfect for big, dark
beers, and wood ageing for anything up
to nine months creates further layers
of complexity and character. As for the
drinker, they can expect decadence.
That is the whole, and sole, point of
these releases. Big bottles for sharing big,
opulent beers. Toast your friends, toast
your family, remember fondly lost loved
ones. That's what these beers represent.'

The one I tasted was a 10% bourbon
barrel-aged Imperial Scotch, which had
Bourbon vanilla sweetness, coconut and
woodiness on the nose, with a big creamy,
dreamy mouthfeel, followed by malt
sweetness, vanilla softness and some
alcohol burn. A rich and unctuous beer
that will get even better with age.

Goes well with… Sharing with a friend after a strenuous dog walk

BURNING SKY
Monolith

8% Occasional

Firle, East Sussex
burningskybeer.com

Time and Brettanomyces make their mark on this barrel-aged dark beer

Burning Sky's founder Mark Tranter made his name at Dark Star, but in early 2013 he left to plan starting his own brewery. He also went over to the USA and visited various breweries. By the end of the year Burning Sky was already being seen as one of the most exhilarating breweries in the country.

'I was proud of the part I played in what I achieved,' he once told me of his time at Dark Star. 'It was a real wrench to leave, but one of the reasons for getting out was that I didn't want to look back and regret not doing things. I had an itch I wanted to scratch. I also wanted to do this brewery properly and didn't want to sit in a van dropping a nine (gallon cask) here and there. I wanted a decent sized brewery and everything has to be good.'

Monolith was first made in 2014 just after the first wooden *foudres* were delivered. The aim was to produce a barrel-aged dark beer married with Brettanomyces and then aged in a Chianti *foudre* for eight months. The result is a beer as dark as the soul of a demagogue with toffee, treacle, smoke, cherry and wood on the nose and a perceptible glaze of acidity and booziness joining in. Carbonation is soft, a prickly pepperiness says 'hi' and a wine-like headiness joins in, and then it is vanilla, chocolate, cherries, liquorice and a stroke of creaminess before heading for a dry and bitter finish. Different Monoliths have included raspberries and more recently one has spent several months with 300kg of elderberries, which Tranter says, 'is almost like a red Burgundy'.

Goes well with... A robust beer demands a robust dish, so try matching it with cassoulet

CONISTON BREWING Co.
Nº9 Barley Wine

8.5% Seasonal

Coniston, Cumbria
conistonbrewery.com

*Rich and lavishly flavoured
golden Barley Wine*

Barley Wine: a sonorous and sombre name for a beer style, a name that suggests venerability, the ales of olde England and the sound of the coachman's horn as the stagecoach and horses clatter into an inn's pebbled yard. From out of the carriage emerge its sore and weary occupants, to be served with a Barley Wine that shimmers and simmers with depth and potency.

Sadly this is an unlikely image, as by the time the term Barley Wine was starting to become commonplace amongst the language of British breweries towards the end of the 1800s, the stagecoaches had long gone and railway lines stitched their way across the country.

Given that it lost its railway line and station in the 1960s, the Lake District village of Coniston might like to consider reinstituting a stagecoach service, whose passengers could this time be served with Coniston Brewery's potent, gold-coloured Barley Wine, which is brewed once a year. According to the brewery founder Ian Bradley, 'we wanted a golden Barley Wine, so as usual we contacted David Smith, our consultant of nearly 30 years, and asked him to formulate a recipe. He came back with a simple but effective one – Maris Otter, crystal malt and our old faithful Challenger hops.'

Matured for several months, No 9 is a smooth and soothing beer, which pulsates with a rich fruitiness in the company of notes of marzipan, a herbal hoppiness, a sense of the world at ease and overtones of Cognac. It is a potent beer that demands to be sipped and considered with a serious sense of study while waiting for the sound of the coachman's horn.

Goes well with… What else but a well-matured Stilton

DIGBREW
Waka/Jawaka

8% Occasional

Digbeth, Birmingham
digbrewco.com

Double New England IPA with earthy, tropical fruit and peppery notes

This is a Double New England IPA with a difference. Instead of being liberally dosed with American hops, it has four English varieties: Harlequin, CF 182 (Opus), Jester T45 and Olicana T45. According to head brewer Andy Whyte, 'we were eager to explore what we could do with British hops, so Charles Faram provided us with some samples from the latest efforts in their hop breeding programme so we could perform some dry hopping trials and see what jumped out at us.'

The result is a commanding beer with notes of earthiness, pepper and restrained tropical fruit on the nose, an austere nose compared to the noisy zinginess that comes with American hops. The tropical fruitiness surges on the palate, booms away like a cannon, and there is a moussec-like mouthfeel before finishing as dry as a day in the Sahara.

'The first batch was a really exciting moment,' recalls Whyte. 'We were flying blind to a certain degree. Although we had done dry hopping trials, I had never personally worked with these varieties, some of them are so new that they are yet to be put through their paces while others hadn't even been named. Tasting the beer for the first time brought on a lot of feelings, but mainly encouragement. We felt encouraged in our processes, but also encouraged for the future of British hops.'

Initially brewed as a collaboration with Michelin-starred chef Brad Carter, the regularity of this beer will be determined by the supply of these new hops. For the moment Digbrew are the only UK brewery to use British hops in this style of beer, but I would expect that to change, such is the restless nature of British brewing.

Goes well with… A spicy pulled pork cob

FULLER SMITH & TURNER
Golden Pride

8.5% Core

Chiswick, London
fullersbrewery.co.uk

Classic, gold-coloured Barley Wine that was first brewed in the Swinging Sixties

Golden Pride is one of those beers that sits there quietly, allows itself to be deep and thoughtful while other beers, brash and bold, proclaim their modernity, shout loud and long. But then sometimes you wonder if these newcomers will stand the test of time as Golden Pride has. After all, its heritage dates back to the 1960s when it replaced a 7% beer whose sales were beginning to weaken. Meanwhile, its name was an obvious reference to the brewery's flagship beer, London Pride.

Poured into the glass, it is not so much golden as a sleek, Burgundy red, the kind of colour you would expect one of the great wines to have, while the gravitas of the beer saw it compared to a Cognac by the great beer writer Michael Jackson. On the nose there is malt, a hint of toffee, currants, sultanas (almost veering towards a territory taken up by fruit cake); it is a warm and inviting aromatic profile. It is rich and malty on the palate, full-bodied, with a bitterness from the hop in the finish; there is more fruit cake as well as a hint

of cherry followed by a bitterness and dryness in the finish that lingers and prepares the mouth for another sip.

This is a legendary beer, a beer that can fuel late-night conversations and decisions about the next day, a beer whose survival we can toast, and a beer that talks to us about a gentler way of living, a carnival of flavour that brings the drinker into the full colour and glory of this most exquisite of Barley Wines.

Goes well with... A rich, ripe Camembert at its most succulent

FULLER SMITH & TURNER
Vintage Ale

8.5% Seasonal

Chiswick, London
fullersbrewery.co.uk

A joyful Vintage Ale that becomes more complex over the years

London Pride and various other regulars might be the bread-and-butter beers of Fuller's, but come the early autumn it's the annual release of Vintage Ale that quickens the pulse of dedicated beer lovers. First created in 1997 by then head brewer Reg Drury, with the aid of assistant brewer John Keeling, who took Drury's job when he retired, this is a beer with a unique recipe every year, with the brewers aiming to use the best and most interesting hops and barley available. It is also a beer that changes and becomes more complex with age. Over the years I have enjoyed several tastings of various vintages, including a memorable one in 2006 of the first ten.

2021 saw the release of the 25th Vintage, an amber-copper delight with the softness of fruit loaf on the nose, bara brith even, alongside orange marmalade and hints of raisins and currants. Drinking it is a joy, with each sip revealing a rich and harmonious play of flavour on the palate including notes of toffee, light caramel, a deep muscat-like citrus and a sherry-like fruitiness. The bitterness in the finish lingers alongside a bracing dryness that just encourages you to carry on thrilling the palate.

Back at that 2006 tasting, Keeling recalled the first Vintage Ale from 1997: 'Reg and I wanted to create a truly outstanding beer. This was not about volume it was about producing a one-off Vintage Ale. At the time we didn't know how successful the beer would be.'

This is beer as a luxury item and we are all the better for it.

Goes well with… Contemplation, study and appreciation of the finer things in life

HARVEY'S BREWERY
Prince of Denmark

7.5%   Core

Lewes, East Sussex
harveys.org.uk

*A fulsomely flavoured
and potent dark beer*

I have always thought Prince Hamlet to be one of the most infuriating and dithery characters in Shakespeare, or as a voiceover went in the 1948 film version of the play: 'This is the tragedy of a man who could not make up his mind.' Damn right there. However, there shouldn't be any doubt as to the character and commitment to certainty when it comes to tasting Harvey's gorgeous Prince of Denmark, a potent, rich and fulsome dark ale, which, if you were in a Shakespearian mode, you could ask, 'is this a Porter or an Imperial Stout which I see before me?'. Prince Hamlet would presumably have sat on the fence when considering this question.

However, for once I am in agreement with Hamlet and I also think that this beer could be an Imperial Stout or a dark ale or even a strong Porter, but whatever the answer it is still a fulcrum of darkness and potent flavours that swirl about on the palate as if on a merry-go-round of taste, dizzying with the joy it brings. It is as dark and unyielding as a moonless night that cloaks itself on the earth, while aromatics of treacle toffee, mocha coffee, milk chocolate and a delicate smokiness, suggestive of the wisps of woodsmoke that drift about a town on a cold winter's night, surge out of the glass. Sip this and consider it slowly as more chocolate, coffee, treacle, ripe dark plum and caramel combine in the creamy mouthfeel, before a finish of dryness and bittersweetness. This, unlike the eponymous prince, is a beer that has made up its mind – and so will you once you begin studying it.

Goes well with… Dessert, either a tiramisu or more simply a homemade apple pie

HOGS BACK BREWERY
Aromas Over Tongham

9% Seasonal

Tongham, Surrey
hogsback.co.uk

Complex and elegant, this strong ale is a must-have for the colder months

There is something poignantly nostalgic about the aromatics emerging from a glass of this potent Barley Wine. There is toffee, a hint of marzipan, stewed stone fruit (plum crumble?), the chime of orange liqueur and an earthy woodiness. It's the kind of aroma that suggests Christmas Day or an evening in during the kind of winter night that we never get anymore. A nostalgic array of aromas for the kind of time we never really had and wouldn't have liked if we did have.

Let's turn that around though and leap from the mourned to the modern. There has been a massive growth of interest in traditional beer styles amongst brewers in the UK and Europe and this is the kind of beer that has sparked the interest – a malt-led strong ale that has characteristics of an Old Ale as well as a Barley Wine. It is fiery in its alcohol on the palate, has lots of rich and smooth malt, some peppery and citrusy hop character and a richness reminiscent of the grandest of ports, while the bitterness in the finish mingles with more of the fruitiness.

According to head brewer Miles Chesterton, 'it was originally conceived as a fortified Barley Wine, to be brewed in small batches and matured in the brewery cellar, like a fine wine. We used to brew it once every two to three years but now it's annually. The beauty of it is how it matures over time to give a different drinking experience. Although it is always brewed to the same original recipe, each vintage develops its own characteristics as it ages.'

Buy two, drink one and save the other for the future to come.

Goes well with... Christmas pudding and the compliments of the season

LACONS
Audit Ale

8% Frequently available

Great Yarmouth, Norfolk
lacons.co.uk

Intriguing strong ale with links to Oxbridge colleges

An Audit Ale was a strong beer brewed annually for some of the more traditional colleges in Oxford and Cambridge and then usually drunk by the dons at high table. Given its strength, as well as all that port and wine, it must have made for a merry night, with plenty of learned discussions along the lines of medieval monks' discussions on how many angels you could fit on the head of a pin. At least one college, Queen's in Oxford, had its own brewery where its Audit Ale was produced until it closed in 1939, though other audit ales were brewed by commercial concerns such as Lacons. The practice of brewing these ales died out after the Second World War, but several breweries have since delved into the archives to brew one. Great Yarmouth-based Lacons' award-winning Audit Ale is based on the beer the original brewery of the same name, which was closed in the 1960s by Whitbread, used to make for various Cambridge colleges.

Sleek copper in colour and packaged in a handsome 750ml bottle, it has a sweet, Demerara-like note on the nose, the kind of ghostly aroma you might get if you were to boil some sugar in water. There is also a flurry of berry notes, berry jam (blackberry perhaps?) and an amiable undercurrent of citrus. First sip reveals a sweetness and fruitiness, hints of caramel, toffee and blackberry, with its 8% ABV deftly camouflaged, while a rousing bitterness lingers in the finish. It's one of those beers to share with a friend or bring out at the end of a dinner party to go with the cheese and a discussion of how many angels you can get on the head of a pin.

Goes well with... Philosophical questions that end up going nowhere but are good fun nonetheless

MARSTON'S BREWERY
Owd Rodger

7.4% Frequently available

Burton upon Trent, Staffordshire
marstonsbrewery.co.uk

A strong dark ale from the one-time capital of British brewing

British brewing history is crowded with all sorts of tall tales, which thankfully over the last few years have been brought down to earth by the work of several beer writers specialising in history.

Maybe there is a need for further research into Marston's claim of Owd Rodger's origins, with the brewery alleging that the recipe is thought to be over 500 years old. I must admit I find that claim to be rather fanciful especially as Ian Webster in his book *Brewing in Burton Upon Trent* claims that it was first brewed in 1908 (brewing of it being suspended during the First World War). Then there is the issue of what style category Owd Rodger comes under. I recall it being part of the Barley Wine family, then Old Ale, while current branding has it down as a strong dark ale, which seems to be a fair compromise.

Whatever the issues over origins and categories, this is a pleasing and potent beer that sits well in the glass whenever the mercury has dropped and the nights have drawn in. It is dark mahogany in colour and its nose is resplendent with rich caramel, toffee and dark fruit (such as ripe plum and raisins); there is also a suggestion of liquorice. On the palate there is more of the dark fruit, a malt-derived sweetness (in fact it is quite a sweet beer), a smooth mouthfeel and a well-integrated bloom of alcohol before it finishes with a light bitterness. Old school and all the better for it.

Goes well with... Staffordshire oatcakes stuffed with fried bacon and grated Cheddar and then grilled

MOUNT ST BERNARD ABBEY
Tynt Meadow

7.4% Frequently available

Coalville, Leicestershire
mountsaintbernard.org/tynt-meadow-ale

A devotional kind of beer brewed and enjoyed by Cistercian monks

Trappist ales are the ultimate beer collaboration (or perhaps they are a contract that the devil doesn't impose for once), taking place between the secular world of brewing and the spiritual one of the monks who oversee the process. They are the ancient traditions of monastic brewing made flesh once more. Belgium is ground zero for such beers, the holy sepulchre even, if you want to feel a bit devotional, with the eyes of the beer world steadily fixed on such iconic breweries as Orval, Westmalle and Westvleteren. When you visit Belgium and order a Trappist ale, it is brought to your table in a chalice-like glass that wouldn't have been out of fashion with King Arthur and his lordly knights.

However, the last few years has seen a growing group of Trappist beers being brewed outside the Low Countries, in Austria, Italy and the USA. Then there is this one from England, which came about when the Cistercians at the abbey of Mount Saint Bernard in Leicestershire discovered that their forebears had made beer in the 19th century. So off they went in 2018 and produced the first English Trappist ale, as well as becoming the 12th Trappist brewery in the world.

Strong in alcohol and dark chestnut-brown in colour, this is a satisfying beer whose aroma is suggestive of chocolate, liquorice and ripe dark fruits such as plums. This distinctive character continues on the palate alongside a slight hoppy pepperiness before finishing dry and slightly bitter. A beer that is full of grace and flavour and which both saints and sinners will hail and enjoy.

Goes well with… Slices of roast ham that have been glazed with orange marmalade and English mustard

NEON RAPTOR BREWING
Minotaur Shock

8.2% Occasional

Nottingham
neonraptorbrewingco.com

*An expressively aromatic
Double New England IPA*

This is a thoroughly modern Double New England IPA, a beer of the now, whose aromatics leap out of the glass with the acrobatic style of a Minoan bull jumper. There is tropical fruit, sweet strawberry, ripe stone fruit and citrus and that is just on the nose. Once it awakens the palate there is more of this ripe fruitiness (berry/tropical/stone fruit/citrus), a mid-palate bittersweetness and a dryness in the finish that is bracing and tingling, somehow reminiscent of the feeling you experience when licking a peach skin. There's a slickness and a herbaceous herbalism and an urge towards fruitiness, which makes it as easy to drink as a glass of milk.

Part of the character of this beer comes from the liberal use of the Lotus hop (alongside Citra, Simcoe, Chinook and Mosaic), which is, according to brewer Tom Ainsley, 'an under-appreciated newish hop. We were very keen on trying Lotus hops as they'd been getting great write-ups just around the same time everyone started going crazy for Strata. When we first brewed it we thought it was head and shoulders above our other DIPAs and as good as ones that we'd had on our travels to other breweries. We felt great about it and were so happy that everyone agreed.'

As for the name of the beer, you might think of a connection to the mythological beast of ancient Crete, but according to Ainsley it is named after an electronic music producer of 'bleepy, slightly gentle but always interesting tracks. It's background music but interesting, and kind of what you want with this beer. You can drink it with friends and just enjoy it as you're chatting, or you can concentrate on it and appreciate more layers.'

Goes well with… The bold and vibrant flavours of Thai cuisine, especially a classic dish such as Pad Thai

NORTH END × YEASTIE BOYS
West Moon Old Ale

10.5% A one-off but available at the time of writing

UK and New Zealand
yeastieboysuk.myshopify.com

A magnificent, strong, aged ale that celebrates memory, loss and friendship

This is a unique collaboration that spans the world and tells a tale of memory and loss and friendship. It was brewed and matured at North End Brewing in Waikanae, New Zealand, in conjunction with the UK arm of the Yeastie Boys, who started life down under. It is an incredibly potent Old Ale, brewed in September 2019, put into oak barrels with wild yeast two months later then bottled in July 2020, before being released in February 2021.

This is no ordinary beer and in the traditional style of Old Ales, which were often produced to celebrate special milestones, it has been brewed in the memory of North End Brewing's owner and brewer Kieran Haslett-Moore's late father, Paul, who is on the label holding Kieran as a baby.

Poured into the glass, it is still and limpid with a gentle carbonation. The colour is reddish chestnut, like a well-burnished cabinet in a stately home seen behind a rope and guarded by a smiling archangel. On the nose there is the patina of age, alongside cherry, charred wood, fruit cake, a hint of Marmite, Brett funkiness, the heady fumes of alcohol plus caramel as the beer warms up. On the palate there is a rich and fiery jam-like sweetness, an austere woodiness, sweet caramel, cherry, vanilla, dried fruit, old leather, a pepperiness and hints of sherry nuttiness while the dryness is spartan in the finish. This is a marvellous beer with which to celebrate both a bittersweet memory and a global collaboration and friendship.

Goes well with… Toasting the memories of lost loved ones

ORKNEY BREWERY
Skull Splitter

8.5% Core

Stromness, Orkney Islands, Scotland
orkneybrewery.co.uk

Complex and palate-caressing Wee Heavy

If, like the alcohol watchdog the Portman Group did in 2008, you think that the name of this beer refers to its strength and its ability to render the drinker senseless, then you would be barking up the wrong tree (though this is difficult on Orkney as the islands famously have very few trees). As the colourful label demonstrates, it is actually named after the 7th Viking Earl of Orkney, Thorfinn 'Hausakljúfr' Einarsson (*c.* 947–963 CE), who was nicknamed 'Skull Splitter', presumably because of his prowess on the battlefield (though given the strength of the beer you might have a splitting headache if you drink too many of them).

It was first brewed in 1988 by the brewery's original founder Roger White and it is a beer that has survived over 30 years of changing tastes and trends in brewing in the British Isles. It has also remained a classic example of a strong Scotch Ale, or Wee Heavy, a rich and fulsome beer that is designed to be savoured and drunk as if it were a fine wine or malt.

When poured into the glass it is a gleaming, deep ruby in colour, attractive and engaging. On the nose there is an abundance of dried fruit, fruit cake perhaps, and a hint of the spice cupboard. It is rich and aristocratic on the palate, with more fruit cake and dried fruit, elements of sherry-like sweetness and a smooth but integrated booziness that leads to a dry and bittersweet finish.

Goes well with… A ripe Stilton and a favourite book

POMONA ISLAND
I Feel Weasels On All Sides

8.5% Occasional

Manchester
pomonaislandbrew.co.uk

*An easy-drinking, well-hopped DIPA
from Manchester*

This is a DDH DIPA. For those of us who aren't that good with acronyms, this means that the beer in your glass will be a double dry-hopped Double India Pale Ale.

That's the difficult part over with. Now we can enjoy an orange-gold delight that is traditionally hazy. On the nose there is a breeze of lemon lozenges, a light citrusy sweetness alongside a brooding tropical fruitiness, almost as if the constituents of the hops used have come face to face with an essence of fruitiness. The palate has more tropical fruit alongside a hint of soft coconut fruitiness followed by a gentle sweetness before a joyful dryness in the finish. For an 8.5% beer the alcohol is well integrated, which makes it easy to drink.

DIPAs are a natural part of the craft beer order these days, potent reminders of the joys of hoppiness, with part of the attraction of Weasels being the use of cryo pop hops in the blend. Despite sounding like a band put together for the Eurovision Song Contest, this addition gives the raw flavour and aroma of hops to a beer, having being released onto the market by

**I FEEL WEASELS
ON ALL SIDES**
DIPA

USA-based Yakima Chief Hops in 2017, with the company claiming that they add 'a true "pop" of aromas and flavours in beer' (or maybe you'd like to think of them acting almost like a stock cube).

As for the process it is relatively simple with whole leaf hops being separated into lupulin (the hop acids and the essential oils) and bract (the outer leaves of the hop flower) and then put into a hop pellet with the essential oils and resins preserved. In other words, more hoppiness without the associated bitterness.

Goes well with... A juicy steak done just the way you like it

RIDGEWAY BREWING
Imperial Barley Wine

10%   Seasonal

Reading, Berkshire
ridgewaybrewery.co.uk

*A rich and languid Barley Wine
with a bracing bitterness*

Sit yourself down, relax, throw the weight of the long day off your shoulders and pour yourself a Barley Wine. Better still, reach for a bottle of Ridgeway Brewery's Imperial Barley Wine, which at 10% is the kind of beer that should envelope your weary self with the comfort of a loving hug. Barley Wines are the beer world's version of a comfort zone, a warm-hearted and snug experience, the day winding down with each sip.

First brewed in 2012 by Oxfordshire-based Ridgeway founder Peter Scholey (Brakespear's last head brewer before its closure in 2002), this is a potent, light-coloured example of the style, with a flurry of caramel, pepper, spice and barley sweetness emerging from the nose; there is more of the same on the palate alongside a bracing bitterness and a long, dry finish. It is a beer whose depths of flavour are almost unfathomable and would be a welcome companion on a raw winter's night.

'I've always thought that the real skill in brewing strong beers is to produce something that remains drinkable,' says Scholey. 'It's dead easy to brew something that tastes great for a third of a pint and then becomes steadily harder and harder to finish. Brewing art is at play where you've had three Barley Wines already and really fancy another one. This beer doesn't warn you of your folly. "Warmly deceptive" would be the words I would use to describe the mood of this beer. Not as deceptive perhaps as its Imperial Russian cousin but I made this beer and it still catches me out.'

Goes well with… A bowl of Flemish beef stew and a hearty appetite

ROBINSONS BREWERY
Old Tom

8.5%   Core

Stockport, Cheshire
robinsonsbrewery.com

*Venerable strong ale that
commemorates a brewery cat*

A brewery cat was once a common sight, the four-legged sentinel of the grain store hunting down those mice that thought themselves imperious and invincible as they wended their way through bags of malted barley. Modern sensibilities might think the idea of a cat patrolling what is part of a place of food manufacture a bit unhygienic and against the very essence of health and safety, but a cat was the most efficient way of keeping down destructive pests.

Every time you drink a glass of Robinsons' comforting and soothing Barley Wine (or is it an Old Ale?), you are both recalling and toasting the memory of Old Tom, who was the brewery cat when the beer was first brewed. He was so obviously revered that his name was given to the beer. Even more surprisingly, the beer has survived since its debut in 1899, unvanquished and still a valuable part of this Stockport brewery's heritage.

Whatever beer style you want to assign to Old Tom, this is very much a sipping, contemplative and ruminating beer, a dark mahogany-coloured jewel from which warming aromatics of dried fruit (raisins, currants), caramel, toffee, alcohol and a port-like fragility emerge, rich and symphonic in their impression. There is more dried fruit, a caramel-led sweetness, a vinous character even, alongside an earthy hop impression before the finish delves into a realm of spiciness, dryness and bittersweetness.

An ideal beer with which to toast your good fortune on a stormy night as you sit in a beloved armchair and watch the future reflected in the flames of an open fire.

Goes well with… A juicy venison burger with added Cumberland sauce and a couple of hours afterwards to take a nap

SAINT MARS OF THE DESERT
Our Finest Regards

9% Occasional

Sheffield
beerofsmod.co.uk

*A complex Barley Wine that
shows off what malt can do*

This is a fulsome Barley Wine, dark
mahogany in colour with a firm crema-
coloured head of foam. It broods in the
glass, mysterious but also glamorous, a
beer sleek and sensuous in its rich malt
character. Just take the time to inhale
and recognise toffee, caramel, a nuttiness,
chocolate, molasses and coffee – if a nose
could be said to be dark then this is it.
On the palate there is more of the coffee,
a nutty chocolate mix, caramel, toffee,
a roasty toastiness and a bittersweet
and dry finish that lingers on and on.

This deep, thoughtful beer used to
be made under the same name by Saint
Mars of the Desert's Dann Paquette
and Martha Simpson-Holley when
they were based in the USA and brewed
as The Pretty Things. Now they're in
Sheffield, and according to Paquette it is
a dream come true to brew it in the UK.

'It was inspired by strong British ales
like Thomas Hardy's, Fuller's Vintage,
J W Lee's Harvest Ale and the fantastic
malts from the UK: amber, Maris Otter
and the barrel-roasted malts at Fawcett's.
Trips to the annual Old Ale festival

at the White Horse in London also
played their part! American breweries
make a different sort of Barleywine,
basically another IPA but sticky and not
like this. This is meant to be a tribute
to barley and it changes every year
because I always think I can do better.

'This is a beer that should show
everything that grain has got going for it
and more. Should coffee, chocolate, toffee,
caramel, molasses, sultanas be thrown in
beer? Hell no! Here's why – barley is all of
that and so much cooler. Here's proof!'

Goes well with... North African lamb tagine

SALT BEER FACTORY
Tram

8% Core

Saltaire, West Yorkshire
saltbeerfactory.co.uk

*A lusciously fruity
Double New England IPA*

This delicious little number is called Tram
in relation to a special type of woven silk
rather than a type of public transport. This
is mainly because the brewery's location
is in the UNESCO World Heritage
Village of Saltaire where there is an
historic 19th-century textile mill where
Tram silk was no doubt made. However,
you could be forgiven for thinking of a
double meaning as Salt and its taproom
is housed in a former tram shed.

There's an equally appealing amount of
thinking needed when you come to Tram's
beer style. Yes it is an IPA, but as is the
norm these days, craft brewers are coming
up with so many different variations of
the style that it's hard to know whether
the beer in your glass is a West Coast IPA,
milkshake IPA or, as in the case of Tram, a
Double New England IPA. However, firmly
sitting on the fence I find it best to leave
the philosophy to others and just enjoy the
beer, which is what I have done with Tram.

Gold in colour, this is a juicy and
refreshing beer which pulsates with an
array of fantastically appealing aromas
of tropical fruit and citrus, including

mango, peach, papaya, grapefruit and
banana. Each refreshing sip delivers more
of this luscious fruit bowl of flavours
and sensations, alongside a gentle
bittersweetness and a lip-smackingly
dry finish. Oh, and yes it is hazy, but as
Salt's head brewer Colin Stronge told
me about this trend, 'I think hazy beers
are here to stay, even if they are never
the predominant selling style nationally.
In craft circles the extra mouthfeel and
body have opened up the IPA style and
changed perceptions of what they can be.'

Taproom philosophers take note.

Goes well with... Shellfish, especially grilled scallops

SIX° NORTH
Chapeau

9.5% Core

Laurencekirk, Aberdeenshire, Scotland
sixdnorth.co.uk

Luminous and lustrous strong Golden Ale which is dry hopped with Citra

Top of the world, tip of the hat, whatever way you want to frame it, Chapeau is a deliberate and loving nod to the joys of Duvel's Triple Hop series, which saw the Belgian brewing group use American hops for several well-hopped versions of its strong Golden Ale. For Six° North founder Robert Lindsay, the Citra variation, which eventually became the main hop for the series, was a prod in the back and a declaration of love for what Moortgat was doing.

'Duvel had just released their Triple Hop with Citra,' he recalled, 'and the first time I tasted it I thought, "wow". The big brewers in Belgian at the time rarely played around with American hops and the balance they had found with the yeast was excellent. This style fitted perfectly into our ethos so we wanted to emulate it. By calling our beer Chapeau, it was "tip of the hat" to Duvel.'

Lindsay recalls being exceptionally pleased with the first brew of Chapeau, pointing out that the dry hopping with Citra really helped the beer to shine on the palate and produce a lustrous liquid in the glass. 'We could still see where our inspiration had come from but this was very much a beer with its own identity,' he says.

Pouring a gleaming pale gold, there is an immediate blossom of tropical fruit on the nose, ripe and sweet, followed by that familiarly jazzy spiciness so redolent of Belgian yeast. On the palate it is smooth and spritzy, with more of the tropical fruit sweetness alongside a hint of tart lime before it finishes dry and luminous.

Goes well with... Either a farmhouse Cheddar or a gorgeous sunset

STANNARY BREWING
Repeat Offender

8.1%   Seasonal

Tavistock, Devon
stannarybrewing.shop

Dry-hopped DIPA brimming with tropical fruitiness

It's a familiar story in the world of independent brewing. Boldly flavoured and vividly hopped beers have been tasted and fallen in love with, sometimes on a visit to the USA, other times on a more modest journey to the likes of London, Bristol or Manchester. However, once back home the hunt for similarly exciting beers in local pubs is fruitless and you decide you will just have to brew them yourself.

This is the origin story of Tavistock-based Stannary, as co-founder Garry White explains: 'We started the brewery because we couldn't get hold of the hop-forward beers we loved to drink in our local pubs and bars, so we began making them as home-brewers. Then one night over a few IPAs we decided to start up a brewery of our own and from that moment Stannary was born.'

Repeat Offender is a dry-hopped DIPA and the first of the style that they brewed back in 2016 when they were founded.

'DIPAs were probably in their infancy as far as UK breweries were concerned when we started back in 2016,' says White. 'Cloudwater were releasing their DIPA series and we managed to grab a bottle of the DIPA Mk2, and it blew our minds.'

Part of the Anomalies range and released twice a year, it is orange gold in colour with a shaded haze. The nose is ripe orange and mango alongside an equally ripe peachiness, perhaps one that has been cut in half with the aromatics rising to the heavens. More tropical fruit and stone fruit engage the palate with gusto, alongside a bittersweet graininess and a persistent juiciness, before it finishes dry with more of the tropical fruit coming back.

'For me,' says White, 'with DIPAs and other big ABV beers it's about drinkability and we are always looking to make our big ABV beers as balanced and drinkable as any other beer we produce.'

Goes well with… The saltiness and sweetness of beef panang

SWANNAY BREWERY
Old Norway

8% Occasional

Birsay, Orkney Islands, Scotland
swannaybrewery.com

Rich malt, vibrant hoppiness and a lingering finish make for an elegant strong ale

It's a long way from San Francisco to the Orkney Islands, but for brewery founder Rob Hill distance was no object when he developed this potent Barley Wine. According to Hill's son, Lewis, who joined the brewery after returning home from university, 'Old Norway is a recipe of my dad's. I believe the inspiration was Old Foghorn from San Francisco's Anchor, hence it being spelt Barleywine on the label. It was off our five-barrel plant and would have been pretty tough to brew owing to our small mash tun and the amount of malt required to hit the ABV (it was originally 9%). It was brewed in the winter time when we had less demand for "regular" beers. I remember trying it from the vessel but also drinking from a pin at my dad's house with a storm howling outside. The first hit is luscious and warming with so much depth and body.'

Bruised gold in colour, Old Norway has an elegant and eloquent nose of sweet malt, which is balanced by the rough and tumble of hop fruitiness (Cascade, Citra, Nelson Sauvin and Simcoe all go into the kettle), which

helps to prevent it from being over-sweet. There is more of the rich malt on the palate, a deep and soulful richness, with the vibrancy of stone fruit and earthy herbal notes, before a lingering finish that is both bittersweet and lightly fruity.

This is definitely a beer for an Orcadian winter, as Lewis Hill seems to relish: 'As with all our stronger beers this is perfect for an Orkney storm, when it is pitch black outside, howling wind, horizontal rain, wood fire and a warming drink.'

Goes well with... Cheese, naturally, perhaps the creamy, rich and aromatic Strathdon Blue made in the north of Scotland

THORNBRIDGE BREWERY
Bracia

10% Occasional

Bakewell, Derbyshire
thornbridgebrewery.co.uk

One of Thornbridge's most distinctive beers, featuring Italian chestnut honey

I first tried this chestnut honey dark beer at the 2008 awards dinner organised by the British Guild of Beer Writers. It was matched with a tiramisu and everyone on my table agreed that it was a perfect match and also the best beer of the night. It is not always available, but when it is there is a definite cause for celebration. According to Thornbridge production manager Dominic Driscoll, 'it was a beer quite some time in the making. One of our then brewers Stefano Cossi had a plan of making a historic type of beer but also wanted to use some Italian chestnut honey, which was very different to the type of honey we were used to.

'The first difficulty was getting some of the honey over to us. A friend of one of the brewery founders, Simon Webster, was involved in an Italian steel business based in Sheffield and regularly brought product in so we arranged for some of the honey to sit alongside the next consignment. It arrived and we brewed the beer for the first time. It was different to any beer I had ever tasted before and still retains that. The complexity of the malt bill is excellent and the honey gives a unique taste that I really love.'

It is a beer that is easy to wax lyrically about. Beneath its crown of crema-coloured foam, it is as dark as the most moonless of nights. Both the nose and palate feature notes of coffee beans, chocolate, almond paste and a fiery bitterness with a tongue-tingling bite on the end of the palate. Then you can also think of sambuca, chocolate-coated coffee beans and the bitter bite of chestnut honey, which adds a herbal-like sweetness to the beer. Simply stunning and well worth keeping an eye out for when Thornbridge brew it next.

Goes well with... Tiramisu

THORNBRIDGE BREWERY
Halcyon

7.4% Seasonal

Bakewell, Derbyshire
thornbridgebrewery.co.uk

*A golden beauty of an Imperial IPA
bursting with hop character*

One of Thornbridge's earliest Imperial
IPAs (as DIPAs were once called around
2009/10), this is a strong and silent kind
of beer, pristine and secure in the glass,
but happy to flex its hop-flecked muscles
if called upon. In recent years it seemed
to wander off on its own and get lost
in the outback of speciality IPA when
it became the base beer for a couple of
Thornbridge's fruit IPAs featuring mango
or pink grapefruit (its ABV has also
descended from the original 7.7% to 7.4%).
These were excellent beers but I wanted
the stand-alone Halcyon. Thankfully, my
wish was granted and it has returned to
its rightful place as one of the brewery's
regular limited editions, a situation
that is much to be celebrated given the
joyous complexity that the drinker enjoys
when faced with a brimming glass of
this gleaming, light-gold treasure.

    Given the use of hops from the USA,
New Zealand and Australia, you would
not be far wrong if you thought that
the nose was a cavalcade of sprightly
tropical fruitiness as the soft dust of ripe
mango, freshly cut pineapple and brittle

grapefruit combine with the plangency
of an almost earthy graininess in the
background. On the palate there is more
grapefruit, pineapple, mango and ripe,
sweet mandarin in league with a cry of
graininess before a dry and rusticated,
bitter finish. This is a complete beer, a
treat of a beer that plunges the drinker
straight into a newly opened bag of
hops at the brewery before they are
thrown into the brew to be sacrificed
to the cause of taste and aroma.

Goes well with…   Grilled cubed pork that has first been marinated in lemon juice, garlic, salt, lemon, paprika and cumin

TRAQUAIR HOUSE BREWERY
Jacobite Ale

8% Core

Traquair, Borders, Scotland
traquair.co.uk/brewery

A rich, spicy and tangy ale brewed in one of Scotland's most historic houses

Tradition is at a premium in the stone-built confines of Traquair House Brewery near the River Tweed. Situated at Traquair House, which is the ancestral home of descendants of the Stuarts and the oldest inhabited stately home in Britain, modern-day brewing began in 1965 when the then laird rediscovered the old brewhouse with its mash tun, open coolers and wooden stirring paddles in perfect condition. It had lain unused since the 1880s, but within a short while brewing had recommenced. The laird died in 1990, but his daughter then took over the brewery's running and it continues to forge its own path.

Jacobite Ale is a rich and smooth spiced ale first brewed in 1995 (coriander is the spice). It is as dark as an old mahogany sideboard and makes its mark immediately with a powerfully fragrant, spicy, almost perfumed nose offset by an undertow of sweet maltiness. In the mouth it's refreshing, herbal, spicy, with hints of liquorice, milk chocolate and a citrusy orange marmalade character in the background; smooth and semi-creamy in feel, with a spirit-like fieriness, this is a big bruiser of a beer with its spicy, tangy finish lingering for a long while.

On the style front this is more like a modern Belgian Brune than a Scottish ale, though its long-serving brewer Ian Cameron once told me that he looked to history rather than across the Channel when designing the beer: 'I was looking through old recipes such as cock ale and oak bark ale. We couldn't use the cock ale so I thought I would use a small amount of crushed coriander seed instead.'

Goes well with... A hearty helping of game pie with mashed potato and spiced red cabbage on the side

TRING BREWERY
Death or Glory

7.2% Seasonal

Tring, Hertfordshire
tringbrewery.co.uk

Brewed once a year, this is a full-bodied and muscular dark Old Ale

This dark mahogany-coloured strong ale is brewed once a year, an annual treat that usually begins on 25 October in commemoration of the fateful charge of the Light Brigade during the Crimean War. Its name comes from the regimental motto of the Queen's Royal Lancers, whose antecedents took part in that futile cavalry charge. There's another connection: the idea for the beer was conceived in the early 1990s by a then member of the brewing team, a former lancer.

'The first brew was intimidating as we had never brewed quite anything as robust in the brewhouse, though we had confidence that we'd do the lancers proud,' recalls brewery founder Mark Shardlow. 'As we do today, the first casks were laid to rest for an extended maturation in the brewery cellar, allowing complex esters to develop in the sweet Old Ale before tapping. The month-long ageing was worth it. The resulting ale was sweet, yet not too cloying, and in fact deceptively easy drinking.'

A gleaming dark mahogany in colour, shining like the hope of a long gone day, it is full-bodied and muscular and has a charge of dried fruit on the nose alongside a wheeling cavalcade of nuttiness, malt, chocolate, orange marmalade, marzipan, caramel and treacle. The palate has a similarly virtuous mixture of flavours, making for a judicious balance of fruit and sweetness, followed by a dry and bittersweet finish. It is rich and eloquent in the way it presents itself, encouraging end-of-the-night thoughts of contemplation by the fireside as the weather outside rants and roars as if eager to charge into the jaws of the enemy's cannon.

Goes well with… A rereading of Tennyson's *Charge of the Light Brigade* and contemplating its folly

TWISTED WHEEL BREW CO
88 Miles Per Hour

8.8% Occasional

Warrington, Cheshire
twistedwheelbrewco.co.uk

*DIPA that will have your tastebuds
tapping their toes with abandonment*

Picking a beer from an unknown brewery
can be entirely random. Some might go
for the branding, others the beer style,
but for me seeing a can of Twisted Wheel
whilst in North Wales took me back to
my schooldays in the area and the culture
battles between northern soul fans
(Twisted Wheel was a famous northern
soul club) and hard rockers (then punks).
The fact it was a DIPA was also a boon.

I also thought that the beer's name
was something to do with northern soul's
frenetic style of dancing, but, according to
Laura Dearman, whose parents founded
the brewery, 'the inspiration first came
from catching the clip of *Back To The
Future* where the DeLorean needs to
travel at 88mph to initiate time travel.
We wanted to create a beer that could
have the same effect on the drinker!'

Amber orange in colour, the beer has
stone fruit and tangerine notes on the
nose, a fresh assemblage of fruitiness that
tasks the nose and then the palate to think
deeper about what it is experiencing. The
palate has pineapple, some coconut, stone
fruit and grapefruit, all merged together

like a great living monolith of flavour.
There's also a tangy, piney sweetness
while the finish is juicy, dry and bitter.

This is a full-bodied and expressive
DIPA, one of several the brewery
makes, though Dearman explains that,
'the current brew is the first and only
brew of to go out to trade so far but the
team have been very happy with the
results. We initially brewed this beer
as a one-off special, but who knows,
if it proves popular we may bring it
back in the future'. Or should that be
back to the future?

Goes well with... Several mature cheeses, including Cheddar, Stilton and a gnarly goat's cheese

VOCATION BREWERY
Smash and Grab

8% Seasonal

Hebden Bridge, West Yorkshire
vocationbrewery.com

*Tropical fruit salad aromatics and a
dry and comforting bittersweet finish*

Fruity or fruitiness are often bandied about in descriptions of well-hopped beers with the ease of an indulgent and kindly headmaster handing out numerous prizes at the end of summer term. 'This IPA has tropical fruit emerging from the glass ... while this one has citrus ... and that one over there has a hint of blueberries and stone fruit and well done everyone.'

This fruitiness for all is probably an easy description for drinkers who are still not sure about beers that use North American and Antipodean hops, but there is also a vagueness in the use of the term, a similar issue that comes when a beer's epithets includes malty or juicy or spicy. Clarity is needed, perhaps without descending into a parodic tasting note that confuses everyone and educates no one.

Take Hebden Bridge-based Vocation's ample DIPA Smash and Grab, which you could easily and lazily and without any consequences term as fruity in both its aromatics and flavours. However, if you start to pick apart its character

and minutely examine its aromatic profile, there is a surge of freshly cut mango, ripe guava, freshly peeled lychee and squeezed grapefruit, a pliable impression of fruitiness. Then there is more of this tropical fruit salad on the palate, a cereal-like graininess in the background with hints of a restrained caramel sweetness before it finishes dry and comfortingly bittersweet.

This is a potent and luscious beer of which brewery founder John Hickling says, 'we wanted to brew a really uncompromising Double IPA – true to style, big on hops and alcohol, and bold in flavour.'

I think he succeeded.

Goes well with... Grilled lamb sausages, or surprise your dinner party friends by matching it with a crème brûlée

WILD CARD BREWERY
DIPA

8.1% Occasional

Walthamstow, London
wildcardbrewery.co.uk

Potent DIPA with a well-maintained bitterness and dryness in the finish

Hops are the alpha and omega of an impactful DIPA, the beginning and the end of all reason and the rapture that's captured within both the aromatics and the presence on the palate. For Wild Card's award-winning head brewer Jaega Wise, with the brewery's first DIPA, 'we wanted a really bold and overtly juicy beer with a strong ABV and thick texture, but ultimately it should also be a smooth drink despite the booze. When we first tasted this beer, we were absolutely ecstatic. Very high ABV beers are notoriously difficult to get right. There was just a general feeling of "nailed it" amongst the team.'

Amber orange in colour, the beer pulsates with the aromatics of tropical fruit and citrus (especially grapefruit) on the nose, thanks to the use of American hops, which are also used for dry hopping (though different versions of the beer use different varieties). As well as grapefruit there is also freshly sliced ripe mango and the kind of juiciness and palate pleasing that fresh pineapple brings. These fruit notes are repeated on the palate alongside suggestions of papaya and orange and a resiny, pine-like note, all kept in order, well-integrated and creating a whirl of flavour on the palate. There is also a well-maintained bitterness and dryness edging towards the finish, all of which makes for the kind of conjuring trick in which an 8.1% beer vanishes as swiftly as if it was a 3% table beer.

Other versions of the beer have seen it extensively double dry hopped, as Wise explains: 'We've brewed this beer loads of times, with each version moderately tweaked. However, the essence and flavour profile of this beer has always remained the same.'

Goes well with… A rich and meaty lamb stew

BOTTLE SHOPS IN THE UK

South-West

BARNSTAPLE
The Crafty Beer Shop
thecraftybeershop.com

BRISTOL
Two Belly Cheese & Beer Shop
twobelly.co.uk

EXETER
Hops and Crafts
shop.hopsandcrafts.co.uk

FALMOUTH
Lauter Bottleshop
lauterbottleshop.co.uk

NEWTON ABBOT
**Maltings Taphouse
and Bottleshop**
themaltingstaphouse.co.uk

PLYMOUTH
Vessel Beer Shop
vesselbeer.co.uk

TRURO
Red Elephant Beer Cellar
redelephantbeercellar.co.uk

London & South-East

BRIGHTON
Seven Cellars
sevencellars.co.uk

BURY ST EDMUNDS
Beautiful Beers
beautifulbeers.co.uk

NORWICH
Sir Toby's Beers
sirtobysbeers.co.uk

PECKHAM, LONDON
Hop Burns & Black
hopburnsblack.co.uk

SOUTHAMPTON
Bitter Virtue
bittervirtue.co.uk

ST ALBANS
The Beer Shop
beershophq.uk

TUNBRIDGE WELLS
Fuggles Bottle Shop
fugglesbottleshop.co.uk

Midlands

BURTON UPON TRENT
Brews of the World

CHELTENHAM
Favourite Beers
favouritebeers.com

CLEETHORPES
Message in a Bottle
miabcleethorpes.net

COVENTRY
Beer Gonzo
beergonzo.co.uk

HEREFORD
Hereford Beer House
shop.herefordbeerhouse.co.uk

LOUGHBOROUGH
Hoptimism
hoptimism.co.uk

NOTTINGHAM
Brew Cavern
brewcavern.co.uk

STIRCHLEY,
BIRMINGHAM
Cotteridge Wines

Yorkshire & North-East

DURHAM
The Hop Knocker
thehopknocker.co.uk

HARROGATE
Husk Beer Emporium
huskbeeremporium.com

ILKLEY
**Fuggle & Golding Tap
House – Bottle Shop**
fuggleandgolding.com

NEWCASTLE
Block & Bottle
blocknbottle.com

SHEFFIELD
Hop Hideout
hophideout.co.uk

SUNDERLAND
Port Bierhaus
portbierhaus.com

YORK
Beer Ritz (online only)
beerritz.co.uk

North-West

DOUGLAS, ISLE OF MAN
Bottle Monkey
bottlemonkey.im

HELSBY, CHESTER
Beer Heroes
beerheroes.com

LIVERPOOL
Haul
haul.beer

MANCHESTER
Beermoth
beermoth.co.uk

STOCKPORT
Heaton Hops
heatonhops.co.uk

ULVERSTON
Beerwolf
wearebeerwolf.com

WIGAN
Northern Beer Temple
northernbeertemple.co.uk

Wales

ABERYSTWYTH
Bottle and Barrel
bottleandbarrel.cymru

BALA
Stori
storibeers.wales

CARDIFF
(Penylan, Penarth, Pontcanna)
The Bottle Shop

CARDIFF
Pop'n'Hops
popnhops.myshopify.com

LLANELLI
**Beer Park Bottle Shop
and Tasting Room**
beerpark.co.uk

MONMOUTH
The Crafty Beer Guy
www.facebook.com/CraftyBeerGuy

PENRHYN BAY, LLANDUDNO
Craft Beer Cave
www.facebook.com

Scotland

ABERDEEN
Hop Shop Aberdeen
hopshopaberdeen.com

DUNFERMLINE
The Caledonian Craft Beer Merchant
thecaledoniancraftbeermerchant.com

EDINBURGH
The Beehive
thebeerhive.co.uk

DUNBAR
Beer Zoo
shop.beerzoo.co.uk

GLASGOW
Valhalla's Goat
valhallasgoat.com

GLASGOW
Wee Beer Shop
weebeershop.co.uk

PERTH
Craft Beer Bottle Shop
cbbsperth.co.uk

Northern Ireland

BELFAST
The Vineyard
vineyardbelfast.co.uk

INDEX OF BREWERIES

John Bryan, Oakham Ales

Simon Webster and Jim Harrison, Thornbridge

Dom Erik, Father Michael, Father Joseph, and Brother Robert, Mount St Bernard Abbey

CAMRA Books

The Family Brewers of Britain
ROGER PROTZ

Britain's family brewers are stalwarts of beer making.
Some date back as far as the 17th and 18th centuries and have survived
the turbulence of world wars, bomb damage, recessions, floods, and
the hostility of politicians and the temperance movement. This book,
by leading beer writer Roger Protz, traces the fascinating and sometimes
fractious histories of the families still running these breweries.

RRP **£25** Hardback   ISBN 978-1-85249-359-2
RRP **£17.99** Paperback   ISBN 978-1-85249-377-6

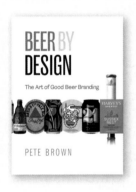

Beer by Design
PETE BROWN

The design of a beer label, pump clip, bottle or can has to do a lot of
work to stand out, get noticed, and suggest to the thirsty punter that
here is a beer they will enjoy. In this lavishly illustrated book, acclaimed
beer writer Pete Brown traces the history of beer label design back to
the UK's first-ever trade mark and beyond. He explores the conventions
of successful beer design (and how they are now being shattered)
and explains the tricks and secrets of successful design in a compelling
and highly readable narrative.

RRP **£15.99**   ISBN 978-1-85249-368-4

Modern British Beer
MATTHEW CURTIS

This book is about why modern British beer is important.
Over the course of the past two decades the British beer scene as we
know it has changed, forever. Matthew Curtis gives a personal insight
into the eclectic and exciting world of modern British beer from a
choice of 86 influential brews; from how they taste, how their ingredients
are sourced, to the engaging stories of the people behind the scenes
working hard to bring exciting beer to drinkers all over Britain.
This book is a fantastic starting point to explore British beer with
an exciting location closer than you think.

RRP **£15.99**   ISBN 978-1-85249-370-7

Modern British Cider
GABE COOK

Cider is one of the world's oldest drinks, with a heritage dating back at least 2,000 years. It formed an integral part of the landscape, economy and culture of many rural parts of the UK for centuries before being commoditised by industrial-scale production. Cider now faces a new change in the drinking landscape of Britain – the rise of craft drinks, which brings with it modern, discerning drinkers with different needs, habits and spending opportunities. Acclaimed cider expert Gabe Cook celebrates the heritage, diversity and innovation within the wonderful world of British cider today.

RRP **£15.99**   ISBN 978-1-85249-371-4

World Beer Guide
ROGER PROTZ

The world of beer is on fire. Traditional brewing countries are witnessing a spectacular growth in the number of beer makers while drinkers in such unlikely nations as France and Italy are moving from the grape to the grain. Drawing on decades of experience, Roger Protz takes readers on a journey of discovery around the world's favourite alcoholic drink – uncovering the interlinked stories behind the best breweries and beers across every continent in the world.

RRP **£30**   ISBN 978-1-85249-373-8

London's Best Beer, Pubs & Bars 3rd Edition
DES DE MOOR

The essential, indispensable and award-winning guide to one of the world's great beer cities is back with a fully revised and updated 3rd edition. From traditional pubs serving top-quality cask ale, to the latest on-trend bottle shop bars, and funky brewery taprooms in Victorian railway arches, London is now bursting with great beer and this book will direct you to the very best.

RRP **£16.99**   ISBN 978-1-85249-360-8

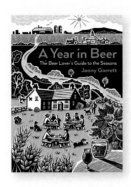